DATE DUE

OCT 1 1 2002			

THE NEW LISTENER'S COMPANION
AND RECORD GUIDE

B. H. HAGGIN

THE NEW
LISTENER'S COMPANION
AND RECORD GUIDE

HORIZON PRESS • NEW YORK

FOREWORD TO
THE NEW LISTENER'S COMPANION
AND RECORD GUIDE

As against the writing that encourages the reader to find the meaning of a piece of music in its historical background, this book begins by encouraging him to find it in the internal operation of the piece. Thus it asks him to do as a listener what E. M. Forster once prescribed for the critic: to consider the work as an object, an entity, and discover the life in it. And two chapters on musical procedures and forms, in which the author describes the life, the internal operation he perceives in certain pieces of music, will help the reader to do this for himself with the other music discussed in the book.

What the reader discovers in this music from his own listening will provide him with the means of testing the evaluations in the survey of the literature of music that follows the introductory chapters. This survey offers a reasoned exercise of judgment and taste by the author, which—since it is reasoned —is not dogmatic, and in fact induces a similar exercise of judgment and taste by the reader. And this is true also of the chapters on performance of music, on jazz, on the critical writing that has been done on music; and of the new sections dealing with recorded performances of the music discussed in the book.

CONTENTS

PART ONE

CONTENTS

PART TWO

PART ONE

1

INTRODUCTION: THE READER

AND THE CRITIC

The first chapters of this book are what I have thought would be helpful to someone who has just begun to be interested in music—interested, for one thing, in discovering whether he gets from music anything like what he gets from a novel, a play, a poem, a painting. They include a description of musical procedures and forms from which he should not be deterred by the quotations in musical notation: all he is asked to do is to try letting his eye follow as he listens—something he will, I think, find not only possible, but helpful in impressing what he hears on his mind. The knowledge of the procedures and forms will be helpful in the same way; and an additional benefit from this material will be detailed acquaintance with several great pieces of music. But he can, if he prefers, skip Chapters 3 and 4.

After these first chapters the book offers a critical survey of the literature of music, addressed not only to the newly interested reader but to anyone—whatever his musical experience and understanding—whose interest in music gives him a further interest in what critical perception may reveal in it. I have written in the expectation that he is going to do his own listening and reach his own conclusions about what he hears; and that I will merely be pointing out things for him to listen to and evaluate. Which is to say that I will be performing the function of the critic; and I think it would be good for me to state at the outset what I understand this function to be.

The critic is a music-lover and listener like his readers: he is the expert and professional listener, who is assumed to have greater powers of perception and judgment than the amateur, and therefore to be able to make his readers aware of things in the music which they mightn't notice by themselves. He functions as a sort of guidepost, saying in effect: "I hear this happening at this point"—after which his reader listens and may say: "Yes, I hear it too." But he also may say: "No, I hear *this*." That is, the critic uses his powers to animate those of his reader—but only to animate, not to dictate: what he says about a piece of music is true for the reader only if it is confirmed by the reader's own ears. And each critic writes for the group of people who have found his perceptions and evaluations sufficiently confirmed by their own experience.

Underlying what I have just said is the fact that criticism does not, as some people think it must, offer the one possible and correct opinion, arrived at by measuring the piece of music with a set of established caliper-like esthetic principles for determining the good and the beautiful. The piece of music is a special kind of communication; the critic reports the effect of that communication on a mind operating not with impersonal esthetic principles but with personal sensitiveness, perception and taste; and the communication may impress different minds differently. The critic, then, reports not what is true, but what is true for him, and what becomes true also for the reader who finds it to be so when he listens to the piece.

All this to prepare the reader for the discovery in this book that I too have, as a critic, done my own listening and evaluating—the discovery, that is, of opinions which occasionally differ from those of other critics and even from that awesome authority, accepted opinion. Accepted opinion finds greatness in every note set down on paper by a great composer like

4

Bach or Mozart; I hear in some works—and must report hearing—dull products of a routine exercise of expert craftsmanship. Accepted opinion holds some symphonies and concertos of Brahms to be works of tremendous profundity, and there was a time when they impressed me that way; but today I hear in them only the pretension to profundity. And on the other hand I esteem Tchaikovsky, to whom accepted opinion condescends.

There would be no need of preparing the reader for such dissents in a book about literature. But anyone conditioned by the announcements of music on the radio, the notes on record envelopes, the program notes at concerts, the reviews of these concerts in newspapers, needs to be prepared for the shock of a questioning of the accepted valuation of a theoretic exercise by Bach, a potboiler by Mozart, an imitation of Beethoven by Brahms, a piece of slick trash by Puccini or Ravel.

In sum: I am bound to report what I hear; and the reader then is free to find what I say to be true or not true for him. That is our relation in this book.

I should perhaps mention that if I take more space for Berlioz than for Haydn it isn't because I consider Berlioz greater than Haydn: the space in each instance is what is required by what I think needs to be said about each composer. And the same for differences in treatment of the composers—e.g. the inclusion of detailed analysis of particular works, or of quotations in musical notation, in one instance and not in another.

And I should, finally, speak of the difficulties in writing about music—primarily the difficulty in using words about a means of communicating what words cannot communicate. I operate on the assumption that it is legitimate to speak of the *Benedictus* of Beethoven's *Missa Solemnis* being about the blessedness at the heart of things, even though precisely what Beethoven "says" about this blessedness is something to be learned only from the music.

5

2

THE MEANING OF MUSIC

I said that a piece of music is a communication. And if you are one of those to whom a Beethoven symphony is a lot of meaningless noises, you may say: "Tell me what it communicates"—meaning of course "Tell me in words." But the simple inescapable fact of the situation is that what Beethoven says in those sounds cannot be told in words.

Someone observed once that art is not superfluous—by which he meant that the artist produces it to communicate something he can't communicate in any other way. You can see this most clearly in poetry: the particular images and overtones of sense and feeling from the lines

> When to the Sessions of sweet silent thought
> I summon up remembrance of things past

are communicated only by this particular assemblage of words; and you won't get them from a statement in other words like "When in hours of meditation I recall the past."

So with painting. In one of his finest essays, *Music at Night*, Aldous Huxley writes about two paintings of the Virgin, one by Piero della Francesca, the other by Tura—about how they observe the same current symbolical conventions but differ "in the forms and their arrangement, in the disposition of the lines and planes and masses," and how as a result of this pictorial difference they "say" different things. Huxley describes what he thinks those different things are; but the point of his essay

6

is that words cannot really tell us what the two paintings "say," and that we can learn this only from the paintings—from Piero's "welding together of smooth and beautifully balanced solidities," from Tura's intricate lines and writhing surfaces—themselves.

This is true also of the grave, powerful, massive emotions to which, says Roger Fry, we are compelled by a Cézanne still-life—by the way a few apples and pears, commonplace objects entirely without emotional associations, are "reduced to pure elements of space and volume" and "coordinated and organized by the artist's sensual intelligence." That is, Fry can describe those emotions as grave, powerful and massive; but we can discover what they really are only from that organization of elements of space and volume on the canvas.

So with the piece of music, an organization of sounds which don't, like words, refer to external objects, but do have internal coherences that are meaningful to an ear sensitized to them. Huxley's example in his essay is the *Benedictus* of Beethoven's *Missa Solemnis;* and he says correctly that it is a statement about the blessedness at the heart of things, but that no words can give us any knowledge of what Beethoven felt this blessedness to be—that we can learn this only from the music.

Actually, Cézanne compels us to those grave, powerful, massive emotions not just with one painting of apples and pears but with many; and the state of inner illumination and superearthly exaltation that Beethoven attained in his last years is communicated to us not just in one piano sonata or string quartet but in a number of works. And from this you may understand that our interest in a work of art is an interest not just in its meaning but in this meaning as embodied, made explicit in the organized detail of the work of art, and as newly and differently embodied and made explicit in the organized detail of each work of art. We are interested in those grave, powerful, massive emotions as they are communicated by each different painting of apples and pears by

7

Cézanne; in that state of inner illumination and superearthly exaltation as it is communicated by each different piano sonata or string quartet of Beethoven.

If then you don't understand what Beethoven "says" it is because the sounds he uses are not a meaningful language for you; and the thing to do is to learn this language as you would any other. If you enjoy the music of Kern and Rodgers that is because its musical language is the one you do understand—the one you learned, as you did English, by hearing it from earliest childhood. Probably, if you had heard Beethoven as early, as much, and as long as Kern and Rodgers you would understand him as well; and if you want to acquire an understanding of Beethoven's vocabulary and ideas (for actually his language is the basic one of all Western music, popular and serious) you will have to live with them and get to know them as well as those of Kern and Rodgers.

Which is to say that you will have to listen to Beethoven's music, and keep listening. That, fortunately, is all you will have to do: music is easier than French in this respect. With French you have to learn the things the words refer to, and the grammar that organizes them in statements; but the meaning of a statement by Beethoven is an internal coherence of the sounds that you will apprehend directly from them by listening to them, or not at all.

And so try the experiment of listening to the beginning of the third movement of Beethoven's Trio Op. 97 (*Archduke*)—just the two statements of the piano that are echoed by the violin and cello, no more; and just once. Listen to it once again the next night, and every night for a week or two or as long as you care to continue the experiment. The passage may say as little to you after a month as it did the first night—in which case you will have to accept the fact that Beethoven and you are not for each other. But on the other hand it may, one of those nights, suddenly come alive for you and begin to make a definite though indefinable sense; and this will be the beginning of an understanding of music, the opening up

8

of a new world of artistic experience as rich and stimulating as that of literature or painting. One thing is certain, however: if you don't get the meaning of Beethoven's statement from the statement, you won't get it from anything else.

There are some whose disappointing experiences with music lead them to argue that a piece of music must have within itself the evidence of its having been produced by a certain human being in a certain time and place, and to conclude from this that if they were told something about the composer and his period they would be better able to understand his music. And there are books which "treat music in the terms of the men who created it." Now certainly the Cézanne painting of a few apples and pears was not produced by a disembodied ability to put paint on canvas: each of the countless decisions to choose *this* bit of paint and place it in *that* relation to the other bits on the canvas was a decision by the whole man, involving all his experience, thought, emotion, insight, and involving also the ideas about painting, the general ideas, and all the other things that had influenced him as a human being and artist. And certainly this was true of the Shakespeare sonnet from which I quoted a couple of lines. But the result in the end was an organization of elements of space and volume on the canvas, an organization of words on the page; and to know what was involved in the process is not the same thing as to experience the effect of the painting or the sonnet that resulted from the process; nor is it necessary or helpful in experiencing that effect. The effect is produced on one's mind by the organization of pictorial elements on the canvas, the organization of words on the page, and by nothing else; and one experiences it solely by looking at the one and reading the other. Similarly, whatever the biographical and historical influences involved in the process that produced the opening statement in the third movement of Beethoven's *Archduke* Trio, the result of the process was an organization of sounds with an effect which you can experience not by reading about the biographical

9

and historical influences but only by listening to the organization of sounds in the statement.

To repeat: just as the way to understand a poem is to read it, and the way to understand a painting is to look at it, so the way—the only way—to understand a piece of music is to listen to it, and to keep listening.

This is also the way to deal with the difficulty that arises when you listen beyond the opening statement in a piece of music. A poem lies before you on the page; and you can read each line as slowly and as many times as you need for the rhythmed sound, the images, the overtones of sense and feeling to register on your mind. A painting hangs before you on the wall; and you can look at it as long as you need to take in all the details and their organization and be affected by them. But the sounds of a piece of music succeed each other in time—too quickly for your ear to catch some of the details or your mind to grasp them fully and relate them to others; with the result that instead of a coherent succession you may hear only a number of unconnected fragments. And the remedy for this is again to keep listening.

One way is to listen to the entire piece: with each hearing you will catch more of the details you missed and fit them into their places in what will become an increasingly coherent succession. Another way is to listen to the opening statement— of, for example, that third movement of the Beethoven trio— and then to a little more, repeatedly, until this additional passage is familiar and makes sense not only by itself but in relation to the first part; and to keep adding a little at a time to what you already know, until you know the entire piece.

If you want help—the help that will point out the details your ear may have missed, the large formal design you may not have been aware of—and if you want this help from a book, then you will have to do something that will cost more effort. For you will come up against a major difficulty for both the writer and the reader of a book about music—the difficulty of correlating printed word with living sound.

A statement about a passage of music which the reader hasn't heard can have no more real meaning for him than a statement about a line of poetry he hasn't read or a detail of a painting he hasn't seen. But whereas the writer can quote the line of poetry or reproduce the detail of the painting, he cannot provide the sound of the passage in the symphony. The only thing he can do is to help the reader to find it on a phonograph record, giving the passage in musical notation to make it easier to recognize and grasp. This isn't easy for the writer even when it is possible; and it calls for effort by the reader. But if the effort isn't made the statement is just words, which the reader can repeat, but without really knowing what he is talking about.

And so if you want to know more than you can discover by your own listening, you can read the next two chapters; but then you will have to make the effort involved in hearing as you read. If that effort is more than the additional knowledge is worth, you can skip the next two chapters.

3

MUSICAL PROCEDURES

AND THE FORMS THEY PRODUCE

"What she wants other people to know," Edmund Wilson wrote once about a novelist, "she imparts to them by creating an object, the self-developing organism of a work of prose." What a composer wants other people to know he too imparts to them by creating an object, this one the self-developing organism of a work of musical sound. What kind of object and organism, created out of what substance and by what procedures, you can discover by listening to examples; and two good ones to begin with are Bach's *Passacaglia* and the Prelude to Wagner's music-drama *Tristan und Isolde*.

You can, if you wish, merely listen to them in the ways I described in the last chapter—all the way through repeatedly, or a little at a time—and become increasingly aware of what happens in the course of each piece. Or you may want me to point out what happens—in which case you will have to do a little more than just listen: you will have to gear your listening with my statements, and for this purpose have your eye follow musical notation as your ear follows the sound, the more easily to grasp the musical detail and fix it in your mind.

Even if you intend to follow the second course of action it is a good thing to begin by listening straight through the two pieces to get an idea of certain general characteristics. For one thing, that the object is made of sound which progresses in time (hence the term *movement* of a symphony), and which conveys meaning of the indefinable kind I discussed earlier. Hence that the progression in time reveals gradually not only a developing form in sound but a developing meaning—a train of musical thought. And that the object in the end has a size and weight commensurate with the magnitude of the thought it embodies.

The next step is to listen to detail and observe by what operations the object is produced and the thought proceeds. Listening again to Bach's *Passacaglia* you can this time hear that the grave opening statement

is repeated—and not just once but a second time, a third, a fourth (stop here for the moment). And you discover from this that musical thought, unlike the thought of prose, proceeds by repeating itself—in some instances by repeating itself exactly.

Having said this I must add a qualification. The opening statement of the *Passacaglia* is repeated without change; but each time you hear something new with it, which makes the repetition a *variation*—the same thing said in a different way. Here are the repeated statement and different accompanying material of the first four variations:

Variation 1

theme marked by asterisks

This progression in terms of a melodic figure is *figuration*.

Variation 2. Continuation of the figuration of Variation 1.

13

Variation 3

Variation 4

The *Passacaglia*, then, is produced by the operation of the variation procedure, and is one of the *variation forms*—the one with a continuous succession of variations on a brief repeated theme called the *ground-bass* (though it doesn't stay in the bass).

Another thing you discover from these first variations is that music, unlike prose, can say more than one thing at a time, and that what you hear most often is not a line of sound but a texture. When there are several clearly defined lines or *voices* moving at the same time, as in these variations, you have *counterpoint*, and the texture is *contrapuntal*. And at any point in the progression if you read vertically instead of horizontally the combination of sounds at that point is a *chord*, and the succession of chords is *harmony*.

Still another thing to observe in these first variations is that while the theme maintains its unvarying form and pace, the varying accompanying material becomes increasingly animated, and its texture increasingly dense and complex, with a resulting effect of increasing momentum and intensity. The cumulative impact of the repeated ground-bass, the crescendo

14

of intensity in the accompanying material—these together produce the effect of the passacaglia form.

When now you listen further in Bach's *Passacaglia* you discover that the intensity doesn't increase in one single unbroken crescendo—that it is alternately built up and lessened, until it is eventually carried to a concluding maximum.

In Variation 5 it is lessened:

theme itself varied

Also the figuration is carried into the ground-bass itself; and thus you discover that the theme itself can be varied.

But in Variation 6 the ground-bass is unvaried again, and the flowing accompanying material begins to build up the intensity that is further increased by the denser textures of Variations 7 and 8.

In Variation 9:

theme itself varied

the figuration is again carried into the ground-bass itself; and the momentarily lessened intensity builds up to the force of Variation 10.

In Variation 11 you hear the ground-bass transferred for the first time to an upper voice, with a single line of flowing accompanying material down below. Additional voices create

15

a denser texture and greater urgency in Variation 12; but there is sudden quiet in Variation 13:

in which the intricate texture varies, envelopes, and obscures the ground-bass.

In Variation 14:

the quiet continues, the figuration in which the ground-bass is involved is simpler.

In Variation 15:

the quiet becomes hushed, the figuration even simpler.

16

The hush is broken by Variation 16:

in which the ground-bass is unvaried and forceful below the explosive figuration. The intensity is maintained in Variation 17, with its brilliant accompanying figuration, and further in Variation 18:

Then, in Variation 19:

the intensity begins to increase; and in Variation 20, with its denser textures, the crescendo of intensity builds up to its maximum point in the powerful conclusion.

When the thunderous final chord of the *Passacaglia* breaks off you hear the first half of the ground-bass once more. Over it Bach has written in the score *Thema fugatum*, which tells you that the theme, after having been subjected to the procedure of variation in a passacaglia, is now to be subjected to the procedure of *fugue* in a fugue. That procedure is to discuss a theme in several lines of thought that proceed simultaneously —which means that fugue is a contrapuntal procedure, and the fugue a contrapuntal form. The theme discussed is the *subject;* the lines of thought are *voices;* and a fugue is in two or three or four or more voices.

17

The fugue which follows Bach's *Passacaglia* is in four voices; and the discussion begins with an *exposition* in which one by one the voices enter with a statement of the subject. Usually the first voice enters alone; then, when the second enters with the subject, the first continues with the *countersubject;* then, when the third enters with the subject, the second continues with the countersubject, and the first with material that fits in with both; and so on. In the present example the subject is stated even the first time with the countersubject; and each time the voice that had the subject continues with the countersubject, while the voice that had the countersubject continues with a second countersubject.

Here is the sequence of entries in the exposition of this fugue of Bach:

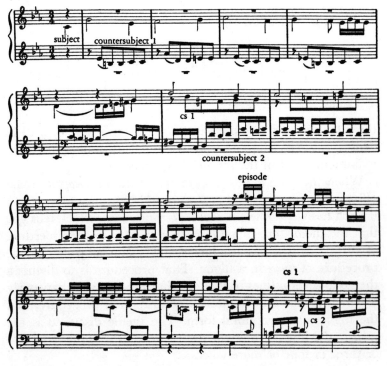

You will have noticed how again, with the increasing animation and density of the contrapuntal texture as the voices enter, there is increasing intensity. And in the further course of the discussion you will hear the alternate building up and lessening of intensity that you hear in the *Passacaglia*.

Something else to notice is the momentary digression, here called an *episode*, after the second statement of the subject, which delays the third statement and adds to its effect when it arrives. This effect of the return to what was departed from is an important one in music, as you now discover when you listen to the further course of the discussion in Bach's fugue— i.e. to the further statements of the subject separated by episodes—and hear the increasing impact of the return to the subject after each longer and weightier episode, and the climactic effect of the last return to a statement of the subject which develops into a great concluding summation, or *coda*.

19

And now let us consider the other piece from which you were to discover how music operates and what the operations produce. The Prelude to *Tristan und Isolde* is the musical equivalent of a prologue spoken before the curtain rises to inform and prepare you for the drama that is to come—which is to say, a preliminary statement and discussion of several musical themes that will figure prominently in the course of the music-drama. Two of these themes are heard in the opening statement of the Prelude:

There is a pause; then the statement is repeated—not exactly, like the theme of Bach's *Passacaglia*, but with a change—at a higher level of pitch:

The effect of this change is to qualify the original meaning of the statement, to develop it, to carry the musical thought further—as against the variation's saying the same thing in a different way.

Again there is a pause; then another, distended, more forceful repetition at a still higher level of pitch, developing the thought further:

Another pause; then [2] of the last statement is repeated:

then only its concluding two notes—first by the violins:

then by the flutes:

and finally, very emphatically, by the entire orchestra, which carries the line of thought to a momentary conclusion:

Out of the opening statement, then, there has been elaborated, by the procedure of repetition with modification, a musical paragraph—the beginning of an organism which now extends itself by the same procedure as new ideas enter and are developed.

Thus, with the conclusion of the first paragraph this idea:

is developed:

and then is qualified by a new idea and its development:

to the point where another idea enters and is developed:

and continues with this:

And now [3] returns (oboe, clarinets, horn) with increasing sonority and intensity, to bring this second line of thought to its momentary conclusion.

There is a pause in which [3] is reflected on:

These reflections increase in urgency and are carried to an emphatic conclusion; at which point [4] re-enters (oboe, English horn) to set the progression of thought in motion again.

As before, [4] continues with [5] (flute, oboe, English horn, clarinet), whose developments, increasing in intensity, again lead to the re-entrance of [3] (violins, cellos), which also increases in intensity, to the point where the intensity lessens as a new idea enters:

Its developments bring references to [2] (horn, English horn), and work up to the impassioned re-entrance once more of [3] (strings), which now in turn works up to increasingly powerful proclamations of [1] (horns) and [2] (trumpets). This is the climax of the discussion; and from the point of maximum intensity it subsides into quiet recollections of the opening statements, which eventually lead to a hushed transitional passage (cellos and basses) and a pause for the rise of the curtain.

In this piece you have heard one idea stated and repeated with modification to the point where another idea was stated and repeated with modification to the point where still another was so stated and repeated, and so on in the progression of the self-developing organism. Also, you have heard again, as in the Bach fugue, ideas returned to after being departed from, and the end, after the climax, return full circle to the quiet statements of the beginning. These are things you will hear in most of the music you will encounter. But usually with this difference: that the circular deployment of the material of the organism will have a more clearly defined schematic pattern—the pattern of one or another of the forms we shall examine in the next chapter, which may be called *cyclical* forms (in accordance with the dictionary definition of *cycle*).

The Prelude to *Tristan* has demonstrated that there is form in music that is purely organic, like the form of prose. But the pieces you will hear in the next chapter will demonstrate that there are also the forms of music that are schematic, like the forms of poetry.

The schematic patterns are something for you to be aware of, as you are aware of the pattern of a sonnet. But there is a danger of thinking of form in music as being only schematic pattern. And I had you listen to the Prelude to *Tristan* to make you aware of form as something organic, and to impress upon you the necessity—when you are listening to a piece that is in a schematic form—of taking in all the organically related substance that deploys itself within the schematic pat-

23

tern, as you take in all the organically related substance that deploys itself within the pattern of the sonnet.

And there is one other thing to impress upon you. Someone told me once how at college he had found the first quarter-inch of a number of records almost destroyed by all the students who had played that much and no more in preparation for theme identification in their music appreciation courses. A few themes were all that these students got to know of those pieces of music, and all they thought there was to know about any piece of music; and other people have got the same idea from books like the one that offered the themes of a number of symphonies as "just what the listener wants to know, and all that he, lay or expert, *needs* to know: the stuff of which symphonies are made." What your guided tour through the Bach *Passacaglia* and the Prelude to *Tristan* should have made clear is that you must hear not only the themes but what is elaborated out of them and what happens between them.

4

MUSICAL FORMS—II

The simplest cyclical form is one with only one cycle—one departure and return. It can be expressed as *A B A;* and it is called *ternary form* or *three-part song form.* If you listen straight through the second movement of Schubert's String Quintet Op. 163 you will hear a succession of three large sections: the first slow and quietly sustained, the second agitated and vehement, but quieting down at the end for the repetition of— which is to say, the return to—the first.

Something else to notice is that there is also a cycle of keys: the first section is in E major; * the second in F minor; and when it quiets down it maneuvers a return to E major in the third section. Because there is this organization of—and by—keys in the cyclical forms, they are also *harmonic forms.*

And now when you listen the second time give your attention entirely to the substance that deploys itself within the cyclical pattern—the substance that makes the movement one

---

* C major:

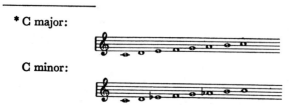

C minor:

The two series of sounds thus related in the major and minor scales can begin with **D** or **E** or any other note.

25

of the most sublime and most affecting utterances in all music. As the movement begins:

notice the dense and rich texture, which is extraordinary and possibly unique (I can't at the moment recall anything like it); and notice also how this texture works—how, as the sustained melody and harmony of the second violin, viola and first cello progress, their meaning is amplified and intensified by the brief expressive figures of the first violin, the plucked notes of the second cello. And when, after the vehement middle section, there is the return to the opening section:

notice that the first violin and the second cello now play intensifying variations of their original parts, which transform the brief figures of the one into passages of the utmost poignancy, and the plucked notes of the other into passages of great dramatic force. Eventually the variations subside into the original figures and plucked notes for the conclusion of the movement.

And so from this piece you learn that the variation procedure is sometimes applied to the repetitions in cyclical forms.

Our next piece of music, the third movement of Mozart's *Eine kleine Nachtmusik*, illustrates one of the ways the cyclical pattern we have just considered can be less simple: each section of the large cycle *A B A* is itself a smaller cycle; and the pattern of the movement can be expressed as

$$A \qquad B \qquad A$$
$$\overline{a\ b\ a} \quad \overline{c\ d\ c} \quad \overline{a\ b\ a}$$

More exactly, the movement is a *minuet with trio* (accept the term *trio* without the historical reason for it); and with the cycle of keys, and the traditional repetitions of the smaller

27

sections in the performances you will hear, the pattern becomes

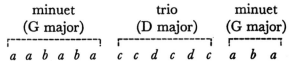

	minuet (G major)				trio (D major)					minuet (G major)		
a	a	b	a	b	a	c	c	d	c	d	c	a	b	a

As you listen, then, you hear first *a:*

which is repeated; then *b:*

leads back to *a;* after which *b* is repeated, and again leads back to *a*.

Now the trio, in which *c:*

is repeated; then *d:*

leads back to *c;* after which *d* is repeated, and again leads back to *c*.

And now the minuet again, without repetitions.

I have used this simple, small-scale example because it exhibits the pattern so clearly and can be given in full detail. Now listen to the third movement of Schubert's String Quar-

28

tet Op. 29, a more expansive and elaborate example—elaborate, among other things, in the wonderful shifts, or *modulations*, of key that are characteristic of Schubert. Because it is more elaborate I can give you only the beginning of each section and let your ear go on from there to complete it.

This is how *a* of the minuet begins, in A minor:

a is repeated; then *b*:

builds up to a climax and pause for the return to *a*. But when [1] is heard from the cello this time, it is with the D changed to D sharp, which brings the breathtaking surprise of C sharp minor instead of the original A minor for [2], after which there is a shift back to A minor. *b* is repeated, and again returns to *a*.

Now *c* of the trio, beginning in A major:

29

c is repeated; then *d:*

1st violin   etc.

which after several shifts of key returns to the A major of *c*, though not to its opening statement. *d* is repeated, and again returns to the A major of *c*.

And now the minuet again, completing the large cycle.

Our next piece of music, Mozart's Rondo K.511 for piano, illustrates another way in which the cyclical pattern can be less simple: the piece comprises not one cycle but two; and the pattern can be expressed as *A B A C A*, with *A* each time in the key of A minor, *B* in the key of F major, and *C* in the key of A major. Each of these sections, moreover, is itself a smaller cycle; and a coda sums up at the end. The complete scheme, then, is

$$
\begin{array}{cccccc}
A & B & A & C & A & \text{Coda} \\
\overline{a\ b\ a} & \overline{c\ d\ c} & \overline{\text{only } a} & \overline{e\ f\ e} & \overline{a\ b\ a} &
\end{array}
$$

And you hear first *a* stating the exquisitely contoured and poignant melody which the piece keeps departing from and coming around back to (hence the term *rondo*):

p   *cresc.*   etc.

Then *b* develops the thought in C major:

mf   etc.

returning to *a* and A minor—but to an *a* with its contours elaborated and its poignancy intensified by the variation

30

procedure:

and this is the point at which to mention that the return is made each time to a new variation of the original *a*.

Now *B:*

which ranges extensively through its cycle of substance and keys before returning to another variation of *a*.

And now *C:*

which ranges even more extensively through its cycle of substance and keys before returning to still another variation of *a*. And the successive variations of *a* that you hear in this last cycle of *A* reach a maximum of impassioned intensity in this final one:

After which you hear last references to *a* in the coda's concluding summation.

Our next piece of music is the first movement of Mozart's *Eine kleine Nachtmusik*, to illustrate another way in which the single large cycle may be less simple than the one we began with.

In the first section of the cycle you hear a sequence of ideas and their developments. First an opening fanfare:

31

which claims attention for

which pauses expectantly for

which is broken into by this transition:

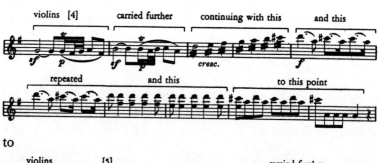

to

which leads to

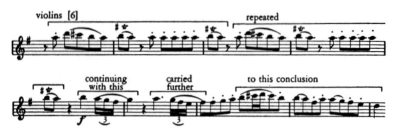

which is repeated and extended:

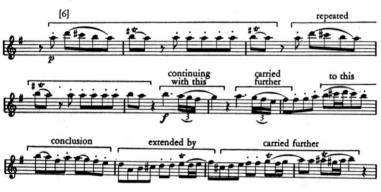

after which this:

concludes the sequence, which may be repeated in its entirety, but usually is not in performances nowadays.

In the second section of the cycle some of the ideas of the first, taken out of their original context, yield new developments which combine with new ideas to form a new sequence of organically related substance. Thus the opening fanfare:

now claims attention for

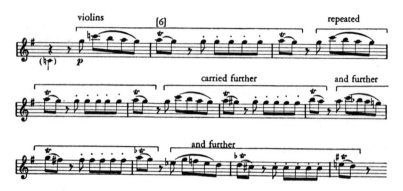

and then

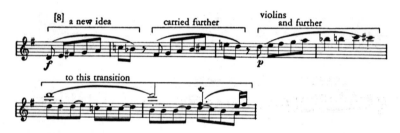

prepares you for the return to

which begins the restatement, with slight modifications, of the sequence of ideas and their developments in the first section.

At the end of this restatement [7] is changed and extended:

and leads to a little concluding flourish:

In this cycle the section in which the ideas are first stated and developed is the *exposition;* the section in which some of them are further developed is the *development;* the section which restates the ideas and developments of the exposition is the *recapitulation;* and the extension of [7] at the end of the recapitulation is the beginning of a little coda.

It is the middle section, with its development of ideas from the first section, that provides one difference from the simple cycle we considered first. And another difference is the cycle of keys: the exposition, beginning in G major, modulates to the *dominant* key, D major (the point of modulation being the C sharp in the transition from [4] to [5]); the development modulates further—to C major, A minor, G minor—until in its last two measures the dominant of G major (the chord on the fifth step of the scale) prepares you for the return of that key with the recapitulation; and the movement now remains in G major to its conclusion.

As before, I have used the simple, small-scale example from *Eine kleine Nachtmusik* because it exhibits the pattern so clearly and can be given in full detail. Now listen to the first movement of Schubert's Piano Sonata Op. 78, in which the cycle, by virtue of its scale and expressive content, is in effect a dramatic narrative, with the exposition presenting the elements of the drama, the development presenting their dramatic involvements, the recapitulation of the original substance of the exposition having the effect of a resolution of those involvements, and the coda providing final conclusions.

The implications of the tranquilly, spaciously meditative opening statement, in G major:

35

are developed for some time; then a more animated statement, in D major:

is developed with increasing liveliness to moments of force,
which break off for quiet statements again:

and the meditative tranquility of the exposition is established
with seeming finality by the references to [1]:

which bring it to a close.

We are, therefore, entirely unprepared for what we hear
now in the development: the meditative opening statement
with the iron-like power it acquires from being hammered
out fortissimo in G minor, the tensions this creates in its
rhythm, the tensions in the imitations of this rhythm by bare
octaves in the bass, the eruptions of these octaves that carry
the passage up to a proclamation tremendous in its sonority
and distentions. The tension is relaxed momentarily in a quiet
development of [2], only to be built up as before to a similar
climax, and to be relaxed again in a similar quiet interlude.
Then treble and bass octaves in imitation hammer out that
development of [2] with increasing intensity, which suddenly
relaxes in another quiet and poignant development of [2]; and
this eventually brings the return to [1] for the recapitulation

36

of the original substance of the exposition, now entirely in G major, and the more affecting for the dramatic involvements that have intervened. The sequence ends, as before, with [4]; after which the brief coda builds up last references to [1] into a powerful concluding summation.

This three-part cycle is the distinguishing feature of the grouping of movements which achieved definition at the hands of Haydn and Mozart, and which was given different names in accordance with the instruments it was written for: *sonata*, when it was written for one instrument or two; *trio*, when it was written for three; *quartet*, when it was written for four; *symphony*, for the then newly standardized symphonic orchestra that we know; *concerto*, for a solo instrument and orchestra. The cycle is therefore referred to as *sonata form;* but since it is the normally prescribed form for the first movement, it is also referred to as *first-movement form;* and since the first movement is normally in quick tempo, for which the Italian direction *allegro* is used, it is also referred to as *sonata-allegro form*. The terminology is inaccurate and confusing, since sonata form is not the form of the entire sonata or symphony but only the normal form of its first movement; since it may also occur in other movements; and since one of these may be the slow movement of the work. And there is further confusion in the fact that the sonata, symphony, trio, quartet and the rest constitute *the sonata forms*.

In one of *the sonata forms* of Mozart or Haydn we find three or four movements—that is, separate and complete organisms, unrelated in substance (the carrying over of themes from one movement to another is begun by Beethoven), diverse in character, yet bound together in one way that we shall see in a moment, and intended to complement each other and produce the effect of a single artistic experience. The diversity is in part one of tempo: normally the first movement is fast, though sometimes preceded by a slow introduction; the second is slow; the last is again fast; **and** when there are four

37

movements a minuet with trio—later a faster *scherzo with trio*—precedes the last movement, though sometimes it precedes the slow movement. What binds the movements together is key: in addition to the unifying cycle of keys in each movement there is a unifying cycle of keys in the group of movements. Thus, the first movement of *Eine kleine Nachtmusik* is a cycle which begins and ends in G major; the second movement is in the same way in C major; the minuet movement is again in G major; and so is the finale. In Schubert's Piano Sonata Op. 78 the cycle of keys is G major, D major, B minor and G major; in his Quartet Op. 29 it is A minor, C major, A minor and A major (a work in a minor key sometimes ends in major).

The forms used in the movements are for the most part the cyclical forms we have been examining in this chapter. The distinguishing feature of the sonata forms is the cyclical first-movement form, or sonata form, or sonata-allegro form normally prescribed for the first movement; and prescribed for the minuet or scherzo movement is the cyclical minuet or scherzo with trio. The other movements have more latitude: in the slow movement we find sometimes simple ternary form, sometimes first-movement form; in the finale sometimes a rondo, sometimes first-movement form. Moreover, cyclical forms are not the only ones that are used: sometimes we find a slow movement or finale in variation form.

The only variation form we have examined is the passacaglia; and of this one there is only one example in the literature of the sonata forms: the finale of Brahms's Symphony No. 4. It has one interesting feature: the return of the theme after Variation 15; the return of Variations 1, 2 and 3 after Variation 23; and the return of the theme a second time at the beginning of the coda—all of which introduce a cyclical element into the variation form.

The variation form that you will encounter more frequently in the sonata forms is the one called *theme and variations*, in which the theme that is varied is not a single brief statement

38

but a longer sequence of statements. The third movement of Beethoven's *Archduke* Trio, the first piece of music I suggested you listen to, provides an example.

The theme, as usual, is in two parts, the second of which answers and completes the first. The first is played by the piano:

and repeated by the violin and cello. Then the second is played by the piano:

with only its conclusion repeated by the strings. And there are similar repetitions of the two parts in each of the variations which elaborate the theme in different figurations.

Here is the beginning of Variation 1:

Then Variation 2:

39

Then Variation 3:

Then Variation 4:

And now there is a return to the theme, with the effect such a return has after intervening involvements. But as the theme proceeds this time it is altered by the change of the original F sharp to F natural:

and by further changes in the second part, which expands into an extensive, wide-ranging coda with implications of summation that reach sublime conclusions.

This is an example of the introduction of the cyclical element into a variation form by the return to the theme at the end. And another example of this that you might listen to is the concluding variation movement of Beethoven's Piano Sonata Op. 109, in which the last variation—extraordinary in the increasing momentum of its increasingly rapid figuration that finally effloresces into trills—subsides into a simple restatement of the sublime theme.

Beethoven also provides impressive examples of the combination of variation and cyclical form in which the theme and its variations alternate with a recurring statement or section that remains unvaried. One of these examples is the exalted third movement of the Ninth Symphony.

After a couple of introductory measures you hear

which is the first in a sequence of statements that constitute the theme. Its conclusion leads to

which in turn leads back to a variation of the theme:

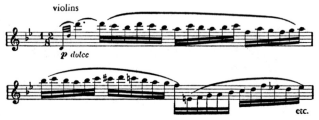

Again [2], unchanged except that it is in G major instead of D major. When it ends you expect the second variation of the theme; what comes instead is a fugal discussion of [1a], which ranges widely before it finally leads to the variation you expected:

41

And this time the conclusion of the variation leads to this solemn call:

which introduces the extensive final summation of the coda.

You have just had an example of a fugal episode occurring in a movement of one of the sonata forms; and you will find other such episodes in the second movement of Beethoven's Seventh Symphony, the second and last movements of his *Eroica* Symphony. And not only episodes but entire movements: his Piano Sonatas Op. 106 (*Hammerklavier*) and Op. 110 end with fugues; his Quartet Op. 131 begins with one.

In addition, the second and last movements of the *Eroica* provide extraordinarily impressive demonstrations of something that has been evident in the other pieces of music I have presented—in the occurrence of the cyclical element in the fugue, of the variation procedure in cyclical forms. That something is the freedom with which the organism operates within the schematic pattern.

Strictly speaking, the second movement of the *Eroica* is in ternary form; but it is ternary form that is considerably more than *A B A*—the more being what happens after *B*. You hear, then, a gigantic opening section (*A*), beginning, in C minor, with

continuing with

and ending with

then the middle section (B), in C major:

and a return to [1], which leads not to [2] and [3] but to this powerful fugal episode:

which builds up a tremendous climax that breaks off for a momentary reference to [1]. This too is broken into by another forceful outburst, which eventually quiets down into a poignant accompanying figure for [1]:

which this time does continue with [2] and [3]—the ternary pattern being completed at last. And the end of [3] brings

43

the beginning of a sequence of affecting details in an unusually extensive coda.

And so with the last movement. After a boisterous introductory passage you hear a two-part theme:

followed by several variations. Then the theme is combined with a new two-part melody:

which leads to a fugal discussion of a subject derived from the theme:

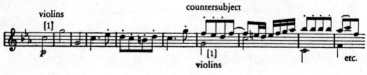

This reaches a climax which breaks off for the return of [2], which then is varied. The variation builds up to a vigorous statement of [1] in combination with a new tune:

This is developed and brought to a conclusion; then you hear [2] again, leading to another fugal discussion—this time of [1] inverted:

It is carried to a climax and a conclusion; then, after a pause, comes a melody which you recognize as [2] made solemn and sublime by the slow tempo and poignant harmonization. It is repeated in grandly proclamatory style; then there is a quiet transition to

another variation of [2], which builds up to a climax that breaks off for the hush before the joyous outburst that brings this extraordinary movement to an end.

To these two examples I add one more: the great concluding variation movement of Beethoven's Piano Sonata Op. 111. After the wonderful theme:

45

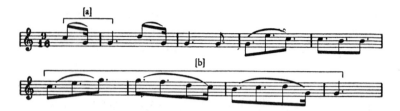

you hear a series of variations which eventually build up to a halt on a sustained trill with references to [a]:

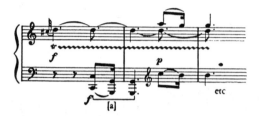

This is the beginning of a wide-ranging digression—concerned with [a], then with [b]—which eventually ends in a return to the theme, heard now over fast-moving figuration, and gradually building up in intensity to a joyous and exalted climax that breaks off for another sustained trill—this one creating a dazzling ethereal radiance for a last superearthly statement of the theme.

These last three examples should impress on you the necessity I spoke of at the end of Chapter 3—of following attentively the detail of the organically related substance that deploys itself within the schematic pattern. It is this that makes each rondo or first movement *that* rondo or first movement and no other—or, to put it more generally, makes each piece of music unique. And your concern, in listening to music, is with the unique series of events in each particular piece of music.

46

5

BEETHOVEN

The pieces of music I presented in the preceding chapters are some of the greatest works in our musical literature. And remembering how indiscriminately the word *great* is tossed about—how anything and everything presented on the radio is "great music"—I think it advisable to establish what I mean by the word when I apply it to those pieces by Beethoven and Schubert.

In his book on Beethoven, which I recommend as collateral reading, J. W. N. Sullivan discusses Beethoven's music as an expression, in successive works, of a developing personal vision of life—that is, of developing states of consciousness that were generated in him by his external experience, conditioned by his spiritual nature, and made explicit in the terms of his art. "In his capacity to express this content," says Sullivan, "Beethoven reveals himself as a great musical genius, and the content itself reveals him as a great spirit." And concerning this he observes further that "perhaps even Shakespeare never reached that final stage of illumination that is expressed in some of Beethoven's late music."

This tells us not only what makes Beethoven's music great, but what makes the *Eroica* a greater piece of music than the First Symphony, and the Piano Sonata Op. 111 even greater than the *Eroica*. As against the First Symphony—the work of a young man confident, exuberant and untroubled in the exercise of his rich gifts—the *Eroica* is the work of one who has come to know catastrophe and suffering, and who in the blackest moments of his life has found in the resources of his own spiritual nature and creative powers the courage and strength to resist, to survive, to triumph (the heroism which the *Eroica* is concerned with is, then, as Sullivan points out, Beethoven's own). But as against this man for whom suffering is something to assert oneself against, the composer of the concluding movement of the Sonata Op. 111 is one who has come to the final realization of suffering as something to accept, in Sullivan's words, "as one of the great structural lines of human life," and who has attained "that unearthly state where the struggle ends and pain dissolves away."

Sullivan warns against a possible misinterpretation of what he says: Beethoven's music is not to be listened to as a sort of diary of daily events in his life. It tells us not his experience, but his attitude toward his experience; and not his immediate response to any and every happening of the day, but states of consciousness representing a lifetime of continuing perception and response to perception: the joyous exuberance and humor embodied in the Eighth Symphony, the exaltation communicated by the Sonata Op. 111, were not responses to the petty turmoil and wretchedness that filled Beethoven's daily existence at these times. Moreover, to Sullivan's warning I will add a reminder that we are concerned not with the joyous exuberance or the mystical exaltation itself, but with this as it is made explicit and communicated in the organized detail of the piece of music—and not just the detail of one piece of music but the constantly new and unique detail of each of a number of pieces.

The greatest Beethoven—greatest in what he says and in his use of his art to say it—is, then, heard in his last works: the last symphony, the last string quartets, the last sonatas and other pieces for piano, the *Missa Solemnis*. And we are concerned with the superearthly exaltation of his last years as it is embodied not only in the concluding movement of the Sonata Op. 111 but in the concluding movement of the Sonata Op. 109, the third movement of the Ninth Symphony. And not only these but the slow movements of the last quartets: on the one hand the expansively elaborating variation movements of Opp. 132 and 127; on the other hand the *Cavatina* of Op. 130 and the third movement of Op. 135, which exhibit the concentrated brevity of some of Beethoven's late writing (other examples of this brevity are the quietly reflective opening movement of the Sonata Op. 109, and some of the Bagatelles Opp. 119 and 126 for piano). Also the *Kyrie*, *Benedictus* and *Agnus Dei* of the *Missa Solemnis*. And other sections of the *Missa* in which, as in the final choral movement of the Ninth Symphony, the exaltation is carried to ever higher points of jubilant ecstasy.

We are concerned also with what lay behind the final illumination. For one thing, what is communicated by the *Arioso dolente* movement of the Piano Sonata Op. 110, the slow movement—tremendous in poignant expressive implications as in size—of the Piano Sonata Op. 106 (*Hammerklavier*). And for another thing, what is communicated by the grim opening movements of the Ninth Symphony, the *Hammerklavier* Sonata, and—in more concentrated fashion again—the Sonata Op. 111.

And we are, finally, concerned with those "strange seas of thought" in which—Sullivan says of the last quartets—Beethoven discovers "unsuspected islands and even continents," as we come to know them not only from some of the movements of the quartets but from the mystically introspective introduction to the *Benedictus* of the *Missa Solemnis*. And above all from passages in the *Diabelli Variations* for piano—Variation 20:

49

and the suddenly still and distant chords:

that follow the vehement fugue of Variation 32 and lead to the final apotheosis of Variation 33. These passages in the *Diabelli Variations* are perhaps the remotest points Beethoven's mind attained in the regions Sullivan speaks of.

In all these his mind can be followed without difficulty; but the *Great Fugue* Op. 133 and the concluding fugue of the *Hammerklavier* Sonata most listeners find obscure and formidable.

A great spirit and great musical genius is heard also in those two tremendous movements of the *Eroica* Symphony that were presented in Chapter 4, and in its opening movement, a dramatic progression no less tremendous in its urgency, tensions and climaxes, its developing structure, and their cumulative power. And if that great spirit moves us with the range and force of the expressive content of the works of this period, the great musician amazes us with the profusion of musical forms embodying this content, their variety, and on occasion their innovations.

Thus, what is expressed in the successive movements of the *Eroica* is expressed again in the Fifth Symphony, but with differences. The dramatic first movement is more grimly concentrated; and in later movements expressive content dictates

an innovation in structure: the dramatically hushed conclusion of the scherzo movement leads in unprecedented fashion
into the opening triumphant proclamation of the finale; and
later in the finale the development breaks off at its height for
a recapitulation of the hushed transition to the opening proclamation.

Unprecedented too are some of the things that happen in
the Piano Concerto No. 4. The audience assembled in Prince
Lobkowitz's house in March 1807 for the first performance
(with Beethoven himself at the piano) expected to hear first
the usual orchestral introduction that would secure attention
for the eventual entrance of the solo piano—instead of which
it was the piano itself that claimed attention immediately
with its spaciously meditative opening G major statement,
this surprise being followed by the surprise of the strings' B
major answer. And later came the extraordinary and unprecedented dialogue of orchestra and piano in the slow movement, leading to the piano's soliloquy, and to concluding
hushed recollections of the opening dialogue—all of which
make this brief movement one of Beethoven's most affecting
utterances.

There is then the externally imposing, monumental Beethoven of the *Eroica* and Fifth Symphonies, who is heard also
in the joyous Symphonies Nos. 4, 7 and 8; the breathtakingly
energetic finale of the Quartet Op. 59 No. 3; the grandiose
Piano Concerto No. 5 (referred to as the *Emperor*); the dramatic Piano Sonatas Opp. 53 (*Waldstein*), 57 (*Appassionata*),
and 90, Violin Sonata Op. 47 (*Kreutzer*), Quartets Op. 59
No. 2 and Op. 95. And there is the lyrical, meditative Beethoven of the Piano Concerto No. 4, who is heard also in the
Symphony No. 6 (*Pastoral*); the Piano Sonatas Opp. 54, 78
and 81a (*Les Adieux*); the Quartets Op. 59 No. 1 and Op. 74
(*Harp*); the song-cycle *An die ferne Geliebte*.

In addition there is the playful Beethoven who contrives
little surprises and jokes. For example the opening theme of
the finale of the Symphony No. 8 coasting along *pp* until it

51

collides with the *ff* C sharp; the unexpected play with that C sharp in the coda, ending with the unexpected change of key; the two places where the full orchestra breaks off, and first the flutes and strings *p*, then the bassoon and kettledrum *pp* go chortling on. Or in the finale of the Piano Concerto No. 5 the episode in the development in which the piano takes off grandly with the imposing principal theme, but gets into a sort of tailspin of faster and faster passage-work that collapses into decisively final statements of the full orchestra—whereupon the horns enter quietly with a new key in which the piano takes off with the principal theme again, only to get into the same tailspin of fast passage-work that collapses into the same final statements of the orchestra—whereupon the oboe and bassoon enter quietly with still another key in which the piano takes off a third time, only to end up in the same way.

I mentioned earlier—as against the expansiveness of the *Eroica* Symphony—the concentration in the first movement of the Fifth; and other examples are the powerfully concise *Coriolan* and *Egmont* Overtures, the fiercely concise opening movement of the Quartet Op. 95. The slow movement of the Piano Concerto No. 4 is a more unusual and striking example of this concentration and brevity; another is the slow movement of the *Waldstein* Sonata, in which the opening statement returns with an added figure in the bass that builds up tremendous tension and power (if, that is, it is played that way). But there are also remarkable examples of expansiveness to take note of: the endlessly and delightfully inventive second movement of the Quartet Op. 59 No. 1; the second movement of the Quartet Op. 59 No. 3, with a strangeness in its poignancy that leads Sullivan to speak of its "remote and frozen anguish."

The first movement of Op. 59 No. 3 begins in fact with a slow introduction, mysterious and remote, which could introduce one of the last quartets. And this brings us to several other works in which there are intimations of what is to be

52

heard in the music of Beethoven's last years: the *Archduke* Trio, whose wonderful slow movement you are already acquainted with; the Piano Sonata Op. 101 with its tranquil and lovely opening movement and profoundly reflective slow movement; the Violin Sonata Op. 96 with its similarly tranquil and lovely but rather strange first movement and the powerful slow variation in the finale; the Cello Sonata Op. 102 No. 1 with its wonderful slow introductions to the two movements; the Cello Sonata Op. 102 No. 2 with its great slow movement— especially the middle section, and the return of the opening section with the cello's comments on the piano's statements.

Interesting in this connection is the Mass in C, with startlingly beautiful and expressive passages and powerful dramatic strokes, all on the small scale of an early try at something which when attempted again years later would come out with the sustained intensity, grandeur and exaltation of the *Missa Solemnis*.

And finally Beethoven's only opera, *Fidelio*, which in this country (but not in Europe) is generally considered one of his failures, but actually has some of the greatest and most effective dramatic music after Mozart's. Not only Leonore's famous *Abscheulicher! wo eilst du hin?* introducing her noble aria *Komm, Hoffnung*, but the wonderful quartet *Mir ist so wunderbar*, the *Prisoners' Chorus*, the affecting duet *Wir müssen gleich zu Werke*, the tremendous orchestral introduction to the dungeon scene and Florestan's *Gott! welch' Dunkel hier*, the affecting duet and trio and the dramatic quartet that follow, and the sublime *O Gott! welch' ein Augenblick!* at the end.

Of the four overtures Beethoven wrote for the opera the *Leonore* No. 3, one of the most popular pieces in the orchestral repertory, has generally been thought of as the final perfected achievement of which the *Leonore* No. 2 is an earlier, imperfect version; but actually No. 2 uses much the same thematic substance in a completely achieved work that is in its own different ways fully as impressive as No. 3, with some details even more impressive. One of these is the prolonged

53

activity of the cellos and basses at the end of the slow introduction—their progression, in the last two measures, from B
natural to D flat, then back to B natural, and only then at
last to the expected C of the beginning of the Allegro portion
of the overture. Another is the more extensive development
in this portion that reaches its climax in the off-stage trumpet-
calls. And another is the omission of the recapitulation after
the trumpet-calls, in accordance with a dramatic logic which
the *Leonore* No. 3 sacrifices in completing the formal scheme.

As for Beethoven's early works, they begin with his attempts to write in the style and forms established and left to
him by his illustrious predecessors. These attempts produced
on the one hand fluent, characterless imitations like the Piano
Trio Op. 11 and the Piano Quartet or Quintet Op. 16, but
on the other hand works like the Serenade Op. 8 for string
trio in which the eighteenth-century delicacy, grace, loveliness and charm appear to represent something genuinely
felt by Beethoven himself. And also a long series of works in
which his own voice makes itself heard with increasing insistence, authority and impressiveness.

That voice is heard in the imposing slow introduction to
the Cello Sonata Op. 5 No. 2; in the vehement outbursts of
the fast movements of the Symphony No. 1; in the introspective slow movement of the Piano Concerto No. 1; in the dramatic outbursts, contrasts and silences of the first movement
of the Symphony No. 2, the elevation of its slow movement,
the explosive exuberance of its scherzo and finale. And similarly in other works—some of the piano sonatas, some of the
chamber music. In particular the String Quartets Op. 18,
with their pages of engaging writing in eighteenth-century
style, but also their pages in which Beethoven's individuality
asserts itself: the affecting slow movement of No. 1; the graceful opening of No. 3 and its lovely slow movement; the impassioned opening of No. 4, its delightful Andante scherzoso
in place of the usual slow movement, the engaging trio of its

54

minuet movement, its bustling finale; the lilting first movement of No. 5, its charming minuet and fine trio, its energetic
finale; and above all the humorous first movement, fine slow
movement, intricately cross-rhythmed scherzo, and lovely
slow introduction to the engaging finale, that make No. 6 one
of the best of these early works.

And only Beethoven's voice is heard in several outstandingly fine works that we encounter at the end of this early
period. The Piano Concerto No. 3, for example, is pure Beethoven in its powerfully dramatic first movement (e.g. the
piano's first entrance: its three upward-rushing scales ending
with the impact of cannon shots, which lead to its forceful
proclamation of the principal theme of the movement), the
expansively introspective slow movement, the dramatically
eventful finale (e.g. the episode near the end of the development, in which the orchestra's fugato breaks off for the surprise of the piano's hushed A-flat octaves, which lead to the
further surprise of the E-major statement of the principal
theme—all in preparation for the piano's last return to the
principal theme in its original key of C minor).

So with the Piano Sonata Op. 31 No. 2, characteristic in
its imposingly dramatic first movement, poignantly lyrical
slow movement, and dramatically eventful concluding perpetuum mobile. Also the Violin Sonata Op. 30 No. 3, equally
characteristic in its energetic fast movements and gracefully
wistful middle movement.

And so with the Piano Sonata Op. 31 No. 3, characteristic
of the genially relaxed and lyrical Beethoven in its grace,
warmth, good humor and bubbling high spirits. Also the
Piano Sonata Op. 28, sometimes called *Pastoral* because of its
quiet mood throughout, and much of it—especially the first
and last movements—very lovely. And the String Quintet Op.
29, of which every movement is an astonishing manifestation
of Beethoven's matured powers.

55

6

SCHUBERT

What Sullivan says of Beethoven I would say of Schubert: his music reveals him as a great spirit and great musical genius. I am aware of the generally held opinion that credits Schubert with lovely and affecting writing, but the writing of a lyricist without the powers of large-scale content and construction revealed in Beethoven's music—a lyricist whose large-scale works, then, are mere garrulously repetitive, structurally diffuse successions of lovely melodies. But in this instance, as in some others, I would say generally held opinion rests on nothing more authoritative than the unperceptive listening that started it and the inattentive listening that has kept it going—as you have discovered if you listened attentively to what actually happens in the Schubert pieces that were presented in Chapter 4.

In the minuet movement of the Quartet Op. 29, for example, there is not only some characteristically beautiful writing, but—in that unexpected shift to C sharp minor—one of those miraculously achieved intensities of loveliness and expressive force that are characteristic also of Mozart and Berlioz. They are to be heard in breathtaking succession in the last quiet passage just before the end of Mozart's G-minor Symphony, and after the first two simple phrases of the English horn's serenade in the third movement of Berlioz's *Harold in Italy;* and they occur in similar succession in the scherzo movement of Schubert's posthumous Piano Sonata in B flat, in the development section of the first movement, in the development of the first movement of the posthumous Sonata in A. And they are manifestations of powers that place Schubert with Mozart and Berlioz as one of the greatest of musical geniuses.

Similarly, the first movement of the Sonata Op. 78 offers not only, in the exposition, a characteristic example of Schubert's expansively meditative writing, but, in the development, an impressive example of the dramatic power that is no less characteristic—an example, in fact, of the iron-like power arising out of tranquil meditation that is so remarkable in Schubert. One of the most remarkable examples of this occurs in the slow movement of the posthumous Sonata in A: the recitative-like middle section that takes off quietly in a declamatory crescendo to a hair-raising climax. I can recall nothing like it anywhere in music.

And in the slow movement of the Quintet Op. 163 we hear the sublimity of other writing of Schubert's last year—most notably the opening pages of the posthumous Sonata in B flat, which communicate a final illumination such as we hear in Beethoven's last sonatas.

It is true that the first movement of the B-flat Sonata descends from the sublimity of its opening pages. But it rises again to the wonderful concluding reflections of the exposition, and to the later sublimities of the development which lead to those of the recapitulation of the opening pages. And the English critic Tovey is right in finding the weaknesses in works like this sonata to be "relaxations of their powers," and in contending that "neither Shakespeare nor Schubert will ever be understood by any critic or artist who regards their weaknesses and inequalities as proof that they are artists of less than the highest rank"; that "the highest qualities attained in important parts of a great work are as indestructible by weaknesses elsewhere as if the weaknesses were the accidents of physical ruin"; and that Schubert must be regarded, "on the strength of his important works, as a definitely sublime composer. It does not matter when, where,

57

and how he lapses therefrom: the quality is there, and nothing in its neighborhood can make it ridiculous."

That is the way to view the redundancies and diffuseness of works like the beautiful Quartet Op. 161, Piano Trio Op. 100 and Piano Sonata Op. 42. But on the other hand there are works in addition to the Quintet Op. 163 and Sonata Op. 78—works like the *Death and the Maiden* Quartet, the Piano Trio Op. 99, the posthumous Piano Sonata in C minor and Sonatas Opp. 53 and 143, the last two symphonies—which do not demand such indulgence. What they do require is the realization that Schubert's mind operates expansively, and this at all times—whether in an extended progression of thought or a single statement, and whether the utterance is tranquilly meditative or powerfully dramatic. And the further realization that this expansiveness is not slackness—that on the contrary it most frequently operates with tension, and that the result then is highly effective large-scale construction of Schubert's special kind.

Consider for example the best known of Schubert's instrumental works, the first movement of the *Unfinished Symphony*, in which generally held opinion may have caused you to hear only the occurrences of its famous melodies. I have said Schubert's mind operates expansively; all the more remarkable therefore is the fact that the single hushed opening statement of cellos and basses is enough to achieve the purpose of the extensive slow introduction of Haydn and Beethoven. The statement appears to have only that introductory purpose, for it is heard no more in the exposition: we hear next the melody of oboe and clarinet; and noteworthy at this point is how, with the unhurried pace and calm of the sustained melody, there is the movement, the momentum, the urgency that Schubert creates with the figuration and plucked notes of the strings. Noteworthy also is the fact that while the melody itself is expansive its treatment is concise, carrying it directly and quickly to a climax which breaks off for the sustained note of bassoons and horns that is the pivot for one of Schu-

bert's extraordinary shifts of key. And noteworthy again is
how, with the quiet flow now of the famous melody of the
cellos, there is the added movement and tension that Schubert
creates with the syncopated accompaniment of clarinets and
violas. Again the melody is expansive, its treatment concise,
carrying it quickly to a climax which breaks off for last quiet
reflections that bring the exposition to its close. And here we
come to another demonstration of mastery: after an exposition concerned entirely with the woodwind and cello melodies
it is the hushed opening statement of cellos and basses that
returns now to be elaborated with increasing tension into a
development of tremendous dramatic power; and noteworthy
here is the way one of the climaxes breaks off repeatedly to
recall the syncopated accompaniment of the cello melody.
The recapitulation brings a return to the comparative calm
of the woodwind and cello melodies, which has the effect of
a resolution of the great dramatic conflict in the development;
then the hushed opening statement of cellos and basses returns
once more, to be elaborated this time into a powerful coda.

I cannot imagine anything further removed from the diffuseness and slackness generally attributed to Schubert than
what is actually heard in this piece of music: the economy of
its three themes, the conciseness of their treatment, the skill
of their deployment in the formal design, the sustained tension from first note to last in this design—all of which adds up
to one of the most remarkably compact and effective pieces
of large-scale construction in the symphonic literature.

Nor is it diffuseness and slackness that we hear in the gigantic first movement of the Symphony No. 9, but rather an
enormous energy, manifesting itself in an increased expansiveness of the themes and their treatment, a sustained momentum and tension—first in the solemn introduction, then in the
animated exposition with its great pronouncement of the
trombones over the unceasingly driving movement of the second theme, then in the development in which this driving
movement builds up to tremendous climactic references to

59

the trombone pronouncement, and finally, after the recapitulation, in the coda in which group after group of the orchestra joins the huge upward rush to exalted heights. Grandeur is what the expansiveness, momentum and tension produce; and grandeur continues to be the outstanding characteristic of the subsequent movements—above all the extraordinary whirling finale. We hear something like it in the finales of the Quartets Op. 161 and *Death and the Maiden;* but in the symphony the energy and momentum are breathtaking, and the reiterated opening notes of the expansive second theme over the unceasing whirl build up to tremendous pronouncements in the exposition, development and recapitulation, and to final sublimities in one of the greatest of codas.

I have been talking until now about the greatest of Schubert's large-scale instrumental works. In addition there are large works of lesser stature which have beautiful pages—like the Fantasia Op. 159 for violin and piano, the Octet Op. 166 for strings and winds, the Quintet Op. 114 (*Trout*) for piano and strings. And there are engaging minor works like the early Sonata Op. 162 for violin and piano. Also there are the smaller-scale and more intimate examples of his mature writing for the piano, the *Moments musicaux* and Impromptus, most of them as affecting in their loveliness and melancholy as anything Schubert ever wrote. Affecting in the same way is the *Andantino varié* Op. 84 No. 1 for piano four hands; and other fine pieces in this category are the Fantasie Op. 103 and Grand Duo Op. 140.

And there are, finally, the songs. At a time when the instrumental works of Mozart and Beethoven were eliciting from the seventeen-year-old Schubert only inconsequential imitations, a poem of Goethe could elicit such evidence of astonishingly matured imaginative and musical powers as *Gretchen am Spinnrade*. And this susceptibility to poetic stimuli, activating constantly more matured powers, resulted in a steady flow of songs throughout his life. It was a flow which included, inevitably, many that were less impressive than

Gretchen: Conceding that "in his six hundred songs there is, no doubt, as Brahms said, something to be learnt from each one," Tovey points out that "*Erlkönig* and *Gretchen am Spinnrade* stand alone in four volumes of early work," and observes that "even in the later years there are songs . . . from which Brahms could have learned little but the fact that Schubert was always keeping his pen in practice, whether or not he had anything in his head at the moment." But the flow also gave us some of our most treasurable pieces of music—single songs like *Nacht und Träume, Du bist die Ruh', Der Doppelgänger, Der Tod und das Mädchen, Geheimes, Der Jüngling an der Quelle, Das Lied im Grünen,* and the great song-cycles *Die schöne Müllerin* and *Die Winterreise.*

MOZART

From the towering and expansive immensities of Beethoven and Schubert we turn to music one of whose outstanding characteristics is its subtlety in the expression of powerful meanings. We hear in Mozart's music a melancholy, passion and intensity that some of his contemporaries found disturbing, but these powerful emotions expressed with an economy and conciseness analogous to what the mathematician calls elegance—manifestations of a keenness and precision of mind which only Berlioz exhibits in comparable manner and degree. And the English critic W. J. Turner considered Mozart to be the supreme classical artist precisely because in his music intensity and passion are crystallized in the clearest, the most beautifully balanced and proportioned, and altogether flawless musical forms.

Nobody has written with anything like Turner's wonderfully illuminating insight about the special qualities of Mozart's music and the ambiguities they create. For example about the "still, unplumbed melancholy underlying even his brightest and most vivacious moments." Or about the vital energy in which Turner doubts Mozart was exceeded by any other composer: the finale of Beethoven's Seventh Symphony, he contends, produces a bigger volume of noise, but not the quick, tense rush of Mozart's Overture to *The Marriage of Figaro*—the one being like the rumble of thunder, the other like the flash of lightning. "Its effect upon the mind," Turner says of the overture, "is out of all proportion to its impinge-ment on the senses"—something that is true of all of Mozart's music.

It may not be true for some listeners accustomed to the luxuriance and vehemence of Wagner and Strauss; but for others—after that luxuriance—the effect of Mozart's music is the greater for its economy and subtlety. For these listeners there is no need of waiting for Wagner and Strauss: they find Mozart completely adequate for every demand of the drama he is setting. They find this so when they listen to the orches-tra's comments in Leporello's *Catalogue Aria* in *Don Giovanni:* to the discreetly mischievous detached notes of the violins, answered by cellos and basses, at the beginning; the erup-tions of the violins and woodwinds, like bursts of laughter, a moment later; still later the suave phrase with which the violins punctuate *son già mille e tre;* after this the quiet ascend-ing scale of cellos and basses, answered by the descending scale of violins, both like repressed laughter over *In Italia sei cento e quaranta;* and so on. Or the grandly impassioned and lamenting phrases of Donna Anna's *Fuggi, crudele,* the abrupt, energetic and bold phrases of orchestra and singer in Donna Elvira's *Ah chi mi dice mai:* what more modern music could place each character on the stage more effectively? Or Don Giovanni's *Là ci darem la mano:* could Wagner or Strauss have achieved anything as elegantly seductive? Or the solemn D-minor chords with which the overture begins; then the omi-nous dotted rhythm of the strings over which sustained wood-wind chords lead to the poignant figure developed by the violins and interrupted by the vehement outbursts of the en-tire orchestra; then the powerful ascending scale passages, again over the ominous dotted rhythm that continues through the final measures which—first forceful, then quiet—lead to the Allegro portion of the overture: the Prelude to *Tristan und Isolde* does not establish the atmosphere for the drama to come, does not take possession of the listener's mind and emo-tions, more quickly and completely.

63

There are comparable things in *Così fan Tutte:* in the first act the quintet *Di scrivermi ogni giorno!,* the trio *Soave sia il vento,* the aria *Come scoglio;* in the second act the duets *Secondate, aurette amiche* and *Il core vi dono,* the aria *Per pietà,* the duet *Fra gli amplessi.* And in *The Magic Flute:* the ensembles involving the Three Ladies, the ones involving the Three Boys, the arias of the Queen of the Night, Tamino's *Dies Bildnis ist bezaubernd schön,* Pamina's *Ach, ich fühl's,* the trio *Soll ich dich, Teurer, nicht mehr seh'n?,* the fugato of Tamino and the Two Armed Men, Tamino's and Pamina's *Pamina/Tamino mein! O welch' ein Glück!*

But wonderful as all these are, they are surpassed by what is heard in *The Marriage of Figaro:* the three-hour outpouring of incandescent invention—miraculous in its varied loveliness, expressiveness, characterization, dramatic point and wit— that is one of the supreme wonders achieved on this earth by human powers. Nor do I mean only the vocal invention: *Figaro* surpasses the other operas in orchestral writing of the kind I have described in the *Catalogue Aria*—with its three-hour running fire of comment that creates the atmosphere of comedy in which even the serious things happen. And in this connection I will mention Tovey's observation that in the G-minor Symphony Mozart's musical language is, as it is in fact everywhere else, that of operatic comedy—by which Tovey doesn't mean that what is said in this language is humorous: one often, he says, finds the language of comedy the only dignified expression for the deepest feelings. It is in this manner that they are often expressed by Mozart—the result being the ambiguity that is one of his outstanding characteristics, and of which an outstanding example is *Così fan Tutte,* with its apparently farcical action for which Mozart wrote some of his most poignant and sublime music, and with things like the aria *Come scoglio,* whose apparent grand style sometimes invites the suspicion that it is parodying itself.

Nor—to get back to *Figaro*—do I mean only the vocal and instrumental invention of the arias. The work rises to its greatest incandescence in the climactic ensembles—the comparatively brief *Cosa sento!* trio of Act 1 and sextet of Act 3, the extended finales of Acts 2 and 4, of which the one of Act 2 is the supreme achievement of its kind, and incidentally the supreme demonstration of the adequacy I spoke of a moment ago. Nothing could be simpler than

and nothing more modern and complex could express more effectively the Count's and the Countess's amazement at seeing Susanna step out from the cabinet. So with what follows: the bland irony of Susanna's *Signore! cos' è quel stupore?;* the atmosphere of wonder created by the orchestra for the Count's *Che scola!*, the Countess's *Che storia è mai questa,* Susanna's amused *Confusa han la testa;* a moment later the atmosphere of high comedy created by the orchestra for the Count's entreaties, the women's severe *Le vostre follie non mertan pietà;* still later the elaborate and menacing politeness of the Count's *Conoscete, signor Figaro, questo foglio chi vergò?* and the violins' impudent amusement behind Figaro's *Nol conosco;* the stolid stupidity in a state of excitement conveyed by the gardener's *Dal balcone che guarda in giardino,* burlesqued by Figaro's *Via piangione, sta zitto una volta;* and finally the suspense created for the Count's sparring with Figaro by the orchestra's long development of the figure

which swells to triumph for Figaro's *è l'usanza di porvi il suggello.*

The finale of Act 4 is another such succession, for whose conclusion—and the climax of the entire work—Mozart holds

65

in reserve a last marvel. Its overwhelming effect, like that of anything else, comes partly from its context—where it is placed, what it follows. Three hours have been filled with the sorrow of the neglected Countess's *Porgi amor* and *Dove sono;* the agitated awakening emotions of Cherubino's *Non so più cosa son;* the enchanting playfulness of Susanna's *Venite, inginocchiatevi;* the longing of her *Deh vieni, non tardar;* the irony and menace of Figaro's *Se vuol ballare;* the mockery of his *Non più andrai;* the bitterness of his *Aprite un po' quegl' occhi;* the pompous malice of Bartolo's *La vendetta;* the ear-ravishing loveliness of the *Letter Duet;* the wit of Susanna's duets with Figaro, Marcellina, the Count; the comedy of the first-act trio, the third-act sextet, the great finale of Act 2, the finale of Act 4. Three hours have been filled with the orchestra's running fire of comment, which has continued to the last to create the atmosphere of comedy for even the serious happenings: even in the hush of amazement and wonder produced by the Countess's entrance the violins have softly chattered their amusement. But now at last there is an end to all this— a moment's silence; and when the Count begins his *Contessa, perdono* we hear music which speaks of the sublimity of human forgiveness—music which, after what has come before, is overwhelming. It becomes even more overwhelming when it is taken up by the entire group, and when it is carried to a point of superearthly exaltation. Then, in the silence which follows, solemn octaves of the strings gently ease us down to earth again—and to the bustle and fanfares of the final curtain of the operatic comedy. The passage lasts only a few minutes; but those three or four minutes, coming after the three hours, create the most wonderful moment I can recall in opera.

From the comedies of the last years of Mozart's short life (he died at thirty-five) we turn back to the *opera seria* he wrote at twenty-five—to *Idomeneo*, in which, says E. J. Dent in his illuminating book on Mozart's operas, we "see the young Mozart at his greatest heights." Dent speaks of the

work's nobility and dignity of conception, its intense serious-
ness, the "monumental strength and . . . white heat of passion
that we find in this early work of Mozart's and shall never
find again"; and this turns out to be an accurate description
of what we hear: the grandly impassioned gestures with
which the overture begins, the continuing urgency of its so-
called second subject in A minor, the breathtaking shift to C
major; the powerfully expressive detail with which the orchestra points up the recitatives; the noble style of the beautiful
arias; the dramatic use of coloratura style—most notably the
descending staccato scale in Electra's final aria that suggests
the laughter of a demented creature; the power of the great
quartet, and of the chorus *O voto tremendo!*

For the rest there are two more comedies to take note of.
One, the full-length *The Abduction From the Seraglio,* composed
a year or two after *Idomeneo,* has some lovely and charming
music in addition to the great bravura aria *Martern aller Arten.*
The other, the one-act *The Impresario,* composed the same
year as *Figaro,* has a delightful overture and superb vocal
writing in its two arias and trio.

I have called Dent's book illuminating; and nothing in it
is more so than his observation that "the theater is the sphere
in which Mozart is most completely himself; his concert
works—concertos, symphonies, quartets and sonatas—are all
fundamentally evocations of the theater." The truth of this
statement is most evident in the concertos: the special circumstances which produced them made them the most ex-
plicitly dramatic in character of Mozart's instrumental works.
And those circumstances also made them the most elaborately
contrived, the richest in substance, the most complex in form,
the most fascinating and exciting and in all ways impressive
to listen to.

Mozart produced most of his greatest concertos for the occasions at which he presented himself to the public as the
greatest musician of his time—exhibiting the capacities of the

greatest performer, in music that exhibited the capacities of the greatest composer. He wrote a concerto as an actor might write a play for himself to appear in; and the form he produced was in effect the musical equivalent of a play. Listening to the opening movement of one of the piano concertos we first hear the orchestra perform with increasing suspense in anticipation of the moment when it bows itself from the center of the stage, so to speak, and the piano makes its first entrance, to hold attention for a while with graceful, lovely melodies, dazzling passage-work, exchanges with the orchestra, and eventually to work up to a brilliant exit, at which point the orchestra prepares for the piano's next entrance, and so on—the piano's last such entrance being made for the *cadenza* that exhibits the pianist's powers of improvisation, after which the orchestra brings the curtain down on the movement. And we hear similar dramatic alternation of orchestra and piano in the slow movement that presents the piano in Mozartian sustained vocal melody, the finale that often presents it in Mozartian high spirits.

(Parenthetically, for those who read Chapters 3 and 4, I add a more detailed description of the form of the Mozart concerto which other readers can skip. The first movement is an adaptation of the procedure of the earlier ritornello concerto originated by Italian composers and taken over by Bach. In the first movement of Bach's *Brandenburg Concerto* No. 2 or his D-minor Concerto for clavier or violin, we hear an opening statement by the orchestra that keeps returning after alternating passages for the solo instruments—this constantly returning statement of the orchestra being the *ritornello*. What Mozart does is to have the alternation of ritornello and solo passages take place within the succession of exposition, development, recapitulation and coda in the first movement of the symphony: the exposition begins with the orchestra's opening ritornello and is completed by the first solo section; the recurrence of the ritornello brings the second entrance of the piano for the development and the recapitulation; the

68

next recurrence of the ritornello, interrupted by the solo cadenza, provides the coda. You will note that in this scheme of Mozart's there are fewer alternations of ritornello and solo passages that are more extensive and elaborate than in the Bach concerto; and another thing to note is that this heightens the dramatic effect of the course of events in the symphony movement, makes it more externally explicit. That is, the more extensive and elaborate opening ritornello delays the entrance of the solo instrument, and in so doing builds up suspense in anticipation of this entrance—very much as the minor characters in a play may create suspense in anticipation of the first entrance of the principal character. And so with the later recurrences of the ritornello. Interesting in addition is the distribution of substance between orchestra and piano, the changes in distribution in the recapitulation as against the exposition. In the exposition some, but not all, of the ideas stated in the ritornello are repeated by the piano, which introduces additional ideas that were not stated in the ritornello. In the abbreviated recapitulation some of the ideas of the exposition are restated and some are not; and an idea originally stated by the orchestra may now be restated by the piano, possibly in a different order and context, and with modifications of the idea itself. All this was contrived by Mozart for sharp-eared listeners who were expected to remember the original progression of material in the exposition and to appreciate the changes and surprises in the recapitulation.)

The purpose of the form being to impress the listener, its fascination is, first, in what Mozart contrives for this purpose. But there is in addition a special fascination in the sense it gives of the immediacy of Mozart's presence: in the piano's every phrase of melody, every passage of brilliant figuration, every trill, every ornament, we are aware, almost as his own listeners were, of Mozart himself—showing everything he is capable of, attempting to impress, to dazzle, to overwhelm, and succeeding with an apparently inexhaustible flow of the

69

unique poignant loveliness, the gaiety, and on occasion the power. These are the fascination of any one example of the form; but what is fascinating in one after another of the marvelous works is the seemingly unending variety of the invention with which Mozart fills out the same established scheme, goes through the same established series of steps in a way that is newly interesting and impressive each time, and on occasion—writing for an audience familiar with the established scheme—plays with this audience a little game of now doing what it expects and now surprising it with what it does not expect.

Thus we get the extraordinary first entrance of the solo violin in the Concerto K.219 (Mozart was also an accomplished violinist): the orchestra finishes its introduction; we expect the violin to enter at the same lively pace; and instead it begins a breathtakingly beautiful and poignant slow melody which progresses through a half-dozen measures to a conclusion and a pause; after which violin and orchestra break the spell by resuming the original lively course of the movement. And on the other hand, at the beginning of the Piano Concerto K.271 we get the surprises that represent Mozart's love of fun: the orchestra begins imposingly, but before it can finish the piano jumps in to complete the statement; again the orchestra tries, and again the piano interrupts, after which the orchestra is allowed to proceed without further interruption to the final flourish, the final bow of its ritornello; but while it is still bowing the piano bursts onto the scene with a brilliant trill that leads into its opening statement.

The Violin Concerto K.219, which Mozart wrote at nineteen, the Piano Concerto K.271, which he wrote at twenty-one, are among the first great examples of the form; and from these and other early examples we learn that the difference between Mozart at twenty and Mozart at thirty is not, as we might suppose, the difference between Mozart immature and Mozart mature. In the Violin Concertos K.218 and 219, with their characteristic mingling of high spirits and poignant loveliness; in the Violin Concerto K.216, with its especially delightful first movement, its Andante movement whose long flow of sustained melody leaves one spellbound; in the Piano Concerto K.271, with another especially delightful first movement, one of Mozart's deeply affecting C-minor slow movements, and an exuberantly gay finale whose "rush" leaves one breathless—in these early works we hear the essential Mozart expressive content and Mozart form completely and astoundingly matured. What time brings is enrichment, elaboration, subtilization, which rise on occasion to sheer incandescence; that is the difference between the first movements of K.216 (1775) and K.271 (1777), and the first movement of the Piano Concerto K.453 (1784); between the slow movement of K.271, and the C-minor slow movement of the Sinfonie Concertante K.364 for violin and viola (1779); between the slow movement of K.216, and the Andante movement of the Piano Concerto K.467 (1785); between the finale of K.271, and the finales of K.466 (1785) and 488 (1786).

Enrichment, elaboration, subtilization, then, give us the later great examples of the form—the Piano Concertos K.450, 453, 456 and 459 (1784), K.466, 467 and 482 (1785), K.488, 491 and 503 (1786), and K.595 (1791). And incandescence gives us the individual movements and entire works, among those great examples, that are some of Mozart's supreme utterances in instrumental music.

Thus K.453 has a first movement that is one of the supreme examples of Mozartian instrumental high comedy—though one in which characteristically the gaiety is mingled with Mozartian poignancy. They are mingled right from the start, in the opening violin theme that begins with grace and elegance, continues with a poignancy the more intense for the exquisite contour of the embodying phrase, and is punctuated by mocking flutters of the woodwinds. A moment later the bassoon chortles on comically after the flourishes of the full orchestra stop, leading to another exquisitely contoured and poignant statement of the violins (at this point in the recapitu-

71

lation Mozart contrives a couple of his little surprises and jokes: when the orchestra's flourishes stop it is not the chortling bassoon but the piano that continues them, leading not to that statement of the violins but to a sharply contoured theme which the piano itself stated in the exposition). And such alternations continue throughout the movement.

This first movement of comedy is followed by one of Mozart's most affecting and most extraordinarily organized slow movements. A poignant opening statement recurs several times, pausing each time before a long sequence of thought takes off from it; overlaid on this pattern of arrangement are alternations of orchestra and piano, and a cycle of keys; and after the piano's cadenza the woodwinds' last enunciation of the opening statement is completed, with sublime implications, by the piano. Then the finale: a genial theme and several variations, one of them suddenly hushed and ominous with its minor mode and syncopations; and a coda made breathtaking by the tempo, style, surprises and jokes of a Mozartian operatic-comedy finale.

In the seldom-played K.456 it is the Andante movement that is outstanding, with an extraordinarily beautiful and poignant theme in G minor that is elaborated in several impressive examples of Mozartian variation-writing.

K.466, one of the most frequently played, begins with what is perhaps the most powerful of Mozart's instrumental movements. The power of the hushed D-minor opening passage is an example of effect on the mind out of all proportion to the impingement on the senses: it is achieved by nothing more than the agitated syncopations of violins and violas, the quiet eruptions of cellos and basses, with not even one of the kettle-drum-strokes that punctuate those eruptions in the orchestral outburst a moment later (not only kettledrums but trumpets are added to the orchestra in this work). In the second movement it is the interlude of sustained melody for the solo piano that is noteworthy—more so even than the stormy G-minor episode later in the movement. And then comes one of Mozart's incandescent perpetuum mobile finales, similar to the one in K.271, but its momentum this time unbroken by a minuet, and with a last-minute surprise in the coda: the theme

heard twice before in the movement, is now changed, extended, and unexpectedly answered by the horns' and trumpets'

which becomes increasingly insistent in the crescendo that brings the movement to a close.

Trumpets and kettledrums contribute to the festive brilliance of the first movement of K.467, the gaiety of its finale; but they play no part in the extraordinary Andante inbetween. In this movement the orchestra makes a long opening statement of a succession of ideas, on which the piano then discourses in several sequences of thought that get to be excitingly eventful in the way that is so extraordinary: up above there is the calm of the melody as it proceeds with developing tensions and involvements; while down below there is the agitation of faster-moving accompanying violins and violas, the power of plucked bass-notes; and occasionally there are intensifying comments by the woodwinds. All these, working together, build up tension and impact that make this movement, for all its quiet, one of Mozart's most powerful utterances; and indeed with this power achieved in quiet it is one of the most extraordinary pieces of music he ever wrote.

In the first movement of K.482 festive opening proclamations claim attention for a rich flow of exquisite melodic invention; there is a similar flow of loveliness and humor in the finale; and inbetween is another of Mozart's most affecting and extraordinarily organized slow movements. Muted violins

73

play a long and poignant melody in C minor; when the piano enters it is to play an elaborating and intensifying variation on this melody, reinforced at climactic moments by the orchestra's strings; the winds then enter with an engaging interlude in E flat major; the piano makes a second entrance with another variation on the opening melody, again reinforced momentarily by the strings; in a second interlude, this time in C major, the flute and bassoon, accompanied by strings, carry on a gracefully ornate dialogue; then the piano engages in a powerful dialogue with the full orchestra in another variation on the opening melody; after which orchestra and piano alternate in a coda that ends with a master-stroke: the concluding phrase of the first interlude, with the intense poignancy it acquires from being now in C minor.

In K.488 there is a return to an orchestra without trumpets and kettledrums for the flow of some of Mozart's most ear-ravishing and heart-piercing melodic invention in the first movement, another of his affecting slow movements in minor mode, and the supreme example of his incandescent per-petuum-mobile finale—the most breathtaking in its profusion of ideas, its momentum, its strokes of surprise and humor. The effect of these strokes comes, again, from their context; and Mozart expects us to remember how

proceeded and ended the first time, when he brings it back later in the movement and makes it proceed and end differently—i.e. prolongs it with changes of harmony that create increasing suspense before it suddenly leaps triumphantly into the clear with

Similarly he expects our recollection of the previous two appearances of this blandly, suavely mocking statement:

to enable us to appreciate the effect of its unexpected last appearance near the end of the movement.

The large orchestra is heard again in K.491, contributing to the magnificence that is one of the outstanding characteristics of its first movement, another being its dramatic power—the power, for example, of the hushed C-minor opening passage of strings and bassoons and its forceful restatement by the entire orchestra a moment later; or of the forceful statements and the hushed concluding passage, again in C minor, after the cadenza. This movement towers above the engaging slow movement and the richly elaborated variation finale.

In K.503 too the first movement towers above the others by virtue of a grandeur and majesty that set it apart from other first movements. Thus it begins not with one of their immediately appealing opening themes, but, in the words of Tovey, "with a majestic assertion of . . . C major by the whole orchestra, with mysterious soft shadows that give a solemn depth to the tone." And these mysterious soft shadows of delicate woodwind textures after the initial radiance of the entire orchestra—the second time with a wonderful shift to C minor—are subtleties contrived for the eighteenth-century ear that may escape some listeners of today. Another such subtlety is created with a reiterated rhythmic figure, which in the opening ritornello is carried to a point where it is trumpeted forth on the note G and leads to C minor: when the orchestra trumpets forth those G's again at the beginning of the development, they are answered breathtakingly by the piano's reiteration of the figure on B, in a sudden shift to E minor that is the first of a series of such bold modulations.

Trumpets and drums are not suitable for the first move-

75

ment of K.595, which also stands apart from the other concertos, and in fact from everything else, in its late-in-life calm
(e.g. the opening statement of the violins, punctuated by the
strange calls of the winds), with which it conveys intimations
of agony that preceded calm (e.g. the poignantly altered
repetition of the violins'

a few moments later)—so that as a piece of late writing by
Mozart it has something like the character of a late work of
Beethoven, or Schubert's Piano Sonata in B flat. Something
of this character is heard also in the opening and closing sections of the Larghetto, which has inbetween an eventful, and
in the end impassioned, interlude of sustained melody for the
piano—one of the events being a breathtaking shift in key.
But not in the finale, in which there is only lilting good
humor, with moments of high spirits and fun.

And not, I will add, in another product of the last year of
Mozart's life, the lovely Clarinet Concerto K.622—though
the Mozartian poignancy makes itself heard in the lyricism
and gaiety.

Writing about Schubert I referred to the last quiet passage
just before the end of the finale of Mozart's Symphony in G
minor K.550—a series of textures of sounds with miraculously
achieved intensities of loveliness and expressive force. Hardly
less wonderful is the analogous quiet passage soon after the
beginning of that finale; and there is another series of such
miracles about halfway through the first movement—the passage that leads to the return of the impassioned opening statement. These are incandescent moments in one of the most
extraordinary examples of what Turner spoke about—one in
which the utmost in passion and intensity is crystallized in
the most exquisite of clear, beautifully balanced and propor-

tioned musical forms. Its expressive content and form, in fact, not only set the G-minor apart from Mozart's other symphonies but make it another of the supreme wonders achieved by human powers.

The G-minor is the second of the last great group of three symphonies Mozart composed in approximately two months of the summer of 1788. Its intense melancholy may seem at first to be related to the desperate circumstances of Mozart's life at that time; but the loveliness of K.543—even though it pierces the heart as it ravishes the ear—and the festive majesty of K.551 that has caused it to be given the name *Jupiter* teach us not to attempt such correlations of works of art with the immediate circumstances of the artist's life.

There are flashing miracles again in the finale of K.543— e.g. the series of subtly altered statements of

that lead to the return of the opening statement of the violins. And in the finale of K.551 there is another of those extraordinary rushes of vital energy, expressing itself this time in contrapuntal manipulation of the several themes which Mozart carries to a jubilantly triumphant conclusion.

Of the same stature is the less frequently heard Symphony K.504 (*Prague*) (1786), with the grand opening gestures of a slow introduction that becomes powerfully dramatic before pausing for the brilliant Allegro; with an Andante rich in thematic ideas whose development is made eventful by bold shifts of key; and with a delightful concluding Presto.

Smaller in scale are the earlier movements of the seldom-played K.425 (*Linz*) (1783)—the imposing introduction leading to the brilliant Allegro, the lovely slow movement, the minuet movement. Unexpected, therefore, is the large scale of the finale, its richness of substance and elaboration.

The frequently heard K.385 (*Haffner*) (1782) has a powerful first movement elaborated almost entirely out of its opening statement, followed by a lovely and poignant Andante, a fine minuet movement, and another delightful concluding Presto.

The power of these later symphonies is something we don't find in the earlier K.338 (1780) and K.297 (*Paris*) (1778); but we do find a poignantly lovely Andantino in K.297, an especially lovely Andante di molto in K.338, framed by delightfully high-spirited opening movements and rushing finales.

And like the concertos the symphonies include early small-scale works, K.200 and 201 (1773-4) in which we hear the essential Mozart expressive content and form astoundingly matured: in K.200 the gaiety of the opening movement and rushing finale, the poignancy of the exquisitely contoured muted-violin melodies in the Andante, the pensiveness tinged with sadness in much of the minuet movement; and in K.201 the grace and wistfulness of the opening movement, the poignant loveliness of the Andante, the gaiety of the minuet (e.g.

78

the comical punctuating flourishes of the winds) alternating with the exquisite poignancy of the trio; the high spirits of another rushing finale.

In Mozart's operas, concertos and symphonies we have heard the exquisite textures in which he combines the sounds of strings, of winds, of both strings and winds, of instruments and voices. You will find nothing to equal them (though Berlioz and Debussy will offer something comparable); and since string-quartet-writing is an art of texture you will hear in no other quartets the ear-ravishing use of the medium that you hear in the famous six—K.387, 421, 428, 458 (*Hunt*), 464 and 465—that Mozart dedicated to Haydn, and in K.499, which is of the same period (1782-6). Nor do they, of course, merely delight the ear: their expressive content, as always, touches the heart. And outstanding in these respects are the somberly powerful K.421, the now amusingly high-spirited, now deeply affecting K.458, the less frequently heard K.428 with its grave opening movement, its rich-textured Andante and comedy finale, and K.499 with its richly elaborated opening movement and slow movement, its lovely minuet, and another comedy finale.

But of greatest stature among the works of this category are two of the string quintets, K.515 and 516 (1787). The additional viola, by increasing the sonority and the richness of texture, contributes to the extraordinary power of the first movement of K.515; by darkening the instrumental color it contributes to the somber strangeness of the minuet and first part of the trio, the intensity of the middle part of the trio, the poignancy of the Andante. And the darkened instrumental coloring contributes, as does the key of G minor, to the effect of K.516, one of the best-known of these works, and unique in its expressive content: in no other work of Mozart do we hear such unrelieved melancholy as in the first movement, such poignancy in a minuet, this poignancy carried to such agonized intensity as in the slow movement; and nowhere does Mozart permit himself to speak with the anguish of the slow introduction to a finale whose apparent light-heartedness at first—incongruous after what has preceded it—is qualified as it continues.

Of the great string quintets that are heard less frequently than they should be, K.593 (1790) is especially notable for its deeply affecting slow movement and bustling comedy finale; K.614 (1791) for the unexpected high spirits of its delightful opening movement and finale; K.406 (1787) for its powerful opening movement and contrapuntal minuet movement in C minor, its poignant Andante.

K.406 is an arrangement of the earlier Serenade K.388 for winds, which has less expressive effect than the string quintet version but offers some of Mozart's beautiful writing for wind instruments, both solo and in combination. We hear more of this writing in the Serenade K.361, which has a very fine slow introduction, Adagio, and variation movement; and the brilliant Serenade K.375, which has wonderful details. Beautiful writing for strings and horns is to be heard in the charming Divertimentos K.287 and 334—the first with an extraordinary Adagio in the style of a great vocal aria, the second with some wonderful details in the variation movement. And beautiful writing for three strings in the Divertimento K.563, with its fine slow movement and extraordinary theme and variations.

We hear writing for the oboe that is breathtaking in its vocal style and expressive intensity in the brief Adagio that is framed by charming Allegros in the Quartet K.370 for oboe and strings. And the larger-scale Quintet K.581 for clarinet and strings offers a flow of lyricism, characteristic in its poignant loveliness, that makes it one of Mozart's most beautiful works.

Concerning the Quintet K.452 for piano and winds I am in the awkward position of disagreeing with Mozart, who in a letter to his father pronounced it "the best I have ever written"; since the opening Allegro, to my ears, is inane. But twice even in this movement—near the end of the exposition and the recapitulation—there is a succession of scale passages rushing up to sustained notes which create a texture with wonderful harmonic progressions; there are impressive episodes also in the slow movement; and there are of course wonderful textures of sounds of winds throughout.

The piano is heard with clarinet and viola in the fine Trio K.498; it is heard with strings in the piano trios and quartets, of which the Trio K.496 is the best, and the Trios K.502 and 548 have beautiful slow movements. It is heard also in the sonatas for piano and violin, of which an early group includes the charming K.296, 301, 305 and 306, the impassioned K.304, the lovely K.378; and later ones include the powerful K.379, K.380 with its poignant slow movement, K.454 and 481 with their very beautiful slow movements, and K.526, the finest of the series, with one of the most charming of first movements, a grave, richly elaborated Andante that becomes wonderfully beautiful and deeply affecting, and one of the most brilliant and breathtaking of perpetuum-mobile finales.

For piano solo one of Mozart's finest pieces is the Rondo K.511 that I presented in Chapter 4. And other late works of the same stature are the powerful Fantasia K.475 and Sonata K.457, which are sometimes played, as they were published, together; the Sonata K.576, with some of Mozart's most developed, most complex writing for the instrument; the fine Sonata K.570; the Sonata K.533 and 494, with its remarkable and startling harmonic progressions; the rhythmically intricate Gigue K.574. A little earlier are the powerful Fantasia K.396; the Suite K.399, with its interesting and engaging Mozartian transformations of the styles of the movements of a Handel suite. And still earlier are the fine Sonatas K.333 (with a startling development in the Andante), 332, 311, 310; the engaging K.283; and K.282, with its astonishing Adagio first movement. Of the best-known Sonata K.331 I find the minuet movement more estimable than the opening theme and variations and concluding *Rondo à la turca*.

81

In addition there are the fine Sonata K.448 for two pianos; the engaging Sonatas K.381, 358 and 357 for piano four hands.

Most of Mozart's church music, finally, was written in his youth while he was in the service of the Archbishop of Salzburg; and an outstanding work of this period is the Mass K.317, written when he was twenty-three. It has several sections—the *Kyrie, Gloria, Benedictus* and *Agnus Dei*—which are very beautiful; but most impressive is the *Credo,* with an Allegro opening section that acquires tremendous power from its ostinato instrumental figuration, then a change to Adagio for wonderful passages on the words *Et incarnatus est* and *Crucifixus etiam* and *passus et sepultus est,* and then a return to the Allegro with a lovely episode on *Et in spiritum sanctum.*

Once out of the service of the Archbishop he was kept busy by the instrumental works and operas with which he had to earn a living—too busy to be able to complete the *Mass in C Minor* that he began in 1782. But in its incomplete form it includes a magnificently powerful *Kyrie* with a lovely episode for solo soprano, and the wonderfully beautiful *Et incarnatus est.*

And death cut short his work on the *Requiem,* which was completed in accordance with his sketches and directions by his pupil Süssmayr. This work too has magnificently powerful sections like the *Kyrie* (with affecting passages for solo soprano), *Tuba mirum* and *Rex tremendae;* lovely ones like the *Recordare, Hostias, Benedictus* and *Agnus Dei;* and a *Lacrymosa* which takes its place with things like the Andante of the Piano Concerto K.467—what is extraordinary this time being the way the unceasing two-note violin figure builds up cumulative expressive force behind the affecting vocal parts.

Even this long discussion of Mozart's music leaves undiscussed a large part of his enormous output that I have never heard, and some works, among those I have heard, that a busily engaged eighteenth-century musical craftsman turned out occasionally without inspiration or interest, and with no more inspiration or interest for us than for him. But the works I have dealt with—their use of the medium, and what they express through this use—make that busily engaged craftsman the most extraordinary musical artist who ever lived.

8

HAYDN

Toscanini, excited once about a Haydn symphony he was going to play, exclaimed that he found Haydn more wonderful even than Mozart ("except of course," he added, "the G-minor—and the concertos"). What caused his face to register delight as he listened to a recording of the symphony was the method so well described by Tovey's statements that "the essential character of Haydn's form is dramatic surprise at the moment" and "nothing in Haydn is difficult to follow, but almost everything is unexpected." It is a surprise achieved by variety—a moment-to-moment, point-to-point varying of melodic and harmonic direction, length of phrase, rhythmic grouping and accentuation, volume, orchestral activity, which calls for attentive point-to-point listening.

Here, for example, is the opening statement of the Quartet Op. 76 No. 2:

And here is how the repetition of this statement unexpectedly prolongs its third measure and does a little fooling around in the fifth and sixth before coming to a new conclusion in the seventh and eighth:

For an example of this sort of thing in rich profusion and in a tempo that makes it easy to observe, listen to the introduction to the Symphony No. 104:

85

Listen, that is, to the dramatic surprise—after the radiantly sonorous opening call and answer—of the hushed statement of strings and bassoon in measures 3 and 4. Then the effect—after the C sharps at [a]—of the C natural at [b], and of what this C natural brings: the shift in key from D minor into F major. Then the effect—after the radiantly sonorous call and answer—of the changed hushed answer in measure 9. Then the effect—after the development of the first-violin figure with increasing intensity in measures 9, 10 and 11—of the sudden taking over of that figure by the cellos in measure 12 below sustained notes of the upper strings and flute, with increasing harmonic complexity that is resolved in measure 13. And then the startling effects—after the radiantly sonorous call, back in the key of D once more—of the hushed answer, of the note

G instead of the expected A at [c], of the addition of the remote chord at [d], creating suspense that changes, with the harmonic progressions and the oboe comments in measure 16, to expectancy for the beginning of the Allegro portion of the movement.

This example of the packing in of detail to hold attention from one moment to the next illustrates Tovey's statement that Haydn is a great master working on a very small scale. And it illustrates another of Tovey's perceptive observations— that Haydn's forms become more subtle as his spirits rise. For what we hear in Haydn's instrumental music is a constant playing with the medium and with the listener's mind; and sometimes we hear this process raised to incandescence by his exuberance in the use of his powers for that purpose: on every page we get details which it amused him to contrive on Wednesday to startle his listeners, or hold them spellbound, or make them laugh, on Saturday. Thus the little surprises in the first two movements of the Quartet Op. 76 No. 2 leave us unprepared for the bomb that Haydn explodes in the minuet movement: a canon, with violins leading and lower strings following that make us laugh first with the unexpectedness of the procedure and then with some of the details of the progression. Or, in the Symphony No. 104, when the beautiful Andante movement has completed its formal cycle and we think it is about to end, it goes off on a wonderful wide-ranging digression. And a more obvious bit of musical fooling occurs at the end of the minuet: the silence when we are expecting another trill; and then a soft trill when we expect a loud one. Listening to such mischievously contrived details we are aware of the mind that is operating behind them—which is to say that the course of events in a Haydn symphony or quartet gives us the same fascinating sense of the immediacy of Haydn's presence and activity as we get of Mozart's from one of his concertos.

These are some of the fascinations of any one of the works; but to listen to one after another of the great last symphonies—

the final group, Nos. 93 to 104, that Haydn wrote for his two visits to London, and some that preceded them—is to be astounded by the profusion and variety of invention from this inexhaustibly fertile mind. And astounding in the same way are an even larger number of the string quartets—the many fine works, the works with outstanding individual movements, and the incandescent examples like Op. 20 Nos. 4 and 5, Op. 33 No. 3, Op. 54 Nos. 1 and 2, Op. 64 Nos. 3 and 4, Op. 74 No. 2, Op. 77 No. 2.

Moreover, the symphonies and quartets are only the best-known of Haydn's instrumental works. Recordings have recently begun to make it possible to discover the similar stature and fascination of others that are almost never played in concerts—some of the trios for piano, violin and cello; some of the piano sonatas. Pianists, a notoriously unadventurous species, are content to go on playing the extraordinarily beautiful and often amazing *Andante and Variations* in F minor, and at most the Sonatas in E flat and D.

So with the choral works. We used to hear *The Creation*, with its introductory representation of chaos that is amazing in its daring and power, its other passages that are wonderfully beautiful, and still others that charm us with their innocence and sweetness. And once in a great while there would be a performance of *The Seasons*, with its many lovely and charming pages, and some powerful ones in the *Winter* section. Now, through recordings, we know the *Nelson Mass*, the *Theresienmesse*, the *St. Cecilia Mass*, the *Missa in tempore belli*, all impressive and often superb products of Haydn's fully matured powers.

9

BERLIOZ

By the criteria I applied to Mozart—use of the medium, and what is expressed through this use—Berlioz is another of the greatest musical artists. This estimate is not the generally accepted one you will find in the histories of music and appreciation manuals; it is however what I have discovered to be true from my listening to the music; and I propose to let readers of this book make the same discovery in the same way.

I suggest, then, listening to the song *Au Cimetière* from *Les Nuits d'été*—a setting of this poem by Gautier:

> Connaissez-vous la blanche tombe
> Où flotte avec un son plaintif
>   L'ombre d'un if?
> Sur l'if, une pâle colombe,
> Triste et seule, au soleil couchant
>   Chante son chant;
>
> Un air maladivement tendre,
> A la fois charmant et fatal,
>   Qui vous fait mal,
> Et qu'on voudrait toujours entendre,
> Un air comme en soupire aux cieux
>   L'ange amoureux.
>
> On dirait que l'âme éveillée
> Pleure sous terre à l'unison
>   De la chanson,

Et du malheur d'être oubliée
Se plaint dans un roucoulement
    Bien doucement.

Sur les aîles de la musique
On sent lentement revenir
    Un souvenir;
Une ombre de forme angélique
Passe dans un rayon tremblant,
    En voile blanc.

Les belles de nuit, demi-closes,
Jettent leur parfum faible et doux
    Autour de vous,
Et le fantôme aux molles poses
Murmure en vous tendant les bras:
    Tu reviendras?

Oh! jamais plus, près de la tombe,
Je n'irai, quand descend le soir
    Au manteau noir,
Ecouter la pâle colombe
Chanter sur la branche de l'if
    Son chant plaintif!

Listen to the first three vocal statements to the words

Connaissez-vous la blanche tombe
Où flotte avec un son plaintif/L'ombre d'un if?
Sur l'if, une pâle colombe,/Triste et seule, au
    soleil couchant/Chante son chant;

Immediately striking is the exquisiteness of the vocal melody, of the underlying harmony (e.g. the changes beginning at *tombe*), of the instrumental color. And striking too is the freedom with which the melody moves, grows, takes form—freedom in relation to bar-line and meter; freedom in shape and length of phrase; freedom, then, from the conventional and expected regularities and symmetries. Even in the first statement the deployment of the four measures of vocal melody is irregular in relation to the bar-line (at *la*) and asymmetrical to the seven measures of instrumental accompaniment. In the next statement the melody is repeated, but with elaborating changes: not only the change in rhythm and contour (*un son*) and the exquisite change of F sharp to F natural (on the syllable *plain*), but the additional clause (*L'ombre d'un if*) that makes this statement asymmetrical in shape and length to the first. And in the third statement there are not only further elaborating changes in melody and rhythm but an additional clause that makes this statement asymmetrical to the second.

Clearly this is a progression in which nothing has been set down mechanically or perfunctorily; in which everything, on the contrary, exhibits the operation of a mind unceasingly attentive, active, creative—excitingly so in the placing of the occasional plucked bass-notes, which produce an effect out of proportion to their impingement on the senses. And about this there are two things to say. One is that this mind unceasingly active, which makes Berlioz fascinating to listen to, gives us music that can be described by Tovey's statement about Haydn: "Nothing is difficult to follow, but everything is unexpected." At one point after another the music moves in an unexpected direction, continues with something unforeseen, which turns out to be logical and right; and you will discover that Berlioz is in fact one of the great originals in music, whose thought, language and style are like no one else's before or after him. And the other thing to say is that in each decision to change this note in the melody or that chord in the harmony, to extend this note over the bar-line here or place that plucked bass-note there, we hear evidence that this active mind, as it fills in the musical canvas, so to speak, operates with an ear, a taste, a melodic gift, a harmonic sense, a magic with the orchestra—in short with musical powers—of a most unusual and distinguished sort.

We continue to hear the freedom and freshness of invention in the song's further statements. The melody (*Un air maladivement tendre*) repeats a figure of four quarter-notes against the three-quarter time marked excitingly by the plucked bass; then (*A la fois charmant et fatal*) it takes off, expanding freely over the bar-lines to a high point (*fatal*) from which it descends with exquisite inflections (*Qui vous fait mal* and *Et qui voudrait toujours entendre*); then (*Un air comme en soupire aux cieux*) it is quietly sustained as it rises to an exquisite inflection (*soupir aux cieux*) and conclusion (*L'ange amoureux*).

Now a new section begins (*On dirait que l'âme éveillée/Pleure sous terre à l'unison/De la chanson*): over more agitated eighth-notes in the strings the melody's groups of repeated A's are punctuated in exciting fashion by an irregularly placed and intensely poignant two-note chromatic figure of the wood-winds. This continues, with the addition only of an occasional plucked bass-note (*Et du malheur d'être oubliée/Se plaint dans un roucoulement*); but the conclusion (*Bien doucement*) is made suddenly exciting by quick repetition of the woodwind figure over plucked bass-notes. With increased agitation in the strings the melody (*Sur les aîles de la musique/On sent lentement revenir/Un souvenir*) rises with expansive freedom to a high point of intensity at which there are brilliant woodwind flourishes. Then (*Une ombre, une forme angélique/Passe dans un rayon tremblant*) the melody subsides, with the woodwinds continuing their poignant figure, and with the violins adding gleaming harmonics (at *tremblant*) which continue until the pause before the return of the opening section—this time to the words

Les belles de nuit demi-closes
Jettent leur parfum faible et doux/Autour de vous,
Et le fantôme aux molles poses/Murmure en vous tendant les bras: "Tu reviendras!"
Oh! jamais plus, près de la tombe/Je n'irai, quand descend le soir/Au manteau noir,

It is here, at the beginning of the repetition of the opening statement, that we hear the most extraordinary manifestation of the powers I have mentioned. As the voice, below syncopated woodwind chords, begins its melody, violins and violas add a descending four-note comment, modified at each repetition with overwhelming expressive effect:

I doubt that anyone has ever produced a greater effect on the mind with so little impingement on the senses.

For the rest the opening statements are repeated with only slight changes until *Oh! jamais plus* etc., when the melody's four-quarter figure is repeated over one of Berlioz's enlivening pizzicato oscillations in the cellos, and an ostinato figure in the basses. And the melody itself changes at *Au manteau noir* for new concluding statements to the words

> *Ecouter la pâle colombe/Chanter sur la pointe de l'if*
> *Son chant plaintif!*

with the orchestra speaking poignantly before *Son chant plaintif*, with it, and after it.

If one were given nothing but this song to judge from one would have to say the man who wrote it was one of the greatest masters. Any of the other songs of *Les Nuits d'été* would compel the same judgment; but I suggest listening further to *Sur les lagunes*—a setting of this poem by Gautier:

> Ma belle amie est morte:
> Je pleurerai toujours;
> Sous la tombe elle emporte
> Mon âme et mes amours.

94

Dans le ciel, sans m'attendre,
Elle s'en retourna;
L'ange qui l'emmena
Ne voulut pas me prendre.
Que mon sort est amer!
Ah! sans amour, s'en aller sur la mer!

La blanche créature
Est couchée au cercueil.
Comme dans la nature
Tout me paraît en deuil!
La colombe oubliée
Pleure et songe à l'absent;
Mon âme pleure et sent
Qu'elle est dépareillée.
Que mon sort est amer!
Ah! sans amour, s'en aller sur la mer!

Sur moi la nuit immense
S'étend comme un linceul;
Je chante ma romance
Que le ciel entend seul.
Ah! comme elle était belle
Et comme je l'aimais!
Je n'aimerai jamais
Une femme autant qu'elle.
Que mon sort est amer!
Ah! sans amour, s'en aller sur la mer!

We shall see later on that one of Berlioz's most remarkable procedures is the repetition at intervals of an unchanged figure or note in the constantly changing context of the developing musical thought; and he does something of the kind in *Sur les lagunes:* the orchestra's powerfully somber three-note figure (in F minor) that establishes the atmosphere of the song in the very first measure recurs at intervals, punctuating the grief-laden vocal statements to the words

Ma belle amie est morte:
Je pleurerai toujours;
Sous la tombe elle emporte/Mon âme et mes amours.
Dans le ciel, sans m'attendre,/Elle s'en retourna;
L'ange qui l'emmena/Ne voulut pas me prendre.

In this opening section we hear again the unceasing creativeness producing the freedom and variety of melodic
rhythm, shape and length, the unexpected shifts in direction
caused, sometimes, by progressions in the harmony (e.g. before
Sous la tombe). And the section ends with two statements that
will recur as a refrain: the plaintive *Que mon sort est amer!*, followed by the passionate *Ah! sans amour s'en aller sur la mer!*
Now a shift to B flat major brings a momentary brightness
in a new section which begins (*La blanche créature*) with tranquilly sustained loveliness, but continues with increasing intensity and poignancy (*Est couchée au cercueil;/Comme dans la
nature*) that becomes heavy, dark grief (*Tout me paraît en deuil*).
The momentum increases with the orchestra's activity: with
the violin arpeggio that introduces *La colombe oubliée*, the two-
note woodwind figures and plucked bass-notes that reinforce
Pleure, pleure et songe à l'absent, in the crescendo of intensity
that continues with *Mon âme pleure et sent/Qu'elle est dépareillée.*
Suddenly there is a moment's silence; then again the refrain
Que mon sort est amer!/Ah! sans amour s'en aller sur la mer! And
again the somber three-note figure, which leads again to the
opening musical statement—this time to the words *Sur moi la
nuit immense.* The statement is again punctuated by the three-
note figure, which leads now to one of the most wonderful
passages in the song. The final C of the figure descends to C
flat, which is repeated by the voice in the hushed *S'étend comme
un linceul* over harmonic progressions on which it pivots to
start the wonderfully beautiful and moving *Je chante ma ro-
mance/Que le ciel entend seul.* This leads to the climactic statements of the song:

Ah! comme elle était belle/Et comme je l'aimais!
Je n'aimerai jamais/Une femme autant qu'elle.

Again the three-note figure, which leads to the refrain. And then a last master-stroke: the three-note figure, previously heard only from the orchestra, is heard now from the voice.

After listening to these two songs you are in a position to understand my lack of awe for accepted opinion. For accepted opinion on Berlioz—in the music histories and appreciation manuals—credits him only with a gift for orchestral color and effect, and has it that he used gigantic orchestras to conceal the poverty and banality of his melody and harmony. Writing of "the musicians of the last century, from Berlioz to Strauss," one excessively esteemed historian spoke once of "orchestral scores which when dispossessed of their tremendous orchestral ornaments show an astonishingly meager invention and vague construction." And another wrote that the full orchestra was Berlioz's principal medium because of his preoccupation "with extreme and gigantic aims"; that he used "huge choral masses" for the same reason; that "he forged anew the poetry of *Faust* and *Romeo and Juliet* to his own ends, and monstrous works came forth, half oratorio, half symphony, half lyrical and half dramatic, all blazing with color"; that he similarly used liturgical texts, in the *Requiem* and *Te Deum*, for "a colossal musical exhibition and show of power."

The composer of *Au Cimetière* and *Sur les lagunes* and the other songs of *Les Nuits d'été* doesn't seem to me to be preoccupied with extreme and gigantic aims or to be using dazzling orchestral effects to conceal meager invention; but what of the works that do use large orchestral and vocal forces? The answer happens to be given in one of Turner's critical articles that I encountered recently, written after his first hearing of the rarely performed *Requiem*. This is the work that is usually pointed to as the example of Berlioz's use of huge forces for extreme and gigantic aims; and Turner writes: "It is true that his Mass calls for sixteen kettledrums; it is true that he asks for four brass bands to be played north, south, east and west of the general body of chorus and orchestra. All these things in the hands of anyone but Berlioz would have resulted in incredible vulgarity; but Berlioz could not be vulgar." When the brass bands in the *Tuba mirum* "burst out into their antiphonal blazing coruscations," says Turner, "it is as though a thousand rockets had gone up over our heads and were bursting into flames"; but this, he adds, is only their first effect: "we soon discover that these extraordinary exhilarating pyrotechnics are charged with meaning, the flames are not mere flames but *expressive, imaginative,* full of poetic significance."

It is good to have this answer to the idea of large means being connected with extreme and gigantic aims. That idea is true of some artists, but not of all; it is true of some painters, for example, but not of every painter who chooses to apply oil paints to a large canvas rather than a pencil to a small sheet of paper; it is equally not true of every composer who chooses to write for an orchestra rather than a string quartet; and, as Turner testifies, it isn't necessarily true even of a composer who elects to write for an orchestra with sixteen kettledrums and four additional brass bands: when that composer is a Berlioz he uses such large forces with the same precision and for as legitimate artistic ends, as small ones. The impression of the *Requiem* given by the histories and music appreciation manuals is of the additional four brass bands blaring away uninterruptedly and blatantly for two hours; whereas actually they are used in only a few sections, and where they do play with full power, as in the *Tuba mirum,* they do not merely blare away but operate with imaginative purpose and effect; in addition to which—and this is something Turner doesn't speak of—they don't always play with full power. Indeed the most impressive evidence of Berlioz's integrity in the matter is the discretion and taste with which he uses them in the *Lacrymosa.*

Introduced and accompanied by an explosively agitated orchestral figuration the tenors begin a beautiful melodic passage in nine-eighth time which moves with Berlioz's characteristic freedom of rhythm, shape and direction; when the sopranos and altos repeat the passage the tenors continue with a counterpoint that is similarly free; and the next repetition by the basses is enriched and given exciting momentum by similar counterpoints of women and tenors, reaching a climax that subsides into a new and quiet section. In this, altos and tenors sing a brief figure that is commented on by the basses—the figure and comment being derived from the opening section. They continue and develop with increasing intensity to a conclusion; then comes a section (*Pie Jesu, Domine, donna eis requiem*) of tranquilly sustained melodic loveliness and exquisite harmonic progressions. From this there is suddenly a return to the explosive orchestral figuration and the tenors' nine-eighth melody of the opening; and it is here that Berlioz begins to use the four additional brass bands: in each nine-eighth measure the third group of three eighths is reinforced by a note or chord from one after another of the four bands—the effect of these cries of the brass being indescribable. And in the repetitions of the melody that effect is heightened: with the repetition by sopranos and altos the brass chords from one after another of the bands are fuller and are intensified by kettledrum-rolls; with the repetition by the basses each reinforcing chord is played by all four bands together with thunderous rolls of kettledrums and bass drums. The momentum and excitement are tremendous; and again the climax subsides into the quiet discussion of figures derived from the opening section, carried on this time in three vocal parts instead of two, hence with greater intricacy of rhythm and texture, and with wonderful comments from the woodwinds. And this time the section ends with a crescendo to a climax in which the additional brass bands join in a tremendous unison proclamation of the nine-eighth melody by chorus and orchestra.

As precisely—and on occasion as exquisitely—wrought are the sections that do not employ the additional brass bands: the radiant *Sanctus;* the *Hostias*, which uses, in addition to

99

strings, only flutes and trombones, but these with astounding originality and impressiveness; the *Quaerens me*, for chorus without any orchestra at all. And of these the most remarkable is the *Offertorium*.

This is one of the great examples—great in scale and effect—of the procedure Berlioz used in *Sur les lagunes:* the repetition at intervals of an unchanged figure or note in the constantly changing context of the developing musical thought. The orchestral part is a fugal development of the long opening statement—a development made increasingly rich and exciting by the constantly fresh and unusual elaborating ideas and figurations that are heard with the successive entries of the statement, but also by the episodes into which the fugal progression digresses: the expansive melody to which the progression rises twice; the poignant quiet melodic passage of the violins that follows this expansive melody the second time, dying out gradually for the next fugal entry; the climax to which this entry rises almost immediately. And throughout all these developments and episodes the chorus repeats at intervals its plaintive

Until the end, when the fugal progression gradually dies out and the orchestra becomes silent, the chorus continues alone with its plaintive figure and also stops, and then something breathtakingly unexpected and beautiful happens: a succession of entries of the chorus's figure, wonderfully changed from minor to major, and accompanied by sustained notes of the winds, create an expanding ethereally radiant texture for the final words; after which the chorus's figure is the *Amen*.

Another remarkable example of the same procedure is the second movement of the symphony *Harold in Italy*—the *March of Pilgrims Singing Their Evening Prayer*. Over a marching bass we hear one of Berlioz's exfoliating melodic progressions with exquisite inflections and unexpected turns that pivot on, and are enriched by, equally unexpected and exquisite moves in the underlying harmony, and are further enriched by the subtly contrived instrumental colors. In this instance the progression is a succession of developing statements, alternately from violins and violas, each taking off from the same beginning but moving unpredictably each time to a different concluding note that is answered by a magical note of the horn with exquisite murmurings of the woodwinds—the magic of the horn note being that it seems to be a different note each time but actually is the same note sounding wonderfully different in the different contexts (something not to be achieved without the powers Berlioz is alleged not to have possessed).

After the fourth such statement the further development of the melodic idea is carried on by cellos, basses and bassoons in alternation with violins and woodwinds, while the solo viola plays the melody it plays in each movement. All this produces a texture with great rhythmic intricacy and increasing intensity, in a crescendo to the point where the opening series of statements begins again, proceeding for a time as before, but then, after the third statement, moving unexpectedly to new conclusions, each punctuated by the magical horn note. Then—over the continuing march of the basses, and with accompanying arpeggios from the solo viola—comes the *canto religioso;* after which the march returns briefly and dies out in the distance.

The other movements are no less remarkable in their different ways. In the third, *Serenade of a Mountaineer of the Abruzzi to His Mistress,* we hear first some preliminary pastoral pipings; then the English horn begins the serenade with two statements of a simple tune that don't prepare us for the sudden succession ear-ravishing melodic inflections, harmonic progressions and instrumental colorings. And in the finale, *Orgy of Brigands,* we hear an activating play with dynamics, orchestral sonority and rhythmic grouping and accentuation that is like a tossing about of thunderbolts.

Those titles of the movements of *Harold in Italy* make the work a piece of *program music*—which I would define as music whose generalized expressive meaning is linked to specific visual images, ideas or incidents. A march, with a middle section in a style with religious connotations to our ears, is made a *March of Pilgrims Singing Their Evening Prayer;* music with pastoral connotations, and a lilting tune, are made a *Serenade of a Mountaineer of the Abruzzi to His Mistress;* exciting play with dynamics, orchestral sonority and rhythmic grouping and accentuation is made an *Orgy of Brigands.*

As in the case of music with only generalized expressive meaning, the interest of program music is not in the images or ideas or incidents themselves but in their musical embodiment. And not only the interest but the value: Berlioz's *Harold,* his *Symphonie Fantastique,* his *Romeo and Juliet*—like Mozart's *Figaro* and Schubert's *Nacht und Träume*—are as good as the music he put into them; and that music, like Mozart's and Schubert's, is not less good for its connection with the literary meanings that stimulated Berlioz's musical imagination and enlarge our musical experience.

The stimulation of Shakespeare's poetry gives us, in Berlioz's *Romeo and Juliet,* a work whose central sections are the supreme, the incandescent achievements of his powers. These sections follow a number of preliminaries: first an instrumental *Introduction,* an Allegro fugato depicting *Strife—Tumult* and breaking off for imposing pronouncements of trombones and bass tuba that constitute the *Intervention of the Prince;* then the *Prologue,* in which a small mixed chorus tells the story that will be told in the later sections of the symphony—of the quarrel between the two families, of the Capulets' ball (the orchestra breaks in with a little of the brilliant ball music that we will hear later), of Romeo in the Capulet garden, Juliet on her balcony, their avowals of their love (the orchestra plays a little of the impassioned music of the *Love Scene* that we will hear later); then *Strophes,* a fervent comment sung by the solo contralto, followed by the chorus's description of the dreamy Romeo being chaffed by his friends, including Mercutio, whose exquisite *Queen Mab* Scherzetto is sung by the solo tenor and chorus (note the characteristic writing for woodwinds); after which the chorus (to music we will hear later in *Juliet's Funeral Procession*) tells of death and the reconciliation of the two families.

This brings us to the first of the sections of the symphony proper that I spoke of a moment ago. Melancholy statements of the violins represent *Romeo Alone,* and lead to one of the great Berlioz melodies: a poignant two-measure statement by oboe and clarinet that is repeated, each time with changes in harmony, orchestration and texture that increase its intensity, to the point where violins and woodwinds take off on one of those Berlioz progressions in constantly unexpected directions and with heart-piercingly exquisite inflections. The sharp rhythm of the ball music, heard as though from a great distance, breaks in for a moment but dies out for the lovely oboe melody of Romeo's *Melancholy.* Then the sharp rhythm breaks in again in a transition to the rhythmically activated orchestral brilliance of *Concert and Ball—Great Festivity at the Capulets'.*

And now comes one of those supreme, incandescent sections, the *Love Scene,* which Toscanini once characterized as the most beautiful piece of music in the world, for reasons that are evident from the start. Strings *pppp* and flutes *pp* create the enchantment of *Capulet's Garden Still and Deserted,* leading to breathtaking distant notes of a horn *pp* and last exquisite comments by the violins; then we hear the young Capulets, on their way home, singing reminiscences of the ball music over a wonderfully beautiful comment of the strings. Their singing dies out in the distance; and the music concerned with the balcony scene begins: murmurings of muted lower strings over which are heard sighs of the English horn and clarinet, and, later, exclamations of the unmuted violins which increase in intensity, then subside and break off for agitated figures of the strings that introduce the mournfully impassioned melody of the muted cellos (reinforced by a horn):

In this melody one hears, unquestionably, the voice of Romeo; and concerning it there is a comment to make which applies to everything that follows. The expressive content of the section is unmistakable: declarations, avowals, the *premiers transports, premiers aveux, premiers serments* described in the *Prologue;* and these are conveyed in musical terms of the most exquisite delicacy which not only characterize the emotions of the young lovers but reveal the delicacy of feeling of Berlioz himself. One can say of this section what Turner said of the *Requiem*—that it provided an opportunity for vulgarity, but Berlioz could not be vulgar.

The murmurings of muted strings, sighs of English horn and clarinet, exclamations of violins are heard again, and lead to a more intensely impassioned statement of the cellos' melody. This subsides into the woodwinds' agitated

which is interrupted twice by declarations of the cellos:

And these, the second time, lead to another exquisitely inflected and heart-piercing melody:

and to this statement:

which keeps returning after numerous episodes, some impassioned, some quiet and lovely, like

and (much later)

Eventually there is a last impassioned reference to the cello melody; this is followed by an agitated passage that works up to a point of great intensity at which it breaks off abruptly: the enchanted night has reached gray dawn, and the last halting, fragmentary references to [1] and last sighing exclamations with which the piece ends.

The *Love Scene* is followed by the orchestral magic of the *Queen Mab* Scherzo—the magic which at once evokes the world of the subtitle *The Fairy of Dreams* with the play of alternating woodwinds and muted strings leading to a rush of muted violins. The rush subsides; the preliminaries are repeated; and eventually the rush becomes the theme of a continuing section, with woodwinds first contributing mere glints of light and later alternating with the strings in the rush and chatter. This first section ends on a sustained trill of the violins, which continues in the next section as an accompaniment to the melody of flute and English horn—an accompaniment to which are added gleaming violin harmonics and, a few measures

105

later, the exciting darting about of the violas in references to the rushing theme of the first section. That first section returns, but only briefly; then distant horns are heard in a new section, their statements punctuated by comments of strings and woodwinds. There is a hush, in which kettledrum-beats begin a crescendo that leads to a blazing up of the entire orchestra; this breaks off for a tremolo of violas *ff*, which drops to *pp* for evocative chords of muted strings and woodwinds; then another section begins: an ostinato of the clarinet over gleaming notes of the harp, which gradually draws additional instruments into a crescendo to a point of breath-taking orchestral splendor. This breaks off for a brief return to the first section; then, suddenly, there is a slowing down, a dying out of the exciting activity, the beginning of the end of the dream: a passage of wonderfully evocative hushed chords of muted strings, then of strings alternating with woodwinds, then string chords punctuated by silvery notes of antique cymbals, leading to staccatos of woodwinds, of plucked strings, of harps and strings, and a pause on a sustained note of the cellos; and then a last rush that brings the extraordinary piece to an end.

No less extraordinary in its own way is the section that follows, *Juliet's Funeral Procession*, which is another great example of the procedure we observed in the *Offertorium* of the *Requiem*, with the chorus repeating its plaintive *Jetez des fleurs!* on the reiterated note E at intervals during the fugal march and the melodic episode played by the orchestra, and then the violins repeating the plaintive E's at intervals as the fugal passage and melodic episode are sung by the chorus.

Extraordinary too is the next section, *Romeo in the Vault of the Capulets:* the opening Allegro agitato e disperato, the sudden silence and solemn antiphonal chords of brass, woodwinds and strings; then, over lamenting figures of muted violas and cellos punctuated by heavy accents of basses, the grandly sustained melody of Romeo's *Invocation*, dying out for a passage in which tentative phrases of the clarinet, recalling the sighs of the beginning of the *Love Scene*, alternate with increasingly agitated exclamations of the low strings in *Juliet's Awakening*, leading to the orchestral outburst of *Delirious Joy, Despair*, which breaks off for the tearing, shattering details of *Last Agonies and Death of the Two Lovers*.

Astonishing, therefore, after all this creativeness and originality, is the conventional grandiloquence of the finale.

Romeo and Juliet is only the greatest of the works of Berlioz that we owe to the susceptibility of his powers to the stimulation of poetry. At the age of twenty-six he produced *Eight Scenes from Faust*—including the beautiful *Easter Hymn* and *Peasants' Chorus*, the striking *Rat Song* and *Flea Song*, the hauntingly lovely *King of Thule Ballad* and *Romance of Marguerite*. These were retained in *The Damnation of Faust* seventeen years later, with the additional music including things as beautiful and impressive as the opening scene, the choral scene introduced by Mephistopheles's *Voici des fleurs* (note, among other details in the exquisite orchestral writing of the concluding *Dance of the Sylphs*, the activity of the harps), Mephistopheles's *Invocation* and *Serenade*, the *Minuet of the Will-o'-the-Wisps*, the trio.

Still later his love of Virgil resulted in the opera *The Trojans*, which has never been performed here by a major opera company, but of which the second part, *The Trojans at Carthage*, is available on records. Throughout there is the quietly beautiful vocal writing characteristic of Berlioz's later years; but neither this nor the lovely ballet music early in Act 2 prepares us for the incandescent septet *Tout n'est que paix* and duet *Nuit d'ivresse* later in the act, the wonderful passage with Mercure's repeated *Italie!* that ends the act, and the *Royal Hunt and Storm* that follows, with its lovely opening section and the marvelously altered repetition of this section at the end.

Another work of this period is the oratorio *L'Enfance du Christ*, with suitably quiet writing for a small orchestra, chorus and vocal soloists. Much of Part 1 is in a mellifluous nine-teenth-century oratorio style; but we begin to hear the Berlioz mind in fascinating operation in the Overture of Part 2, and in the music it introduces: the lovely *Shepherds' Farewell to the Holy Family* and the wonderfully beautiful *Repose of the Holy Family*. And there are moving and beautiful passages in Part 3: the Narrator's description of the journey to Saïs, Joseph's appeals for refuge, the trio for flutes and harp, the concluding vocal passage.

Of Berlioz's last opera, *Beatrice and Benedict*, only the delight-ful overture is played here occasionally. The most frequently heard of the overtures is the brilliant *Roman Carnival;* played less often is the brilliant overture of the earlier opera *Benvenuto Cellini;* and only rarely are there performances of the *King Lear* and *Corsair* Overtures, whose relation to their titles is ob-scure and less important than the working of the Berlioz mind that is intensely interesting in each, especially in their opening sections.

Certainly, in Berlioz's case as in every other composer's, it is possible for someone to know and understand the music and decide that he doesn't care for it. But the actual situation is that many have listened to the music in the expectation of hearing the poverty of invention they have read about, and as a result have heard only what they expected to hear; and that others have listened without such preconceptions, but with habit, and have found it difficult to gear their minds to music so different in every way from the music they were accustomed to. That situation calls for additional listening with ears and mind open to the particular distinctive and unusual things Berlioz has to say. And such listening will, I think, lead most people to the conclusion that his music is some of the most beautiful and moving that has come down to us.

10

BACH

At this point I would like to turn back to Bach, whose *Passa-caglia* I presented in detail in Chapter 3; but before I speak of other great works of his I will make a general observation about his entire output. Or rather—having recently found my point formulated very effectively in one of Turner's arti- · cles—I will let him make it for me.

Quoting Terry's description of the fifty-three cantatas Bach composed between 1736 and 1744 as an "unflagging cataract of inspiration in which masterpiece followed masterpiece with the monotonous periodicity of a Sunday sermon," Turner calls it nonsense and contends that "this 'monotonous perio-dicity' was exactly what was wrong with a great deal of Bach's music." Bach, he says, "had arrived at the point of being able to sit down at any minute of any day and compose what had all the superficial appearance of being a masterpiece. It is possible that even Bach himself did not know which was a masterpiece and which was not, and it is abundantly clear to me that in all his large-sized works there are huge chunks of stuff to which inspiration is the last word that one could apply." What makes it difficult to evaluate the music cor-rectly, says Turner, is Bach's virtuosity; but while the pro-digious technical skill may interest and amaze the academic musician "with the score in his hands and his soul long de-funct," for Turner it is valueless "unless . . . it is as expres-sive as it is accomplished."

This seems to me an excellent description of the essential fact about Bach—that one hears always the operation of prodigious powers of invention and construction, but frequently an operation that is not as expressive as it is accomplished.

The occasion for Turner's remarks was a performance of the *B-Minor Mass*, which is generally regarded as a towering masterpiece from first note to last, but in which I have, like Turner, come to hear only in certain portions what he describes as "those really creative moments which are popularly called inspired." For me they are the second *Kyrie*, the *Gratias agimus*, *Qui tollis* and *Cum sancto spiritu* of the *Gloria*, the *Et incarnatus est* and *Crucifixus est* of the *Credo*, the *Sanctus*, and the *Dona nobis pacem*, all for chorus; and only one aria, the *Et in spiritum sanctum* for bass. But you may find other portions genuinely expressive and moving that Turner and I do not.

Similarly you may be moved by more than what I find moving in the *St. Matthew Passion:* chiefly the chorales, the big opening and closing choruses, the great chorale-fantasia *O Mensch, bewein' dein' Sünde gross* that ends Part 1; also some of the accompanied recitatives of the soloists, but only very few of their arias—the tenor's *Ich will bei meinem Jesu wachen*, the soprano's *Aus Liebe will mein Heiland sterben*, and the alto's great *Erbarme dich*, one of Bach's most inspired moments. Or the *St. John Passion:* again the chorales, the magnificent opening chorus, some of the recitatives and ariosos, and the alto's aria *Es ist vollbracht*.

So with the smaller choral works. The Cantata No. 4, *Christ lag in Todesbanden*, is for me one of Bach's great utterances; but in some of the other cantatas, the *Magnificat*, the *Christmas Oratorio*, the *Easter Oratorio*, it is almost entirely the choral portions, and particularly the chorales, that I find beautiful and moving, rarely one of the arias; and most of these smaller works that I have heard I have, like Turner, found to be mechanical exercises of Bach's technical skill. But here again you may discover more than Turner and I.

And so with the instrumental works—in particular the ones that result from Bach's setting himself gigantic tasks and problems on which to exercise his skill. One of these is the *Clavierübung*, a collection of keyboard music comprising the six partitas, four duets, *Italian Concerto*, *French Overture*, and *Goldberg Variations* for harpsichord or clavichord, and the Prelude in E flat, a number of chorale-preludes and the Fugue in E flat for organ. In his notes for a recording of the entire collection Ralph Kirkpatrick contends that the "keyboard practice" of the title is to be taken "in the sense of an exercise, an activity of the spirit," and cites Bach's own statement that the various pieces have been composed "to delight the spirit of music-lovers." But Bach's way of exercising the spirit was to exercise his craftsmanship; and some of the results offer more to delight an interest in the skillful use of technique than to delight the spirit.

All six partitas are no doubt fascinating to anyone interested in their "astonishing assimilation of French, Italian and German keyboard styles"; but as a mere music-lover I find only No. 1 in B flat, and to a lesser degree No. 3 in A minor, interesting to listen to simply as music. Similarly, the *Italian Concerto* and *French Overture* may excite some listeners with Bach's "[appropriation] to the harpsichord [of] prevailing French and Italian orchestral styles of the preceding fifty years"; but listening to the music I am excited only by the slow movement of the concerto. Again, the organ pieces may interest some people with the elaborately organized "mathematical and symbolic structure" that Bach erects out of the chorales to illustrate the basic tenets of Lutheran doctrine; but what interests me as music is the magnificent opening prelude and only a few of the longer chorale-preludes—the closing fugue being impressive as a piece of fugal construction. The four duets may be "the most highly concentrated two-voice music that Bach ever wrote"; but I find them dull. And while everything in the *Goldberg Variations* may sound like "unsurpassable invention" to some ears, I hear examples of mechanical use of the variation procedure as well as things as wonderful as the three slow variations in minor mode.

Similarly, the *Well-Tempered Clavier*, with its forty-eight preludes and fugues in the twenty-four major and minor keys, includes pieces as charming as the Prelude No. 3 of Book 1, the Prelude No. 12 and Prelude and Fugue No. 15 of Book 2; as quietly poignant as the Preludes Nos. 12, 16 and 23 of Book 1 and No. 14 of Book 2; as impressive and affecting as the Prelude No. 8, Fugue No. 12 and Preludes and Fugues Nos. 4 and 22 of Book 1, the Fugue No. 9 of Book 2. But it also includes many examples of competent construction that are, for me, not interesting pieces of music.

Again, *The Art of Fugue*—Bach's last work, which he left uncompleted—contains some of his most magnificent music (which I suggest your hearing a fugue or two at a time). But of the collection of contrapuntal exercises on a theme of Frederick the Great entitled *The Musical Offering* I find only a few of the canons and the concluding six-voiced ricercare similarly impressive.

Listening to the six sonatas or partitas for unaccompanied violin, the six sonatas or suites for unaccompanied cello, one is aware of Bach's success with the difficult problem he set himself, of contriving for the instrument a melody that would imply its underlying harmonic progressions between the occasional chords. But one is aware also that solving this problem was not equivalent to writing great or even enjoyable music. Or at any rate it is what I am aware of: I hear an operation that is genuinely creative and expressive only in the great *Chaconne* of the Violin Sonata No. 4 (Partita No. 2) in D minor and the superb Prelude of the Violin Sonata No. 6 (Partita No. 3) in E; elsewhere I hear only Bach's craftsmanship going through the motions of creation and producing the external appearances of expressiveness. And I suspect that it is the name of Bach that awes listeners into accepting the appearance as reality, into hearing an expressive content which isn't there, and into believing that if the content is difficult to hear, this is only because it is especially profound—because it is "the passionate, yet untroubled meditation of a great mind" that lies beyond "the composition's formidable technical frontiers."

I might add that the formidable technical frontiers this writer refers to are the difficulties for the present-day violinist or cellist caused by the fact that the pieces were written for performance on an instrument with a flat bridge and finger-board on which the notes of a chord could be produced on the several strings simultaneously, as they cannot be on the present-day instrument with curved bridge and finger-board. The present-day violinist or cellist has to break or arpeggiate the chord, and to distend the melodic phrase to fit the ar-peggiated chord in; and the sonatas are among the accepted test-pieces with which he demonstrates his technical and musical powers to the public—the powers that in this case enable him to create continuity in the distended phrases, to do this with an appearance of ease, and—if he is a Casals or a Szigeti—with an eloquence in the playing that listeners mistake for eloquence in the music.

Among the six sonatas for violin and clavier No. 3 in E major is, for me, one of Bach's finest instrumental works; and there are interesting movements in No. 1 in B minor, No. 2 in A major, and No. 5 in F minor. But the sonatas for flute and clavier and sonatas for gamba and clavier I find uninteresting.

An outstanding work for solo clavier is the Toccata in C minor; and other good ones are the Toccatas in D major and E minor, the Fantasy of the *Chromatic Fantasy and Fugue*. The French Suite No. 5 in G major and English Suite No. 3 in G minor have several moderately enjoyable movements; the others I find uninteresting.

Of the *Brandenburg Concertos* No. 3 in G major is for me the most impressive; Nos. 2 in F and 4 in G are also enjoyable; No. 1 in F has an impressive slow movement; No. 5 in D is only moderately interesting; No. 6 in B flat is completely ,

113

boring. And of the four suites for orchestra the best-known
No. 2 in B minor has charming dance movements; No. 3 in
D major has some others, and in addition the famous melody
known as *Air for G String;* No. 4 in D has a fugal section in
the opening movement and a Bourrée that are fine; No. 1 in
C is for me another boring piece.

Of the concertos for one or more solo instruments the D
minor for clavier (or violin) is one of Bach's greatest instrumental works. In the two fast movements the seemingly inexhaustible flow of inspired invention becomes breathtaking;
and in the wonderful slow movement a grave opening statement by the orchestra is repeated in different keys as a sort
of ground-bass that provides structural coherence for the ornate and wide-ranging melody of the solo instrument.

Another great work is the Concerto in D minor for two
violins, with an endless progression of melody in the slow
movement that makes it possibly the loveliest piece of music
Bach wrote. And the Concerto in A minor and the slow movement of the Concerto in E for violin are also fine.

The other concertos, to my ears, are uninteresting.

That leaves the important category of works for organ—
important because the organ was Bach's most immediately
personal medium, through which he expressed what was
strongest in him: his religious feeling and his feeling for musical architectonics. These give us the great *Passacaglia* that I
presented in Chapter 3; they give us also the great preludes
and fugues—the Toccata, Adagio and Fugue in C, the Toccata and Fugue in D minor, the Fantasia and Fugue in G
minor, the Preludes and Fugues in E flat, A minor, E minor
(Leipzig), B minor, C minor (Weimar), among others. And
inevitably they give us works that are impressive as large-
scale construction but not as music.

We get also the chorale-preludes, which include such wonderful meditations on the texts and melodies of the Lutheran
chorales as *O Mensch, bewein' dein' Sünde gross* and *Ich ruf' zu
dir, Herr Jesu Christ* of the *Orgelbüchlein* (*Little Organ Book*);

Herzlich tut mich verlangen and *An Wasserflüssen Babylon* of the *Miscellaneous Chorale-Preludes; Komm' Gott Schöpfer, heiliger Geist, An Wasserflüssen Babylon* and *Jesus Christus, unser Heiland* of the last *Eighteen Chorale-Preludes.* And supreme utterances like *Nun komm' der Heiden Heiland* and *Schmücke dich, o liebe Seele* of the *Eighteen.*

With Bach's music, finally, we come to the matter of transcription. Since Bach himself made some of his clavier concertos into violin concertos, or a concerto movement into a choral movement of a cantata, there would seem to be no reason against merely orchestrating one of his organ works. And good reasons can be offered for it: the desirability of making the work known to many people who would not hear it played on the organ; the advantage of having the strands of the contrapuntal texture stand out more clearly by means of different orchestral colors than they can be made to do by organ registration. But those good reasons don't include a reason that has been offered in recent years: the orchestral transcription isn't needed to fulfill completely a conception only partly fulfilled in the original organ version. The notion that the composer of two hundred years ago—or even three or four hundred—who didn't have the Philadelphia Orchestra to write for worked in an agony of frustration is as incorrect as the analogous notion would be about the painter of that period: the composer's mind operated in the terms of the musical instruments, language, style and forms available to him, and fulfilled its conceptions completely in those terms. That certainly was true of Bach writing for the organ; it was no less true of Bach writing for the unaccompanied violin. He could have written the *Chaconne* for an orchestra; he could have rewritten it for orchestra after writing it for unaccompanied violin (as in fact he made the Prelude of the Sonata No. 6 into a piece for organ and orchestra, the Prelude to the Cantata No. 29); but since he did neither it is clear that he conceived of the piece entirely in the terms provided by the unaccompanied violin and was entirely satisfied with the fulfillment of his conception in those terms.

Nor is it merely that the Bach piece doesn't need completion by Stokowski to fulfill Bach's conception and produce the effect he intended; it is that the piece as completed by Stokowski does *not* fulfill Bach's conception and does *not* produce the effect he intended. When Bach himself makes a violin concerto out of his clavier concerto, a cantata prelude out of a sonata movement for unaccompanied violin, we hear the same mind, personality and feeling operating in the new work as in the old; and this undoubtedly would be so if he were himself to transcribe one of his organ works for the orchestra of today. What his own orchestral transcription of the work would demonstrate is that a composer's instrumentation is no less an integral part of his art than is a painter's color, his way of scoring no less an expression of his feeling than is his way of writing melody and harmony. This means that even a Schönberg, applying orchestral color to the lines of Bach's texture with precision and subtlety that express his fastidiousness and taste, gives the music the impress of his own mind and feeling. The others—Stokowski, Ormandy, Elgar, Respighi—call to mind a remark of Ernest Bloch about Richard Strauss: "Debussy is like a painter who looks at his canvas to see what more he can take out; Strauss is like a painter who has covered every inch and then takes the paint he has left and throws it at the canvas"; and such transcribers give us Bach with the impress of their own vulgarity. Stokowski's orchestrations and performances, in particular—with their lurid phrasing, their tonal heaving and billowing—give us not the religious feeling and structural power that are Bach's, but the feverish, orgiastic excitement that is Stokowski's.

In other words, a work of Bach as completed by Stokowski fulfills not Bach's conception but Stokowski's, and produces not the effect Bach intended but the effect Stokowski wants. Now composers have always made music out of other composers' music: Beethoven wrote sets of variations on themes from Mozart's *Magic Flute;* Brahms wrote sets of variations on themes of Handel and Paganini; Stravinsky in our own century has made one ballet score out of music by Pergolesi, another by using thematic fragments from a number of pieces by Tchaikovsky as the ideas for a work of his own. And what they have done Stokowski certainly may do. But Beethoven, Brahms and Stravinsky haven't offered their products as fulfillments of the unfulfilled conceptions of Mozart, Handel, Pergolesi and Tchaikovsky; they have offered them as works of their own, to be evaluated as such. And that, it seems to me, is how Stokowski may present what he makes of the works of Bach and the other composers, earlier and later, that he fancies up.

I have been discussing in connection with Bach the problem which arises with other music of his period and earlier periods that we shall be considering very shortly. The musical notation reproduced in this book is a series of directions for performance which tell the players what notes to produce, how loud to make them, how long to hold them, and other things of that kind. Ever since Mozart's and Haydn's time the directions have been increasingly numerous and detailed; but the most detailed directions have to leave something to the player—certain subtle differentiations of loudness, certain time-values a little longer or shorter than written, which cannot be specified in notation, and which the player supplies in accordance with the tradition of performance that he has learned, and with his own judgment and taste. On the other hand the further back we go from Mozart and Haydn the less numerous and detailed are the directions for the player; and even the directions concerning the notes to play are summed up in a form of notational shorthand—the melodic ornaments and figured bass which the player was expected to translate into melody, harmony, rhythm and figuration in the language and style of his period. This shorthand is something most people today, including most musicians, know very little about; but it, and the language and style it summarizes, have

117

to be learned by anyone who wants to play the music correctly. For this is music that does have to be completed in performance; but the completion, the filling in of melody and harmony, must be done in the music's own language and style, not in the language and style of our music of the past two hundred years. Which does not mean, however, that a composer of today may not use sixteenth- or seventeenth-century music as the material for a piece of his own.

11

OTHER MUSIC OF THE
EIGHTEENTH CENTURY

We have been concerned thus far with the work of a few major figures among the composers of the music that falls within the normal range of our interest—European music of the past three or four centuries. There remains for us to explore the large amount of great or moving or enjoyable music produced by their contemporaries, their predecessors, their successors.

Thus, in the early part of the eighteenth century there is the music of Bach's contemporaries—Handel, Vivaldi, Domenico Scarlatti, Couperin, Rameau; and later in the century the music of the contemporaries of Haydn and Mozart—Gluck, Bach's son Carl Philipp Emanuel, Boccherini. The music historians would insist that these are not the only eighteenth-century composers worth your attention: they object to the practice, in the concert hall and the appreciation course, of having a period represented by a few outstanding figures and neglecting the other composers who they insist produced equally good music; and they contend that this has resulted in our knowing only a small part of the masterworks of the past.

Well, in the past few years LP recording has provided the opportunities to hear a great amount of music that previously wasn't performed or recorded; and some of it has indeed proved to be music we had been the poorer for not knowing. But most of the newly revealed masterworks have been products of the well-known outstanding figures rather than of their obscure contemporaries: in eighteenth-century music I can recall a couple of charming quartets by Stamitz and Richter, a couple of arresting symphonies by Brunetti; but the works of major stature that come to mind are Couperin's *First Tenebrae Service*, a couple of Carl Philipp Emanuel Bach's symphonies and a few of his sacred songs, Haydn's masses and some of his unfamiliar quartets. It is true, as the historians contend, that many others besides Haydn used the musical language and style of his time; it is not true that these others produced with them music as good as his: the historians' difficulty is their inability to tell when a language and style are being used in a work of great art, and when they are merely being used, period.

As a matter of fact there are works in which even the great masters use the language and style of their time uninterestingly. They are among the things on LP records that could have been left unrecorded. And we can leave them unheard.

But we do want to hear the magnificent and joyous choruses and beautiful solos of Handel's *Messiah;* the dramatic and imaginative writing, mostly for chorus, of his *Israel in Egypt;* the ear-ravishing lyricism of his *Acis and Galatea;* the similar writing in *Alcina, Julius Caesar, Semele, Solomon,* the *Dettingen Te Deum,* the *Ode for St. Cecilia's Day, L'Allegro ed il Penseroso;* the fine instrumental writing of the *Water Music,* the Concerti Grossi Op. 6, the Sonatas Op. 1, some of the harpsichord suites. We want to hear the poignantly lovely writing of Vivaldi's *L'Estro Armonico, The Four Seasons* and some of his miscellaneous concertos. We want to hear Scarlatti's harpsichord sonatas, fascinating and exciting in their endless invention, their harmonic daring, the power of some of the ones in slow tempo, the verve and brilliance of some of the ones in fast tempo, which utilize the sharp, biting, flashing sounds

of the instrument for their effect. We want to hear not only
the charming harpsichord pieces of Rameau and Couperin,
but Rameau's *Concerts en sextuor*, which have some of this
composer's loveliest music, and Couperin's *Tenebrae Services*,
extended vocal declamations which are made remarkable by
their unique style and expressive force. We want to hear not
just the familiar aria *Che farò senza Euridice*, but the other
beautiful and affecting music of Gluck's *Orfeo ed Euridice*. We
want to hear the works of Carl Philipp Emanuel Bach—
symphonies, sacred songs, a *Magnificat*—that exhibit the operation of a mind excitingly individual, daring and dynamic. And
of Boccherini we want to hear not the Cello Concerto in B
flat that Grützmacher put together with materials from
Boccherini's works, but Boccherini's own quartets, quintets
and trios, which are engagingly and at times excitingly individual in invention and procedures.

12

MUSIC OF EARLIER CENTURIES

It isn't very many years since music, in the concert hall and the appreciation course, began with Bach and Handel, and everything before them was dark and unknown except for the distant gleams of Palestrina and—a few centuries beyond—Gregorian chant. Gradually this situation changed, and the public learned there was a great deal more in those early centuries—though again not as much as the historians claimed.

Today there are LP records which offer, in historical sequence, specimens of the music produced in that period from Gregorian chant to Bach. And while many of the examples of the first types of polyphonic music do no more than satisfy our interest in how the music of the ninth or tenth or eleventh century sounded, there are, as early as the twelfth century, pieces (e.g. Nos. 7 and 8 on Haydn Society 9038) which the ear of today finds esthetically effective. There is no question about the effectiveness of some of the more developed polyphony of Machaut, Dufay, Ockeghem, Obrecht and Josquin des Prés in the fourteenth and fifteenth centuries. Nor is there any such question, later, with the beautiful vocal writing of Lassus and Palestrina, the dark intensity of Victoria. Nor, still later, with the power of Gesualdo, though it is achieved by harmonic progressions that are amazingly bold and strange even to twentieth-century ears. And certainly not with the variety

of beauty and expressive power in the works of Monteverdi
—among others the famous *Lagrime d'Amante al Sepolcro
dell' Amata* and the *Vespers of 1610.*

We find some of the most beautiful and affecting music
of the sixteenth and seventeenth centuries in the works of
English composers—notably the superb *Mass for Four Voices*
and other religious works, the lovely madrigals, the fine instrumental pieces that make Byrd a major figure of this great
period of English music. Dowland, Farnaby, Wilbye, Weelkes,
Bull, Morley and Gibbons are among those who produced
other lovely songs and madrigals, and other fine instrumental
pieces.

We come in this way to another great figure, the last in
English music—Purcell. His individuality and power are
strikingly evident in the famous *Fantasia in Five Parts on One
Note,* one of the Fantasias for strings, all superb pieces, in
whose slow sections we follow a mind that moves in strange,
daring, and at times startling ways—as it does also in the
Pavane and Chacony on Bartók 913. The chaconne's reiteration of a ground-bass is a favorite procedure with Purcell (as
in fact with his English predecessors)—one that he uses with
impressive effect not only in instrumental but in vocal pieces.
Thus, the phrases of *When I Am Laid in Earth* in the opera
Dido and Aeneas succeed each other over the repetitions of a
ground-bass. And so with *O Let Me Ever Ever Weep!* and *Next
Winter Comes Slowly* in *The Fairy Queen,* a work that is overwhelming not only in the profusion but in the expressive
range of its superb writing. And on the other hand *I Love and
I Must* and *Tell Me Some Pitying Angel* are two magnificent
examples of Purcell's powerfully expressive florid vocal style.

I referred a moment ago to the claims of the music historians—the musicologists, as these scholars are called—
about the music of early centuries. Intent on establishing
the value of their explorations and excavations, but reasoning in a world of concept thousands of miles from the facts
they are digging away in, they have produced one of their

pat schematizations: not only, they say, has each period had *its* music, produced by *its* creative energies, and satisfying *its* esthetic needs, but since human creative energies must be presumed to have been equal in all periods, it follows that the music of the tenth or eleventh or twelfth century was the equal of the painting and architecture, and the equal also of the music of the eighteenth or nineteenth century. And so we have had one of these men introducing some recordings of keyboard pieces from 1350 to 1700—most of them insignificant in ideas, structure, and even mere size—with the pronouncement that "the music in this album is not 'ancient music,' stale, dusty, and at best a curio for historically minded snobs. It is no more 'ancient' than Rembrandt's painting or Gothic cathedrals."

Actually, human creative energies have not been equal in all periods, or in all the arts of any one period. We find no important or even interesting poetry in England from the death of Chaucer in 1400 to the publication of Wyatt's poems in 1557; we find only minor poets between Pope and Blake; we find no painting of any consequence in the eighteenth- and nineteenth-century Germany that produced the music of Bach, Haydn, Mozart, Beethoven, Schubert, and other great composers whom we have still to investigate. And the music of an early period that satisfied *its* esthetic needs will not always satisfy ours.

13

BRAHMS

People change for us as we ourselves change in time; the things they said come to make more sense or less; and works of art, which are personal communications of a special kind, also change in significance and value for us. From which it follows that for someone to think less than he once did of certain pieces of music, as I have come to do of certain works of Brahms, is not to be guilty of unnatural behavior, of an enormity beyond comprehension. It probably will happen to you with one composer or another. And the reason it happened to me with Brahms is something to talk about here, because it has to do with the nature of his music.

For many years Brahms's music was for me, every note of it, the greatest of all. Until one day, as I was playing through the slow movement of the Cello Sonata Op. 99 at the piano, I suddenly was aware of hearing not real creative activity but the pretense, the pose of such activity—the pretense of feeling in synthetically contrived themes that were being manipulated by formula to fill out the pattern of the movement. And having heard it here I began to hear it in other works.

I recall a broadcast of a performance of the Piano Concerto No. 2 by Toscanini and the NBC Symphony with Horowitz as soloist. Sounds came through my radio that were evidence of attentive, purposeful activity by Brahms, Toscanini, Horowitz, the orchestra, the audience; but what also came through powerfully was the impression that this was the activity of people under a spell continuing to go through a long-established ritual that was without reality or meaning—performers and listeners going through the motions of esthetic response to a piece of music in which the composer went through the motions of esthetic creation. Anyone not under this spell, anyone able to listen freshly to the agitated statements of the piano that broke in on the quiet opening of the first movement, would, it seemed to me, perceive that they were the noisy motions of saying something portentous that really said absolutely nothing; and listening further he would discover that the entire movement was a succession of such attempts at now one such effect and now another.

Tchaikovsky's comments on Brahms have been quoted as an illustration of one composer's inability to understand and justly appraise the work of another; but actually composers have sometimes written about other composers with the special insight of the practitioner of an art; and when Tchaikovsky criticizes in Brahms's music the conscious aspiration to something for which there is no poetic impulse, the striving for something that must be unstriven for, the conscious attempt at Beethoven's profundity and power that results in caricature of Beethoven, and the operation, for these purposes, of the technical mastery that produces "so many preparations and circumlocutions for something which ought to come and charm us at once"—when Tchaikovsky speaks of all this he is describing what is plain to hear in the works that Brahms wrote, as he himself expressed it, with the consciousness of the tramp of Beethoven behind him.

The superb song *Botschaft* exhibits the genuine emotional impulse and musical gift of a lyricist, a creator of small forms; the *Variations on a Theme of Haydn* is one of the fine works the small-scale artist produces when he employs his technical skill to say the one small thing a number of different ways, and creates a large form by writing a continuous series of small ones. On the other hand the opening movement of Brahms's first published work, the Piano Sonata Op. 1, ex-

126

hibits the labored and bombastic proclamations, the stretches of arid manipulation, that are the results of the small-scale artist's attempt to write greater than he feels and to produce with technique what doesn't issue from emotional impulse. Similar striving for portentous utterance and similar arid manipulation are exhibited by the opening movement of the Piano Concerto No. 1, which grew out of Brahms's first attempt at a symphony after hearing Beethoven's Ninth; by the opening movement of the Symphony No. 1 that he did produce after twenty years' labor with the tramp of Beethoven behind him; by the other concertos, the equally pretentious chamber music and choral works. Nor are the cloying saccharine sweetness of many of the slow movements, the archness of many of the scherzo movements, easier to endure.

As a matter of fact the cloying sweetness and archness are heard also in small-scale works—some of the songs, most of the Intermezzos and Capriccios and other small pieces for piano that are, to my ears, arid artifice dipped in treacle. And as a matter of fact a few examples of large-scale operation come off for me—the finale of the Symphony No. 2, the second and final movements of the Symphony No. 3, and all but the third movement of the Symphony No. 4, whose concluding passacaglia is one of Brahms's finest essays in variation form.

These few symphony movements, then, the sets of variations on themes of Handel, Haydn and Paganini, and some of the songs are the music of Brahms that I have continued to hear with belief and pleasure. But the rest, which is only the pretense of artistic creation to my ears, may be the real thing to yours; and yours are making the decisions for you.

14

WAGNER

In the preceding chapter I spoke of my impression of the musicians and audience at a performance of Brahms continuing, under a spell, to go through a long-established ritual. And it is interesting to find an English critic, Richard Capell, writing thirty years ago about Wagner's success in imposing on the world his own idea of his work as a prophetic mission, in having the music-dramas presented in a darkened theatre "more austere than many cathedrals" and to an audience—formerly a prominent part of the spectacle—that was now "a dark and huddled anonymous throng assisting almost clandestinely at the enacted mysteries." No European music before Wagner's, said Capell, had worked "this quasi-hypnotic spell"; and although esthetic fashions had changed there still remained great numbers of "these 'perfect Wagnerites' who religiously adore many things in Wagner which in detachment could only be considered as incoherent, tautologous, morally reprehensible, or even dull."

Capell was writing as an admirer and enjoyer of Wagner, but one with the detachment that made him aware of what he termed the "radical falsity" of the libretto of the *Ring* tetralogy—"that the simple barbarians of the old saga are endowed by Wagner with a new consciousness and a manner of expressing themselves which are by no means simple—and all the while they retain their antique savagery of action. Wotan's cunning and Siegfried's brutal prowess were all very well before these persons took to heroising themselves, but then they became unpardonable." Thus, the Siegfried who robs Brünnhilde of the ring is "a symbol and an ideal, a demi-god, a savior. He is Siegfried, Wagner's 'ordained man of the future'—and he is nothing but an ordinary looting *soudard*. Similarly, Wotan, 'the substance of the Intelligence of the Present,' turns out to be the substance of a fraudulent army contractor."

Now I once had occasion to remark myself—concerning a performance of *Das Rheingold* that initiated a matinee *Ring* series for perfect Wagnerites at the Metropolitan—that the famous long-sustained opening E flat from the orchestra pit "cast a spell over the people who crowded the auditorium to capacity, a spell under which the visual and aural presentation of a story about mighty beings symbolized to them mighty significances." But, I added, to "one listener whom the E flat did not place under this spell . . . no mighty significances were conveyed by what he saw and heard." And I will add now that none were conveyed to me by the subsequent music-dramas of the *Ring* tetralogy. For me, then, it isn't only the libretto that doesn't work; it is also the music. I am aware of the prodigious musical powers operating in those scores, and the wonderful moments they achieve here and there (to say nothing of the wonderful pages in the other works we shall come to in a moment). But I find that the endless narrative declamation, the endless bombastic proclamation, the endless literal illustration of words and action (of which the *Ride of the Valkyries* is only the worst example), and the occasional tawdriness and cheapness (notably in the final scenes of *Siegfried* and *Die Götterdämmerung*) are as unendurable as the philosophical posturings and the equally pretentious and laughable verbal jargon of the texts (e.g. *Winterstürme wichen dem Wonnemond*, or *Starke Scheite schichtet mir dort*, or *Schweigt eures Jammers jauchzenden Schwall*). But again you may find them all convincing and impressive; and you will act in accordance with your findings, not mine.

The Prelude to *Tristan und Isolde*, on the other hand, from its very first statement, does cast its spell over me—despite which I manage, at its conclusion, to remember to skip the next half-hour or so of boring declamatory narration, explanation and argument to the point where the music of the Prelude returns as Tristan and Isolde drink the love potion. King Marke's fifteen-minute reproach near the end of the second act is something else I skip; but most of the music in this act is marvelous in its luxuriant tonal beauty and expressiveness, rising to sheer incandescence in the part that begins with *O sink hernieder*. In the Prelude to Act 3 we hear one of Wagner's most wonderful pages—wonderful as a musical evocation of the desolate scene and the wounded Tristan's bodily illness and sickness at heart that will be revealed when the curtain rises. And after Kurwenal's conversation with the shepherd and his first exchanges with the awakening Tristan we come to the powerful music of Tristan's delirium, which rises to the climax of his curse of the potion, and ends with the exquisite passage *Wie sie selig*.

Though Tristan and Isolde are—compared with the characters of the *Ring*—human beings, even they are somewhat dehumanized and monumentalized in Wagner's music-drama (the music, says Capell, "is accompanied on the stage by rather more than life-size gestures of actors who, no matter how gifted, never can avoid bringing to mind the Siegesallee statuary"). But Wagner's only comedy, *Die Meistersinger von Nürnberg*, is, for once, concerned with characters who are, act like, and are involved in the situations of, real human beings—with the exception of Beckmesser, who is a caricature, and as such a major and deplorable defect in the work. It is true that, as Capell puts it, "for the pint pot of this comedy Wagner poured out music in quarts and gallons"; but if Wagner is characteristically long-winded in the work, he is also uncharacteristically genial and sunny—except with Beckmesser, in whom he is revenging himself on the venomous critic Hanslick—which is to say that the exhaustingly garrulous outpouring includes a large amount of extraordinarily lovely music. Formerly the only thing one could do was arrive in the first intermission: one missed the good moments in Act 1, but was fresh for the beautiful passages in Act 2—the gay opening dance, the entrance of Pogner and Eva, Sachs's monologue *Was duftet doch der Flieder*, his conversation with Eva, her *Geliebter, spare den Zorn*, the watchman's song, Sachs's cobbling song, and the quiet closing pages after the riot. And after these one still wasn't too exhausted for the lovely things in Act 3—the affecting Prelude, Sachs's monologue *Wahn! Wahn!*, Walter's description of his dream, Eva's *Meister, 's ist nicht so gefährlich*, the ensuing scene of Sachs, Eva and Walter, the baptism of Walter's song, the quintet, the charming dances and songs of the apprentices, the crowd's *Wach auf* in greeting to Sachs, Walter's song. Now, with the entire opera on LP records, one can listen to an act at a time.

Parsifal was presented by Wagner, and still is accepted by the perfect Wagnerites, as a work of religious character; but I find this sensualist's exaltation of chastity decked out in religious mumbo-jumbo repellent, and would expect a religious person to find it offensive. In addition, the long dull stretches in the music reveal an astonishing enfeeblement of the powers of invention and manipulation that are so prodigious in the earlier works. But in the radiant closing pages of the lovely *Good Friday Spell* we hear his language marvelously enriched and subtilized—e.g. the ascending scale of clarinet, bassoon and horn in the seventh and eighth measures from the end.

In addition to the music-dramas there are the five Wesendonck songs, of which *Im Treibhaus* uses the thematic material of the Prelude to Act 3 of *Tristan und Isolde* in a piece of extended vocal declamation that is in its own way as wonderful as the Prelude.

And there is the *Siegfried-Idyll*, the charming orchestral piece Wagner fashioned out of some of the better themes of the final scene of *Siegfried* to celebrate the birth of his son.

15

VERDI

Verdi, unlike Wagner, did not spin vast ad hoc fantasies about the past and future of art to rationalize his own present practice, but simply addressed himself to the task of setting a libretto to music as well as he knew how; he set to music not philosophically pretentious dramas about gods and heroes of Teutonic mythology, but melodramas about passionate Italians and Spaniards; for his dramatic purpose he did not weave leitmotifs into hour-and-a-half progressions of continuous *melos*, but produced series of clearly outlined melodic structures. All this was enough to make him an object of condescension for some; and they found additional reason for condescension in the vulgarity to which they attributed his popularity.

There are, certainly, crudities and vulgarities in Verdi's early exercises of his powers; but one thing to say about this is Francis Toye's observation that the occasional vulgarity of *Il Trovatore* is "a by-product of the vitality and passion without which there can be no great art." Another is that the powers, operating with vitality and passion, give us in *Il Trovatore* such wonderful melodic structures as Leonora's *Tacea la notte placida* and *D'amor sull' ali rosee*, the Count's *Il balen*, Manrico's *Ah! sì, ben mio;* and their composer is not someone to condescend to.

Moreover, even in the still earlier *Macbeth* we get in the vocal and orchestral writing of the *Sleepwalking Scene* an astounding manifestation of the art which later—developed, enriched, subtilized—fills in moment after moment in *Otello* with sustained invention of marvelously wrought details of melody, harmony, figuration and orchestration—such as the orchestral passage leading from Desdemona's *Splende il cielo,* at the end of the choral episode early in Act 2, to her *D' un uomo che geme;* or the developing violin figure and harmonic progressions of Otello's *Dio! mi potevi scagliar* in Act 3. And the man who wrote the chorus's song around the fire, Iago's drinking song, and the duet of Otello and Desdemona, in Act 1; the duet of Otello and Iago, and especially Iago's *Era la notte,* in Act 2; the duet of Otello and Desdemona, Otello's *Dio! mi potevi scagliar,* the trio of Iago, Cassio and Otello, and the final ensemble, in Act 3; Desdemona's *Willow Song* and *Ave Maria,* in Act 4—this man is an artist to whom nobody may condescend.

The art that is incandescent and robust in *Otello* shows a further refinement and subtilization in *Falstaff,* in writing that is all lightness and fluent grace and transparent texture. The writing is largely point-to-point invention for the words; and some of this invention—for example, the opening uproar—is only the product of an experienced artist's resourcefulness; but much of it—for example Falstaff's interviews with Dame Quickly and Ford in the second scene—is a succession of marvels of subtly contrived expressive point, wit and loveliness, whose very subtlety may require repeated hearing for full appreciation. Moreover, the point-to-point invention includes vocal writing as lovely as Dame Quickly's *un angelo che innamora* in her first scene with Falstaff, or Mistress Ford's *Ogni più bel giojel mi nuoce* in her first scene with him, but for the most part also as brief—the two duets and two arias of Nanetta and Fenton being the only examples of extended lyricism. And one thing in *Falstaff* is new: the poignant autumnal quality of much of the music of the last act—for example, Falstaff's *Ber del vin dolce* after the innkeeper has brought him the wine; and the orchestra's phrases accompanying his arrival at Herne's Oak. This music conveys to us for once the emotion of Verdi himself—the emotion, that is, of a man nearing the end of his life.

As for the other operas, we hear in the early ones conventions and formulas of the period to which Verdi's powers give artistic validity and impressive effect. In *Rigoletto* the outstanding example of this is the famous quartet, in which freshly attentive listening enables us to appreciate the individualized writing for the four characters in the dramatic situation that makes it one of the most remarkable ensembles in opera. In *La Traviata* it is Violetta's *Ah! fors' è lui*, with its concluding efflorescence into florid passages that are not mere vocal exhibitionism of the period but an expression of the intensity of her emotion about her meeting with Alfredo, as the florid passages in the following recitative *Follie! Follie!* and aria *Sempre libera* are expressions of her feverish decision to reject love and pursue pleasure. In both operas, moreover, we hear other manifestations of Verdi's powers: in *Rigoletto* not only the Duke's *Quest' o quella*, his *Parmi veder le lagrime*, Gilda's *Caro nome*, their *E il sol dell' anima*, but the tremendous Prelude and the extraordinary first duet of Rigoletto and Sparafucile; in *La Traviata* not only Violetta's *Addio del passato*, her duet with Germont, her *Parigi, o cara* with Alfredo, but the music of the parties in Violetta's and Flora's homes that continues as a background of feverish gaiety for the poignant dialogue and dramatic incidents in the foreground. And in *Rigoletto* there is the *Zitti, zitti* chorus, with a delicacy that foretells the ensembles in *Falstaff;* in *La Traviata* the Preludes to Acts 1 and 3, whose divided violins are an example of the increasingly elaborate and refined orchestral writing we hear with the beautiful melodic invention in *Un Ballo in Maschera* and *Simon Boccanegra*.

It is this orchestral writing that combines with the superb vocal declamation to make *Ella giammai m'amò* in *Don Carlo* one of Verdi's supreme achievements, and that contributes to the impressive effect of the subsequent scene of Philip and the

Grand Inquisitor. And it is this orchestral writing that, with the exquisite vocal writing, gives us the *Nile Scene* of *Aida*.

The same matured powers, the same enriched and refined art, produce the superb *Requiem*. And their final manifestation, five years after *Falstaff*, is the marvelously beautiful *Te Deum*.

16

TCHAIKOVSKY

Tchaikovsky is another popular composer who has been regarded with condescension for which we hear no justification in his music. Listening to one of his ballet scores—*Swan Lake*, *The Sleeping Beauty*, *The Nutcracker* (the entire score of each, not just the usual excerpts)—listening, that is, to the canvas, so to speak, being filled in with detail, we hear in the operation a wonderful precision and taste in the use of the entire complex of musical line, color, texture and mass. And we hear also this mastery of the medium serving dramatic and imaginative powers of a high order—the powers revealed for example in the ominous figure that interrupts the opening melodic passage of *Swan Lake* and is developed with increasing tension over plucked bass-notes and sustained brass-notes; or in the music at the end of Act 1 of *The Nutcracker*, and the Prelude to Act 2, which convey so marvelously the world of a child's dream.

Listening now to Toscanini's or Cantelli's performance of the *Pathétique* Symphony we hear the music, as it proceeds in strict accordance with Tchaikovsky's directions in the score, take shape as something contrived with the same feeling for the complex of musical line, color, texture and mass; and we hear also the dramatic power it has when given these correct and beautifully integrated plastic proportions. We are then able to perceive the effect of the more usual performance that exaggerates every crescendo and decrescendo, every acceleration and retardation (to say nothing of the additional changes of tempo and volume Tchaikovsky doesn't request in his score) and makes every *p* a *ppp*, every *f* a *fff*, in the overemphasis that is traditional in playing Tchaikovsky. We are able, that is, to perceive the distortion of the shape of the work, the consequent falsification of its meaning. It is the traditional overstatement in performance that converts drama and intensity into the melodrama and hysteria for which Tchaikovsky is looked down upon. And this overstatement has become the criterion by which mere statement is judged inadequate for failing to impart to the music "its essential feverish excitement"—which is as though some actor's ranting in Shakespeare had become the criterion by which the correct delivery of the lines were judged inadequate.

Tchaikovsky's music has been treated in this way because of the knowledge about his neurotically disordered personal life; and he provides part of the answer to the contention that knowledge of a composer's life is necessary for complete understanding of his music—a plausible contention until we think of some of the actual cases. On the one hand not one statement of Schubert has been reported to us that reveals the insights communicated in his greatest works; on the contrary, it is from the music that we infer the probability of these insights in the man. And on the other hand it is Berlioz's extravagances of behavior and utterance that are responsible for the ideas about "monstrous works" in which he carried out "extreme and gigantic aims" that people would not have got from mere listening to the works themselves. So with Tchaikovsky: it is, among other things, the neurotic self-accusations of incompetence and insincerity that are responsible for the ideas about the defects and the insincerity of his music that people would not have got from mere listening to the ballet scores, the operas *The Queen of Spades* and *Eugene Onegin*, the Overture-Fantasia *Romeo and Juliet*, the *Manfred* Symphony, and even the intensely subjective Symphonies Nos. 4, 5 and 6 (*Pathétique*).

It is a composer's works that we are concerned with and evaluate, not the circumstances under which they were produced; and by the evidence of the works I have mentioned Tchaikovsky was a superb artist. Nor was he less so for having produced other works inferior to them.

17

MUSORGSKY

One article of Turner published in 1924 that is of particular interest for us today opens with the statement that "the beginning of any live, intelligent interest in any art is the desire to know an artist's work in its pure, unadulterated state as it finally left the hands of its creator." It may seem obvious that one wants to know a painting as its creator painted it, not as it was repainted by someone else, and that the same is true with any other work of art. But it must be equally obvious that Turner had a reason for making his statement—the reason, in fact, that many works of art are presented to us *not* in their pure, unadulterated state as they left the hands of their creators.

Turner cited examples from poetry: Swinburne had exposed editors' alterations of the texts in various editions of Shelley; Sampson's accurate edition of Blake, Grierson's of Donne, had revealed the similar editorial tampering with their poems in previous editions. And the situation in music, he said, was even worse: not only had editors and performers taken even greater liberties with the originals, but there were few critics with the knowledge required to expose them, and even the objections that were made occasionally were ignored. Turner's explanation of this was "the generally lower intellectual integrity of men of music as compared with men of letters," to which I would add the generally lower intellectual sophistication and understanding where music is concerned: those who understand that one mustn't change someone else's painting or poem don't understand that one mustn't change the harmony or texture of someone else's music.

And so we have the many nineteenth-century "editions" of music of earlier centuries in which the editors, not knowing or caring what the music was intended to sound like, "corrected" it to make it conform to nineteenth-century ideas of what music should sound like. We have Gevaert's "edition" of Haydn's Cello Concerto, which in addition to re-orchestrating the work cuts half the recapitulation out of the first movement. Or Leonard's "edition" of Corelli's *La Folia*, which should be called Leonard's *La Folia* since that is what it really is. Or Grützmacher's "edition" of the Boccherini Cello Concerto in B flat, which is actually a work by Grützmacher himself, made out of thematic materials taken from five genuine Boccherini concertos: the themes of Grützmacher's first and third movements are mostly from an unpublished cello concerto in B flat recently discovered in the Dresden Library, but in part also from Nos. 1, 2 and 4 of four concertos published in Paris in 1770-1771, while the Grützmacher middle movement is a free rewriting of the middle movement of No. 3; of the themes themselves not one is even stated by Grützmacher as Boccherini wrote it; and the forms into which the themes are elaborated, the accompaniments and tuttis, the harmonization and orchestration, are entirely Grützmacher's and exhibit no resemblance to Boccherini's own practice. And even the discoverer of the genuine Dresden Concerto in B flat, when preparing the work for publication, cannot forbear to "improve" Boccherini's orchestration.

Moreover, those "editions" are still the ones used in performances today. Though a correct edition of the Haydn Cello Concerto is available, cellists continue to play and record the Gevaert version. Though the Eulenburg score of the genuine Boccherini Concerto in B flat is available, cellists continue to play and record the Grützmacher fake. And in this we see the "lower intellectual integrity of men of music" that Turner spoke of.

But a contributing cause is the lower intellectual sophistication and understanding I spoke of, which is to be seen in this
mixture of sense and nonsense in van der Straeten's *History of
the Violoncello:*

> . . . Very meritorious was Grützmacher's activity as an editor of
> classical works which had been practically lost, especially such
> rare treasures as the concertos by Haydn, P. E. Bach, Boccherini,
> sonatas by Duport, Geminiani and others. Unfortunately he
> treated these masters with little reverence as regards the text of
> their compositions, and in various cases he pieced together "sona-
> tas" from about half-a-dozen original compositions and edited
> them as if they appeared in their original form. In the case of the
> six solo sonatas by Bach, he went so far as to edit a "concert
> edition," in which he crowds additional chords, passages and
> embellishments, distorting these great and fine works in the most
> unpardonable manner. Yet for all that, we must be thankful for
> the many works which he has rescued and made accessible. . . .

Nonsense, since what Grützmacher made accessible was not
the great works but his falsifications of them, which kept—
and still keep—the true works from becoming known.*

---

* There is in addition what is to be seen in the statement on the envelope
of a Westminster recording of the fake Boccherini concerto—that "this,
[Boccherini's] most representative work, is actually a combination of two
scores. As widely performed by Pablo Casals, the two movements in B flat
are spaced by an adagio in G minor. That arrangement is followed here,
though the recently published Eulenburg score restores, as middle movement, an andantino grazioso in E flat. In other textual respects, this treatment follows closely the Casals model." Here the Grützmacher fake—which
Casals and a hundred other cellists played when it was accepted as an edition of a genuine work—becomes the "Casals model"; this "Casals model"
and the work in the Eulenburg score become merely different combinations
of genuine movements from two Boccherini works—the outer movements
in the two combinations being the same, but the "Casals model" substi-
tuting a middle movement in G minor for the one in E flat restored by the
Eulenburg score; and if "this treatment" refers to the Eulenburg work we
are told that except for the middle movement it follows closely the "Casals
model." All this in the face of the statement in the preface of the Eulenburg
score that accuses Grützmacher of combining "wantonly altered parts of
[the genuine concerto] with such from other works of Boccherini and
Orchestra Tutti of his own. . . ."

Which brings me to the subject of this chapter. The occasion for Turner's article was the announcement that the piano-and-voice arrangement that Musorgsky himself made of his opera *Boris Godunov* for publication in 1874 was to be published again, after having been out of print for many years. What had been performed since 1896 and available in published form was Rimsky-Korsakov's revision, in which he corrected what he considered to be "the fragmentary character of the musical phrases, the harshness of the harmonies and modulations, the faulty counterpoint, the poverty of the instrumentation, and the general weakness of the work from the technical point of view," which he contended had been responsible for its failure when it had been produced in 1874. It would always be possible, said Rimsky, to publish a "musicologically accurate edition"; he was satisfying the immediate "need of an edition for performances, for practical artistic purposes, for making [Musorgsky's] colossal talent known"— purposes which he claimed were in fact achieved by his revision. For after he became chairman of the Society of Musical Gatherings in St. Petersburg in 1896, he said, "there sprang up in the Society the idea of a stage production of *Boris Godunov* in my revision." The success of this production led to one by Mamontov's company in Moscow with Chaliapin, after which as part of his repertory the Rimsky revision was produced at the imperial Mariinsky Theater in St. Petersburg in 1904 and came to Paris in 1908 in the Diaghilev production that carried the work to Western Europe and America. And Rimsky's claim to have in this way "[made] Musorgsky's colossal talent known" to a world that otherwise would not have known it is accepted to this day.

But what led to the republication of Musorgsky's original work in 1924 was the loudly proclaimed discovery of some French critics that Rimsky, far from making Musorgsky's talent known, had concealed it with his corrections. In the famous words of Jean Marnold, "Rimsky-Korsakov cuts . . . one, two or three measures as serenely as he cuts fifteen or twenty. At will he transposes a tone, or a half-tone, makes sharps or flats natural, alters modulations. He even corrects the harmony. During the tableau in the cell of Pimen the liturgical Dorian mode is adulterated by a banal D minor. The interval of the augmented fifth (a favorite device of Musorgsky) is frequently the object of his equilateral ostracism. . . . From one end of the work to the other he planes, files, polishes, pulls together, retouches, embellishes, makes insipid, or corrupts. . . ." Imagine the analogous things being done to a painting or a poem: you will see what violation of the integrity of another artist's work Rimsky-Korsakov was guilty of; and you will see also that it was one which no painter, no poet would commit or be allowed to commit.

Nor is it true that Rimsky's revision, or any other edition "for performances, for practical artistic purposes," was necessary. It is Rimsky himself who, in *My Musical Life*, tells us of *Boris Godunov*—i.e. Musorgsky's own revised 1872 version—being produced in St. Petersburg in 1874 "with great success," and of its continuing to be performed once or twice each year until 1882, when, "the Lord knows why, productions of the opera ceased altogether, although it had enjoyed uninterrupted success." Concerning the reasons which only the Lord knew, Rimsky writes that "there were rumors afloat that the opera had displeased the imperial family; there was gossip that its subject was unpleasant to the censors"; but he says nothing about any practical difficulties that made necessary "an edition for performances, for practical artistic purposes." Musorgsky's original would have been as practical to produce in 1896 as in 1874; and if it had been produced in 1896 it would presumably have repeated its success of 1874-1882. And if it *had* been produced by the Society in 1896 instead of Rimsky's revision it would have taken the same subsequent steps as the revision in becoming the version the world would know today.

The real reason for what Rimsky did was very different from what he claimed, and much less to his credit. Musorgsky

143

was one of the two great originals of the nineteenth century (Berlioz was the other), with stature and powers that triumphed over his insistence on learning solely by doing; Rimsky, on the other hand, was a minor talent who tells us he needed the help of codified practice in harmony and counterpoint for "new living currents to flow into my creative work." What was original and powerful in Musorgsky's writing was to Rimsky's ears, therefore, error which he tried persistently and unsuccessfully to get Musorgsky to change. And having been unable to get Musorgsky to change it when alive, he proceeded to change it himself when Musorgsky was dead.

Nor is it true that "there sprang up in the Society the idea of a stage production of *Boris Godunov* in my revision." The idea "sprang up" in Rimsky; and in another man there would have "sprung up" the idea of a production of Musorgsky's original work. By using the opportunity to produce his revision instead, Rimsky succeeded not, as he claimed, in making Musorgsky's work known to the world, but in keeping it from being known to most of the world to this very day. For though he argued plausibly that whenever the world disapproved of what he had done it could return to Musorgsky's original score, which he had not destroyed, actually once the revision had taken root everywhere in opera houses, in singers' repertories, in people's minds, then routine and inertia combined with lack of conscience and understanding to keep it from being dislodged for Musorgsky's original. And we come here to what is more extraordinary even than what was done to poor Musorgsky's work—namely, the way people's minds have operated in relation to what was done to it.

Thus, with the republication of Musorgsky's score in 1924 it was possible for anyone, by playing through it, to discover that everything was wonderfully right and nothing called for correction, and at the end to be left overwhelmed by what he had heard achieved with such originality, power, and absolutely assured mastery. And some did. But there were others

144

of whom one could say what Tovey said of Rimsky himself—
that they were incapable of "telling a blunder from a stroke
of genius or feature of style." And you will find them declar-
ing today that a hearing of Musorgsky's original demonstrates
how much it gained from the editing of a man properly
schooled in his craft—which amounts not just to saying that
something like Rimsky's *Le Coq d'or* is good of its kind, but to
setting it up as the good by which the kind of a *Boris Godunov*
must be judged deficient. Imagine that Van Gogh's work had
been tidied up by some academician, or even by someone like
Sargent; and imagine anyone contending that the restored
Van Gogh originals demonstrated how much they had gained
from the tidying up—contending, in other words, not merely
that Sargent was good for what he was, but that his good
was the good for Van Gogh.

Moreover, if it *had* been discovered that someone had repainted Van Gogh's or any other painter's work, there would
have been no debate over whether the work was more effective with the changes or without them, and whether therefore
they should be retained or removed: it would have been taken
as a matter of course that they had no validity and the original work must be restored. But in the case of *Boris* we find the
celebrated English critic Ernest Newman writing that the
difficulty with *Boris* is one of having to choose not merely
between Musorgsky's own two versions, each complete and
with merits of its own, but from these two and Rimsky's, since
it too is "a good practical proposition" in the theater. We
have had European opera companies producing Musorgsky's
original and going back to Rimsky's revision because it
"sounds better." I have had a man who conducted the
Musorgsky original at Covent Garden a few years ago insist
that the change back to the Rimsky version there had been
a good thing because it had induced the London public to
listen to a great work it had stayed away from before, and
have been unable to get him to understand that this was as
though a museum had induced the public to like an El Greco

145

painting by having someone touch it up to make its forms
and colors more conventional—that what the London public
had listened to was no more Musorgsky's great work than the
prettied-up painting would be El Greco's. And even the most
accurately perceptive and clearest-minded of present-day English critics, Gerald Abraham, in his notes for the HMV and
RCA Victor recording of the Rimsky version, recognizes that
by applying to *Boris* an art whose "essence . . . is brightly
tinted transparency, clear-cut harmonies, and part-writing
realized in primary orchestral colors" Rimsky "imprinted his
own personality over the entire work," but goes on nevertheless to call this result "a fascinating posthumous collaboration
of two very different but very fine musical minds." One would
expect Abraham to recognize the obvious disparity and in-
compatibility of the mind that expresses itself in Rimsky's
"brightly tinted transparency, clear-cut harmonies, and part-
writing realized in primary orchestral colors," with the mind
that produces the somber power of *Boris;* and one would expect him not to want the imprint of a mind like Rimsky's on
a work like Musorgsky's.

Thus it is that although Musorgsky's original has been
known since 1924, and the full orchestral score has been available since 1928, the Rimsky version continued to be given at
the Metropolitan until 1953, when a new manager decided—
with a good sense that must be considered something of a
miracle—that if one is going to give Musorgsky's *Boris* one
should give the *Boris* Musorgsky wrote (and his good sense
extended to having its one weakness, Musorgsky's ineffective
orchestral realization of his "sonorous image," remedied by
improvement of the scoring in accordance with this image,
not some other). Thus it is, also, that in the very year that
the Metropolitan at last produced Musorgsky's original, HMV
in England, making its first complete recording of the work,
recorded the Rimsky version; and an English reviewer thought
this was justified by the fact that the Rimsky version was the
one most people knew—which was like arguing against pub-

lishing the accurate texts of Shelley's poems because most people knew the inaccurate ones. Thus it is, also, that Columbia in this country, which had the recording rights for the Metropolitan's productions, decided not to record its production of the original *Boris*. And thus it is, in sum, that if you should wish to hear the original *Boris* you will even at this late date not find any of it on records.

Rimsky-Korsakov's injury to Musorgsky was not just that he made his falsification rather than Musorgsky's own work what most of the world knows as *Boris Godunov* to this very day; it was also that he gave the world the idea of Musorgsky as a clumsy dilettante. This has caused some people, when they have heard Musorgsky's own work, to hear only a dilettante's inept crudities. And it has provided an excuse for others to do with his music what Rimsky did, with the claim that *they* were doing legitimately and well what he had done illegitimately and badly—the legitimacy consisting in their having returned to the original as the basis of changes which they have assured us adhered strictly to Musorgsky's spirit when not strictly to his letter. But that is what Rimsky claimed too; and actually what they have produced has turned out to be based on the original in much the same way as his version.

Thus we had from Stokowski what he called a "symphonic synthesis" of *Boris*, based, he said, on Musorgsky's original score:

> . . . With generous intentions Rimsky-Korsakov tried to re-orchestrate and re-form *Boris*. Instead he made something far from the spirit of Musorgsky. The original orchestration of Musorgsky shows clearly what he was trying to say, but sometimes he failed to express his musical conception, because he was inexperienced in the vast, subtle and highly differentiated world of the modern orchestra. . . . I have tried to help the orchestra more completely say what Musorgsky was aiming to express, keeping the music in the dramatic sequence of Pushkin's poem and Musorgsky's music. The result is something like a free modern symphony. . . .

But to speak of a number of passages torn out of organic context and patched together in what the blurb-writer for once correctly described as "a series of climaxes of almost intolerable brilliance, color and power"—to speak of this as a symphony or even a symphonic synthesis, with its connotation of organic coherence, was to make nonsense of the term. Nor was there more sense in saying an orchestral arrangement was based on the original score if it went back to the original only to depart from it as far as Stokowski's arrangement did. And Stokowski's claim to be merely helping Musorgsky to achieve what he was unable to achieve completely himself was the claim of a man incapable of telling a composer's unfulfilled conception from his mere failure to compose the vast and subtle sonorities Stokowski likes to produce with an orchestra. Musorgsky's sober orchestration does demonstrate clearly what sonorous image he had in mind—or, in Stokowski's way of speaking, "what he was trying to say"; and it demonstrates just as clearly that what he was trying to say was not what is said by the orchestral luxuriance and glitter, the heaving and billowing sonorities, of Stokowski's arrangement.

Musorgsky may have been incapable of using the orchestra in a way that would project his sonorous image of *Boris* effectively in the opera house; but his contemporaries are unanimous about his powers as a pianist, especially in dramatically and pictorially imaginative invention such as we hear in *Pictures at an Exhibition*. For many years I knew this work only in Ravel's orchestral transcription, which I took for granted was more effective than the original for piano—accepting too uncritically the prevailing idea of our time that the orchestra does everything better. And I retain a vivid recollection of my amazement when at last I heard the original played, and discovered how completely achieved an imaginative creation it is. In this work of his maturity—it is dated 1874—Musorgsky writes at every point, in every detail of melody, harmony and figuration, with the unfailing assur-

148

ance of a man who is absolute master of his style; and in his musical translations of *Goldenberg and Schmuyle, Catacombs,* and *Con mortuis in lingua morta* he writes as a musical artist of the highest rank.

Moreover, listening with knowledge of the piano original I was now able to appreciate fully the imaginative insight and artistic rectitude that made Ravel's version, in its fidelity to the original, almost unique among such orchestral translations. And with knowledge of Musorgsky's and Ravel's achievements I could appreciate fully what other transcribers had done—among them Stokowski, whose version came with the usual statement about the greatness implicit in Musorgsky's mere piano sketch and now completely realized in an orchestration which "aimed to preserve and express the Slavic character" of the work, as against Ravel's "Gallic manner." It was no surprise that a man who heard in Musorgsky's original a mere piano sketch should have fulfilled the conception implicit in this sketch by slashing out whole sections and translating the remainder into the fussy and lush and lurid orchestral sonorities and effects that falsified what Ravel had preserved.

For Stokowski a composer's conceptions are unfulfilled if they aren't realized in Stokowskian orchestral sonorities; for Horowitz they are unfulfilled if they aren't realized in the Horowitz piano fireworks. That means not only Musorgsky but even Beethoven, whose powers as a pianist—one of the most celebrated of his time—also are attested to by his contemporaries, and whose command of the instrument and knowledge of its resources were things his deafness would not affect. But Horowitz thinks otherwise: "It's not that Beethoven's piano writing doesn't sound the way *I* want it to; it's because his writing doesn't sound the way *he* wanted it to"; and the piano writing of Beethoven's last years in particular is for Horowitz a mere groping toward a new style that is not achieved. That, presumably, is what he would say of the passages from the *Diabelli Variations* on pages 49 and 50; but the truth of the matter is that they achieve with precision meanings that are beyond Horowitz's understanding.

But whereas Horowitz is content, fortunately, to leave Beethoven's last piano works unplayed and unrevised, he has made Musorgsky's *Pictures* suitable for performance at his recitals by revising it in terms of the Horowitz way of using the piano—the terms employed in Horowitz's *Carmen* Fantasy and his arrangement of *Stars and Stripes Forever*. And as usual the undertaking is legitimized by a pilgrimage to the original text (which even Rimsky-Korsakov left untouched): we are thus assured that Horowitz has been careful to change only Musorgsky's original work. It was none less than Olin Downes who, as Horowitz's spokesman, assured us that the revision doesn't "introduce any extraneous elements into the music as Musorgsky wrote it," but "is a return to the original text. . . . Following it carefully, Mr. Horowitz has done a little 'piano orchestration' in ways confined to octave doublings, redistribution of passage work between the hands, transpositions of brief passages an octave below or above the original pitch, etc. The effort has been solely to realize the intention of the composer, and to refrain from gratuitous ornamentation or officious 'correction' of any detail of his text as it stands." But my ears, following the recorded performance with the text, note such "officious 'correction' " and "gratuitous ornamentation" and "extraneous elements" as the cut in *The Old Castle;* the omission of the *Promenade* before *Limoges;* the insertion of four measures into a repeat in *Gnomus* from which Musorgsky omitted them; the replacement of bare octaves with rich chords; the completely new figuration in measures 12 to 24 of *Limoges*, realizing the intention not of the composer of *Pictures at an Exhibition* but of the composer of the *Carmen* Fantasy; the changing of a rhythmless octave tremolo in *Con mortuis in lingua morta* to a rhythmed figuration of two upper notes, two lower, two upper, two lower, with a very different effect; the insertion, in the last ten measures of *Con mortuis,* of a reiterated off-beat F sharp in the bass, which introduces rhythmic, pedal, and other effects not intended by Musorgsky.

If, then, you wish to hear a realization of Musorgsky's intention, listen to his own piano version. And if you want an orchestral translation faithful to that intention, listen to Ravel's.

Musorgsky's high-level creative achievements include some of his songs: notably the seldom-heard *Sunless* cycle, with perhaps the finest examples of his fully developed style of subtly inflected vocal declamation; and the better-known *Songs and Dances of Death*, which however until quite recently was sung and recorded only as "corrected" by Rimsky-Korsakov.

18

OTHER MUSIC OF THE
NINETEENTH CENTURY

In contrast to Brahms who produced bad music in the attempt to write greater than he felt, Chopin made a great art of writing small poetic pieces for the piano. I speak, I should say, of the music scraped clean of a hundred years' encrustation of performers' affected, mannered phrasing that has made it seem sentimental and morbid. Even so my use of the term *great* may be questioned—though I don't think there would be any question about the art exhibited in the richly elaborated style of writing and its employment of the resources of the piano, or in the beautiful and subtle invention of pieces like the Impromptu Op. 36, the Nocturne Op. 27 No. 2, the Berceuse, the Barcarolle, some of the Mazurkas—the art exhibited most strikingly perhaps in the Preludes and Etudes, in each of which a piano figuration exercising the hand in a particular segment of piano technique provides the terms with which Chopin creates a piece of music as exquisitely thought and formed as any other. But I think *great* is correctly applied to the Nocturne Op. 48 No. 1, the Polonaises Opp. 44 and 53, the Ballades Opp. 23 and 52, the Sonatas Opp. 35 and 58, the Concerto No. 1—in which there are not only beauty and subtlety but magnificence and power.

We hear another richly elaborated style of writing for the piano used with superb effect by Schumann in his sets of imaginative pieces—*Papillons, Carnaval, Kinderszenen*, the *Fantasiestücke* Op. 12, and parts of *Kreisleriana* and *Davidsbündlertänze;* and in some of his large-scale works—the *Etudes symphoniques*, the Sonatas Opp. 11 and 22, the Fantasia Op. 17, and the Piano Concerto. And this writing for the piano contributes much to the effect of some of the finest songs we have—the great *Dichterliebe* cycle, and among the single songs *Aufträge, Mondnacht, Der Nussbaum, Alte Laute, Du bist wie eine Blume, Loreley, Ständchen, Waldesgespräch, Die Kartenlegerin*. The orchestral works, the chamber music, and almost all the later writing I find less interesting.

What Schumann's songs begin, Hugo Wolf's continue—which is to say that Wolf's writing for the piano again contributes much to the effect of the song, and indeed is often so integrated with the vocal part as to provide the context essential to its continuing sense. Wolf's susceptibility to the stimulation of poetry led him to write almost nothing but songs, and was responsible for what is most remarkable about them—the vocal writing that is like an extension of the words around which the music shapes itself as it points up their meaning. This is true of all the songs; what is true only of some is that the progression which is so remarkably integrated with the poem is in addition a moving or attractive piece of music—like *Anakreon's Grab, In der Frühe, Auf einer Wanderung, Heimweh, Auf ein altes Bild, Die ihr schwebet, Nun wandre Maria, Und steht ihr früh, Herr was trägt der Boden hier?, Auf dem grünen Balkon, In dem Schatten meiner Locken*.

In orchestral music we have in Mendelssohn a minor master who—working on a small scale of emotion and texture—produced the magical overture and the other exquisite pieces for *A Midsummer Night's Dream;* the delightful *Italian* Symphony and scherzo and finale of the *Scotch* Symphony; the fine opening movement of the Violin Concerto; the imaginative *Fingal's Cave* or *Hebrides* Overture.

In opera Bellini exhibits his extraordinary gift for melodic writing in the purely lyrical *La Sonnambula*, and in *I Puritani*, which offers in addition passages of impressive dramatic force. *Norma* I find less interesting; but it has what is perhaps the finest, and certainly the most famous, of his melodic structures, the aria *Casta diva*.

Donizetti too reveals himself as a superb melodist—in the tragic *Lucia di Lammermoor*, and in his masterpiece of operatic comedy, *Don Pasquale*.

Rossini exhibits his powers in operatic comedy not only in the best-known *The Barber of Seville* but in *La Cenerentola*, which has even more impressive writing in his lyric, comic and florid bravura styles—the last in particular often breathtaking in its controlled extravagance. But Rossini had powers for more than operatic comedy, as I discovered only quite recently when Berlioz's comments on *William Tell* led me to listen to a recording of that seldom-performed work, and to be amazed by what had elicited Berlioz's enthusiasm. Concerning Matilda's second-act aria *Selva opaca* he observed correctly that "Rossini has . . . written few pieces as elegant, as fresh, as distinguished in their melody, and as ingenious in their modulations as this one"; and noting in addition the writing for the orchestra Berlioz exclaimed: "This is poetry, this is music, this is art—beautiful, noble, and pure, just as its votaries would have it always." And the passages which follow this one—the duet of Matilda and Arnold, the trio of Tell, Walter and Arnold, the choruses of the three cantons—deserve Berlioz's description of them as the marvel that follows marvel.

In addition to the operas of Bellini and Rossini there are the engaging products of a French minor master—Bizet's *Carmen* and his music for *L'Arlésienne*.

Another French minor master of fascinating originality of mind and style is Chabrier—not in the *España* by which he is known almost exclusively, but in the *Dix Pièces pittoresques* for piano, four of which he made into the *Suite Pastorale* for orchestra; the *Trois Valses romantiques* for two pianos, especially the affecting No. 3; the smaller-scale *Marche joyeuse*.

As for Franck, like Brahms he is most enjoyable when he is

least pretentious—in the *Variations symphoniques* for piano and orchestra, parts of the Sonata for violin and piano, the Prelude and Chorale of the *Prelude, Chorale and Fugue* for piano, the second movement of the Symphony, and *Les Eolides* and *Psyché* for orchestra, though these last two suffer from Franck's repetitious long-windedness. But an observation by Tovey— "The saintliness of Franck shines nowhere more brightly than where his music is most *mondaine*"—describes a combination of qualities that you will hear occasionally and may not like even in these best works.

The Russian nationalists associated with Musorgsky achieved nothing of the stature and power of his work; but the engaging things they did produce are exemplified by the *Polovtsian Dances* from Borodin's *Prince Igor* and the Suite from Rimsky-Korsakov's *Le Coq d'or*.

Even more impressive products of this kind are those of the Czech nationalists. The vein of lovely and richly harmonized melody that we hear in Dvořák's superb *Slavonic Dances* provided much of the substance for his symphonies and chamber music—with the possible exception of the best-known Symphony No. 5 (*From the New World*). And a similar source furnished Smetana with the melodious substance of his beautiful symphonic poem *Die Moldau* and his delightful operatic comedy *The Bartered Bride*.

19

STRAUSS

We come to the end of the nineteenth century and the beginning of the twentieth—to Richard Strauss, Mahler, Debussy.

The powers that operate with youthful vigor and exuberance in Strauss's tone-poems *Don Juan* and *Till Eulenspiegel* exhibit matured refinement and sheer incandescence in *Don Quixote*. This is his masterpiece—inspired in its invention; unflawed by a single Straussian excess or error of taste; every note in the complex texture really counting for something; every detail making its programmatic point brilliantly. So profuse is the programmatic detail, and so subtly achieved at times, that much of it will be caught only by the musically trained listener familiar with the score or capable of reading it as he listens; and other listeners need to have it pointed out to them. This is difficult to do in a book; but here are some of the important things to listen for.

Strauss subtitles the work *Fantastic Variations on a Theme of Knightly Character*, and describes it further as an Introduction, Theme and Variations, and Finale. It makes its points, then, by applying the variation procedure to themes which characterize Don Quixote, Sancho Panza and Dulcinea; and much of the substance of the work is derived from the high-spirited statement of flute and oboe with which the Introduction begins:

This leads to a statement of the violins that will play an important part:

a statement conveying a grace that is a little stiff-jointed and absurd, and whose conclusion:

conveys the fact that things are distorted in the Don's mind. Next a statement of the violas, derived from [1]:

which rambles on until the oboe enters with Dulcinea's theme:

This is interrupted by excited martial calls of muted trumpets over gigantesque mutterings of tubas and string basses that contribute to the absurdity; and now all the thematic substance continues to be heard in an increasingly involved and dense texture representing the Don's increasing confusion of mind, and reaching its conclusion in several loudly proclaimed discordant chords and a final loud and empty note of the trumpets and trombones that tell us his mind has cracked and he has lost his reason.

We are now formally introduced to the chief characters of the musical narrative. First, in the words of the score, "Don Quixote, the knight of melancholy countenance," wonderfully delineated by a theme derived from [1] and [4], in minor instead of major, and played by the solo cello, which represents the Don in this work:

He is described further by [2] and [3].

Then Sancho Panza, who is as wonderfully delineated by a new theme from the bass-clarinet and tenor-tuba, which, with the solo viola, represent him in the work:

And the solo viola adds a few marvelously contrived examples of his homely platitudes.

And now the two set out in the first variation of their musical journey—the Don jogging along in the solo cello, Sancho in the bass-clarinet, with the image of Dulcinea (flute, oboe, muted violins) eliciting chivalresque thoughts from the Don ([2] from the solo cello) to an accompaniment of down-to-earth mutterings by Sancho ([S] from bass-clarinet and solo viola). Suddenly they stop: a slowly circling progression by clarinet, bassoon, violins, violas describes the circling of the distant windmills. The Don (solo cello) gallops to a closer point and stops for another look: the windmills continue their circling. Convinced now that they are giants, he gallops up to give battle: there is a crash, a harp glissando; and a sustained note of the solo cello tells us the Don lies pros-

158

trate, while the windmills continue their circling. Gradually he revives.

And he is off again in the second variation. A vigorous martial variant of [D] pauses before what the Don thinks is an army, despite Sancho's frantic remonstrances ([S] from the woodwinds) that it is a flock of sheep, whose bleatings are now heard. Again the vigorous martial statement, which tells us of the Don's attack; then piteous cries from the scattering sheep; and once more the vigorous martial statement, now proclaiming the Don's victory.

[S] from the bass-clarinet and tenor-tuba opens Variation 3, which is an argument about the life of chivalry, with Sancho expressing doubts and the Don affirming belief. A series of brief exchanges, with [3] from the first desk of first violins repeatedly expressing the Don's growing impatience with Sancho's persistent objections, lead to an extensive statement by Sancho (solo viola) of all his nuggets of homely wisdom. Eventually the Don interrupts angrily ([3] from the violins), quieting down for an affirmation of his belief which becomes impassioned, reaches a great climax, and ends on a sustained chord of finality—only to have Sancho venture another doubt ([S] from the bass-clarinet), which the furious Don silences ([3] from the violins).

And they set out again in Variation 4, jogging along until they see some pilgrims approaching, in whom the Don sees a band of ruffians. He attacks; there is a crash; and a sustained note of the low strings tells us he lies prostrate while the pilgrims recede into the distance. Sancho utters mournful cries ([S] from the bass-clarinet, tenor-tuba and solo viola); when the Don (solo cello) begins to revive, the exuberant bass-clarinet and tenor-tuba express Sancho's joy.

In Variation 5 the Don, at night, keeps vigil in extended declamation of the solo cello, in the course of which his thoughts of Dulcinea make him giddy (harp glissandos, tremolos of the other instruments).

Resuming their journey in Variation 6 the two meet a

159

peasant girl mounted on an ass (parody of Dulcinea's theme from the oboes, with punctuating strokes of the tambourine). She is, says Sancho, Dulcinea transformed by an enchanter. The Don is indignant ([2] from the solo cello); Sancho insists (solo viola).

In Variation 7 the soaring aloft of [2] (strings) and [4] (horns), the glissandos of the harp, the rolls of the kettle-drums, the chromatic scales of the flutes, the rushing and whistling of a wind machine all combine to describe the Don— seated on a wooden horse and fanned by a huge bellows— imagining himself riding through the air, while the note D held throughout by the string basses tells us he never leaves the ground.

Next, in Variation 8, a lilting barcarolle ([2] transformed by solo violin and oboe, with the notes of [D] spaced out by English horn, trombone and strings) gives us the episode of the ride in the boat which capsizes. The notes of [D] plucked by the strings suggest the struggling to shore; then [D] *religioso* from flutes, clarinets and horns constitutes a little prayer of thanksgiving.

Galloping off again in Variation 9 the Don meets two monks (two bassoons engaged in a dry-as-dust theological wrangle) whom he takes for magicians and puts to flight— only to encounter, in Variation 10, a fellow-townsman disguised as a knight, who defeats him in a joust and exacts the penalty that he return home.

And now the finale, which depicts the dejected Don plodding homeward, then his last reflections (solo cello's sustained melody derived from [1]) and peaceful death (solo cello's expiring octave-drop to its final note).

Of Strauss's other tone-poems the earlier *Tod und Verklärung* and *Also sprach Zarathustra* are inferior in musical substance; the later *Ein Heldenleben* has pages of superb writing (the love scene, the hero's works of peace, the conclusion) and other pages of Strauss's worst. As for the still later *Sinfonia Domestica*,

it is only one example of the deterioration in the later Strauss—
a deterioration in the quality of his musical ideas, with no
diminution in the prodigious technical virtuosity and garrulous facility, so that although genuine creative activity
stopped, the production of endless pages of empty tonal
luxuriance went on almost to the day of his death.

This deterioration is heard also in the later operas—in
Elektra, in *Ariadne auf Naxos*, and in the vastly overrated *Der
Rosenkavalier*. Most of this opera is, to my ears, an expertly
made hubbub of sounds with no musical significance in themselves and none in relation to the words and action they carry;
of the rest the Princess's first-act monologue and the third-act
trio seem to me not equal to the demands of the texts; and
the one moment of inspired creation and beauty is the second-
act *Presentation of the Rose*, with its first exchanges of Octavian
and Sophie.

It is the earlier opera *Salome* that offers passages of impressive power achieved by the enormously complex writing—
notably the final scene. But it offers others in which the complexity gets to be a luxuriance out of control of artistic purpose or taste. And it offers also the appalling *Dance of the
Seven Veils*.

In addition, some of the songs—*Ständchen, Freundliche Vision,
Die Nacht, Traum durch die Dämmerung, Ruhe meine Seele, Heim-
kehr*—are lovely.

20

MAHLER

It is with Strauss that one can begin to speak of gigantic means and aims; and even more with Mahler. The aim was expressed once in Mahler's statement: "For me 'symphony' signifies using all the means of available technique to construct a world for myself"; and the means are the huge orchestras, choruses and vocal soloists, the enormous formal structures in which they are employed. But the employment of the huge orchestras is not the opulent daubing of Strauss; rather it resembles Berlioz's practice in the fastidiousness, precision and originality of its use, frequently, of now only these few instruments and now only those few to produce contrapuntal textures as clear as they are complex. Mahler's use of the orchestra is in fact only one part of an entire operation that resembles Berlioz's in the fact that nothing in the music is perfunctory or mechanical: if an instrument plays or an inner voice moves, the activity is never a routine instrumental doubling or filling in of texture, but always something done with attention, thought and purpose. And this evidence of a mind always working—working, moreover, in unexpected, individual, original and fascinating ways—holds interest even through one of Mahler's long-winded twenty-minute symphony movements.

The best introduction to Mahler, I think, is the Symphony No. 4, whose expansively relaxed and genial earlier movements lead to a gay final movement—a setting for soprano of one of the poems in Arnim and Brentano's collection of German folk-song poetry, *Des Knaben Wunderhorn*. The work thus illustrates one outstanding fact about Mahler—that his musical imagination was rooted in the Bohemian folk song he heard in his youth. Much of his creative energy went, as a result, into the writing of songs—the settings of poems from *Des Knaben Wunderhorn*, the *Lieder eines fahrenden Gesellen*, the settings of poems by Rückert, *Das Lied von der Erde*. And another result was the close relation of his vocal and instrumental writing: the folk-song-like character of much of his instrumental lyricism; the introduction of actual song into movements of several of the symphonies. Thus, the dramatic and brooding first movement of the Symphony No. 2 (*Resurrection*) is followed by an engaging *Ländler;* this by a gigantic Scherzo which is an orchestral reworking of the delightful song, *St. Anthony's Sermon to the Fishes;* this by a song, *Urlicht*, in which the contralto sings that "man lies in greatest need," but that God "will light my way to eternal blissful life"; and this by a setting of Klopstock's Resurrection Ode, sung by the soprano and chorus. And in the Symphony No. 3, two vocal movements lead to another consoling conclusion, this one for the orchestra alone, and Mahler's most sublime utterance.

It is these works that I find accessible and moving, not the ranting later symphonies.

21

DEBUSSY

The fastidiousness and precision and originality that Mahler exhibits in his use of the orchestra we hear in even greater degree in Debussy's music, and not only in the orchestration but in the melody and harmony. Debussy is another of the great originals; and he exhibits his originality not only in a substance quite different from that of the music we have been considering until now, but in equally different procedures, and in the completed entities which these procedures result in—entities without the kind of continuity of melody, development and structure we have been hearing. In one of Debussy's mature works we hear a substance of evocative fragments of melody, figuration, harmony and instrumental color; and a fitting together of such fragments in a progression with coherence and cumulative effect.

The originality of substance and procedure begins to show itself in the varied play with the flute theme in the opening section of Debussy's first major orchestral piece, the *Prélude à L'Après-midi d'un faune*, and in the similar closing section; while the expansive melody of the middle section reminds us of the astonishingly conventional and sugary idiom of the music that preceded this piece—such as the *Arabesques* and *Suite bergamasque* for piano.

But there are no such reminders in *Nuages*, whose thematic fragments and precisely achieved subtleties of orchestral coloring evoke marvelously, from the first measures, the still atmos-

phere of the scene of clouds moving across the sky. As for
those orchestral subtleties, note the opening two measures of
clarinets and bassoons alone, then the addition of an oboe,
then its withdrawal; note then the entrance of the English
horn, the addition of flutes and horns, then of the chord of
the muted violins *pp* (with clarinets and bassoons), and with
this the kettledrum roll *ppp;* note in that violin chord:

the change from G natural to G sharp, then the change from
chord to simple octave.

We have here the beginnings of the method that exhibits
its matured development in the rich, complex textures of *La
Mer* (particularly its marvelous second movement), *Ibéria* (particularly, again, its second movement), and the smaller-scale
Gigues and *Rondes de printemps*, in the last of which the idiom
is especially rich, lending itself wonderfully to the purposes
of an aural "image" of spring (*Gigues, Ibéria* and *Rondes de
printemps* constitute the *Images* for orchestra).

The same matured orchestral style is to be heard in the
opera *Pelléas et Mélisande;* and it is in fact the superb orchestral writing that I find effective and impressive in the work,
not the tenuous vocal declamation. Nor do I find this declamation more interesting in Debussy's songs.

As astonishingly original in the light of its conventional and
sugary antecedents is the style of writing for the piano that
we hear fully matured in *Soirée dans Grenade* and *Jardins sous
la pluie* of *Estampes*, in *L'Île joyeuse*, in *Reflets dans l'eau, Hommage à Rameau* and *Poissons d'or* of the *Images* for piano, and
in a few of the Preludes—*La Cathédrale engloutie, La Sérénade
interrompue, La Puerta del vino*. The various elements of that
piano style are elaborated in the Etudes, some of which I
find interesting only in that way (as in fact I do some of the
pieces with titles), but a few of which are in addition engag-

ing and impressive as pieces of music. And *Doctor Gradus ad Parnassum*, *The Snow is Dancing* and *Golliwog's Cake-Walk* of *Children's Corner* are charming.

Of the chamber music the early Quartet, though not one of Debussy's best works, has a second and third movement that are exquisitely wrought and lovely; but the late Sonatas for cello and piano, for flute, viola and harp, and for violin and piano offer what to my ears is style carried to a high point of refinement and subtlety, but with little or no content.

22

MUSIC OF

THE TWENTIETH CENTURY

The originality I have referred to in the work of certain composers was something incidental to their achievement of the works of art their minds were concentrated on. With the twentieth century we come to originality—in melody, harmony, rhythm and form—that was consciously striven for, and that was carried to the point where some composers were no longer in communication with the general music public. And so we come to the problem of modern music and the arguments about it.

On the one hand some have contended that the situation is an old one—that the great composers of the past were obscure to *their* contemporaries—and have argued from this that the music which the public has trouble in understanding today is as good as the music it had trouble in understanding in the past. Mozart has been cited as one composer who starved to death for lack of appreciation; but his great contemporary Haydn flourished handsomely, and actually Mozart's difficulty was not the public's failure to recognize his greatness, which it did recognize, but his own lack of skill—whether he was dealing with a French duke who didn't pay him for his daughter's lessons, or an Austrian emperor who paid him only half the salary he had paid Gluck, or a manager who paid him only half the customary fee for an opera, or a publisher who paid him nothing for some quartets—his lack of skill in manipulating the musico-economic machinery of the period

to convert the public's appreciation into the money that would
have kept him from dying of poverty and overwork at thirty-
five. Beethoven also has been cited: the difficulties his contemporaries had with his last quartets have been offered in
support of the contention that he too died in want for lack
of understanding of his music; but actually he did not die in
want, and not only the financial support he received from his
noble patrons but the sums he was paid by publishers who
competed for his works are evidence of the lifelong contemporary recognition of his greatness even by those who had
trouble with his last quartets at first hearing. Schubert is still
another who is alleged to have starved to death for lack of
recognition; but actually, though he was always poor, it was
not privation but an earlier venereal disease that weakened
his body's resistance to the typhus of which he died; and he
died at the point where his music, which had been appre-
ciated from the start by those who knew it, was beginning to
be sufficiently known and recognized for publishers to ask him
for works (in the year of his death the Vienna correspondent
of the Dresden *Abendzeitung* referred to "the inspired Schubert"
whose "name already resounds from all lips"); so that if he
had lived he probably would have been able in a few years
to command adequate compensation for what was published.
The scurrilous attacks on Wagner have been cited as evidence
of his contemporaries' inability to understand his music; but
he was no less warmly defended, and the Bayreuth Festspiel-
haus is merely the surviving concrete evidence of the enormous
interest, recognition and support that his work commanded
in his own lifetime.

On the other hand some have contended, correctly, that
the situation is new, but have gone on with further conten-
tions that are incorrect. The American composer Aaron Copland, in his excellent book *Music and Imagination*, quotes from
an address at Harvard University some years ago in which
E. J. Dent pointed out that "in the days of Handel and
Mozart nobody wanted old music; all audiences demanded

the newest opera or the newest concerto, as we now naturally demand the newest play and the newest novel," and asked why in music today we demanded the old and were hostile to the new. One reason, said Dent, was the excessive reverence for the classics, which he suspected began in England at the Handel commemoration of 1784 (Germany apparently didn't count). And another reason was the change in public. "In Handel's day there was in all European countries an inner ring of cultivated connoisseurs who were the direct patrons of the composers," whereas "the bourgeois public of the nineteenth century had no tradition of connoisseurship . . . and it had no sense of patronage." This was Dent's formulation of the myth of the golden age of eighteenth-century patronage. The fact was patronage by an aristocracy of birth and rank; the myth converts this into patronage by an aristocracy of mind, spirit and taste; and similarly it converts the change from the eighteenth-century aristocratic to the nineteenth-century bourgeois public into a change from an educated, cultivated and enlightened public to an uneducated, uncultivated and unenlightened one. Actually eighteenth-century patronage of music was part of the ritual of aristocratic existence; and you need only read Mozart's letters to learn that the ritual was practiced by many aristocrats of birth and rank who lacked aristocracy of mind, spirit and taste. Actually too the musico-economic set-up of direct patronage for the creation and performance and hearing of music was replaced largely by the nineteenth-century set-up of the public concert and generally distributed printed editions; and in this set-up the new bourgeois public included people who attended concerts under no other compulsion than their interest in the music—the enlightened interest of the educated, cultivated people many of them were. This public listened to the old music which the new widely distributed editions made it possible to perform; but it listened also to the music that was newly composed; and it continued to listen to both old and new all through the nineteenth century and into the twentieth. If therefore at that point it began to be hostile to the new, the reason cannot have been excessive reverence for the old; it must have been rather the particular nature of those new works of Schönberg, von Webern and the rest—the experiences they offered the ear, mind and spirit, as against the experiences that had been offered by new music until then.

But on this point Copland, in an earlier book called *Our New Music*, advanced another argument. In that book he undertook to describe and explain the changes in expressive content and extensions of vocabulary in modern music, in order to remove from the reader's mind the "fantastic notions" with which he said "newspaper writers and radio commentators who ought to know better" had misrepresented modern music and prejudiced the public against it—to remove, that is, the notions that the music lacked emotion and melody, that it was over-complicated in rhythm and ugly in harmony. In this way he undertook to make it possible for the reader to recognize in the emotion that was merely changed in quality and intensity, in the melody, harmony and rhythm that were merely enriched, the things that made Schönberg and von Webern "*our* music," as natural and acceptable to our ears, as interesting and significant to our minds, as people a hundred and two hundred years ago found *their* music.

And the argument about the extension of vocabulary was stated somewhat differently by Gerald Abraham in his excellent book *This Modern Music*, which provided an admirably clear explanation of the extensions of vocabulary and syntax in the music the public had found incomprehensible. As in the case of a foreign language, Abraham contended, one could not understand modern music merely by listening to it, but had to learn its vocabulary and grammar—though the converse was no less true, that "no amount of knowledge of the why and wherefore of [the] musical speech will make that language your own, as natural to you as Bach's or Wagner's, without a great deal of keen listening practice." But children learn their native language by ear long before they study its grammar; and I know from personal experience that foreign languages are best learned in the same way: after a few months in Vienna, as a boy of ten, I spoke German without having seen a grammar. And this is even more true of music, which, as Abraham himself observed in another connection, "has no sense outside itself": the internal coherence of the progression of sounds is conveyed directly by, and on the other hand apprehended directly from, the sounds themselves as heard. That was how I learned to understand the simplest musical vocabulary and syntax in earliest childhood long before I learned anything about chord progressions; it was how I extended that vocabulary and syntax later to include Debussy, Ravel, early Stravinsky (to *Le Sacre du printemps*), Prokofiev, Bloch. And when that way no longer worked— when in the twenties I began to hear music by Schönberg and others that conveyed no sense to me—I found that no amount of reading of explanations of vocabulary and syntax caused the music to begin to make the sense it had not made. So it has continued to be. When, a few years ago, I began to enjoy some of the later works of Stravinsky I had previously found arid and ugly, it was as a result of listening—listening, it is true, with help, but the help of Balanchine's ballet choreography for the works, not of the incomprehensible explanations by the Stravinskyites or Stravinsky himself. Similarly, when I found Schönberg's *Erwartung* expressively effective, the expressive effect was something imposed on my mind directly by the progression of sounds that I heard for the first time; whereas the principle of organization that Abraham pointed out in a passage of Schönberg's *Five Piano Pieces* still doesn't work for me as a principle of coherent sense in the progression of sounds as heard. And this is true not only of me but of the general public.

Which brings us back to Copland's argument. When the public rejected Schönberg and von Webern it didn't do so under the influence of the critics' misrepresentation of them; it acted on the basis of its own direct experiences of the music; and the critics merely described the experiences they had shared with the non-professional, non-writing listeners. To this day the countless explanations like those by Copland and Abraham haven't induced the public to hear in Schönberg and von Webern "*our* music," as natural and acceptable to our ears, as interesting and significant to our minds, as people a hundred and two hundred years ago found *their* music. But readers of mine have reported finding in Bartok the meaning I have said I don't find—which is to say that where the public has come to accept a composer, there too it has acted on the basis of its own direct experiences of the music.

And so will you act: with twentieth-century as with earlier music my experiences and judgments are offered subject to confirmation by your own ears and mind. I must report that the writing of Alban Berg has expressive accuracy and power for me in relation to the situations and text of his opera *Wozzeck* but communicates no coherent sense to me in self-contained instrumental structures like his Violin Concerto; but you are free to find it as meaningful in the concerto as in the opera. And so with Hindemith: there was no difficulty in understanding the harmonically sour and emotionally dry works that he kept grinding out for many years with enormous technical efficiency, but there was, for me, no pleasure in listening to them such as I have had recently with parts of *The Four Temperaments* and *Symphonic Metamorphoses on Themes of Weber*, whose astonishingly conventional and sensuous idiom raises questions about the earlier sourness and aridity; but you are free to enjoy the earlier works.

Among the century's experimenters and innovators who have proved to be fruitful artists Stravinsky stands out as the towering figure. I mentioned that I have only recently enjoyed some of his later works; I should add that there are some I still don't like, but also that there is one—the ballet score *Le Baiser de la fée* (1928)—that I enjoyed at first hearing. What I liked were things it had in common with his earliest masterpiece, the ballet score *L'Oiseau de feu* (1910); and for some years I failed to perceive what it had in common with the later works I disliked.

One striking thing about *L'Oiseau de feu* is how beautifully it is wrought: we hear, for example, a use of the orchestra as precise and fastidious, to achieve coloring often as delicate and subtle, as Debussy's—the most beautiful example being the transition from the Berceuse to the Finale. And there is the mosaic-like fitting together of substance, instead of its development, that we noted in Debussy. But there is no resemblance to Debussy in the bold, raw dissonance at the end, or in the reiteration of dynamic syncopated figures that builds up tension and excitement in the *Infernal Dance*. And it is the further exploitation of this dissonance and rhythm that we hear in the music for one of the great artistic masterpieces of the century, the ballet *Petrushka* (1911), and that achieves the overwhelming power of the ballet score *Le Sacre du printemps* (1913).

In addition to being beautifully wrought *L'Oiseau de feu* is unusual, for Stravinsky, in its direct expressiveness. And both of these things are true of *Le Baiser de la fée*, but in even greater degree: *Le Baiser*, for me, is Stravinsky's most beautiful score, with an expressiveness that has a wider range than that of *L'Oiseau* and is more touching in the lyrical episodes of the boy and his bride, more powerful in the dramatic episodes of the boy and the fairy. And two other beautifully wrought and directly expressive ballet scores are the genial *Apollon Musagètes* (1928) and the grave and haunting *Orpheus* (1948).

On the other hand we hear in *Le Baiser* the tension-producing syncopations and ostinatos characteristic of Stravinsky's abstract works, like *Danses Concertantes* (1942) and the *Symphony in Three Movements* (1945). And *Le Baiser*, finally, throws light on a practice of Stravinsky that has been misunder-

173

stood—his use of themes and styles of composers of the past. At the beginning of the village scene of *Le Baiser* we hear repeatedly a fragment of Tchaikovsky's piano piece *Humoresque*— but only this fragment, and worked into a context of Stravinsky's own. This is the way he uses the other bits of thematic substance of Tchaikovsky in *Le Baiser;* and it is the way he uses the substance and styles of other composers. It is analogous to the old practice of writing variations on another composer's theme: Brahms writing variations on a theme of Paganini wasn't imitating Paganini but writing music of his own that resulted from letting his mind play with Paganini's theme; and Stravinsky has given us music of his own that has resulted from letting his mind play with themes and styles of composers of the past.

I say "play"; and sometimes it sounds as though it *is* for fun; but in *Oedipus Rex* (1927) we hear in the arias a manipulation of the old styles to achieve not the melodic beauty they achieved originally but a harshly austere and monumental utterance suited to this drama of man pursued and destroyed by implacable destiny.

Gerald Abraham points out in *L'Oiseau de feu* elements derived from Rimsky-Korsakov and other Russian predecessors of Stravinsky; but we hear also what the mind of Stravinsky made of them. Similarly one hears in Prokofiev's *Scythian Suite* things which suggest the possibility that the man who wrote this music about pagan Scythia in 1914 knew the music Stravinsky had written about pagan Russia the year before; but we hear also that these things, if they do represent the influence of *Le Sacre du printemps*, are part of the personal and individual way of writing that Prokofiev exhibits in this and other early works. And it is in fact these early works—the Piano Concerto No. 1, the Violin Concerto No. 1, the *Scythian Suite*, the ballet score *Chout*, the Piano Concerto No. 3—that are the most engaging by virtue of the astonishing imaginative and musical powers that operate with youthful freshness and exuberant creative energy. Not that fine works aren't produced later by the more experienced composer—notably the superb score for the ballet *The Prodigal Son* (1928). And even when, much later, what appears to be operating in some works is the developed craftsmanship that could grind out music on demand, there is also the occasional exception like the Symphony No. 5, unusual and impressive in the sustained and involved construction of its first and third movements.

Another personal and individual way of writing, somber and impassioned, is heard in the music of Ernest Bloch. His finest work is the Piano Quintet; and there are impressive pages also in the Violin Sonata, the Viola Suite, the Hebrew Rhapsody *Schelomo* for cello and orchestra, and *Voice in the Wilderness* for cello and orchestra or piano. The more recent String Quartet No. 2 exhibits a refinement and subtilization of the idiom of those earlier works; and its slow portions offer some of the most beautiful writing Bloch has done.

A work by Janáček with extraordinarily powerful writing in a highly individual language and style is his *Slavonic Mass.*

And an arresting new voice in recent years has been that of Benjamin Britten, one of whose outstanding characteristics is a technical resourcefulness and facility which on occasion has turned out a mere pretense at writing music, like the opera *The Rape of Lucrece,* but which on other occasions—in the *Serenade for Tenor, Horn and Strings,* the operas *Peter Grimes* and *Albert Herring*—has served genuine creative imagination and effort.

In addition there is some of the unprofound and enjoyable music that has presented no difficulties to anyone's ears and mind: Delius's exquisitely wrought *Walk to the Paradise Garden* and *Brigg Fair;* the delightful Sitwell-Walton *Façade;* the engaging piano pieces in Albéniz's *Ibéria;* Falla's engaging ballet score *The Three-Cornered Hat;* Sibelius's Symphonies Nos. 5 and 7; Respighi's *The Birds* and *Old Airs and Dances for Lute,* his *Fountains* and *Pines of Rome.*

23

AMERICAN MUSIC

Virgil Thomson once observed in a review of a work by Howard Hanson that Hanson had written lots of music, which made him a real composer, but that the music was as standardized in expression as it was eclectic in style, which made him not a real creator. I would say this of a great many other American composers, past and present—among them Samuel Barber and Gian-Carlo Menotti. And I would go further and say that some Americans haven't really created anything even in music that has *not* been standardized and eclectic. I felt this about Roy Harris, whose music was heard a great deal a few years ago; and I feel it about William Schuman and others whose music is heard a great deal nowadays.

But the stamp of real creative power is, I think, unmistakable in the music of Charles T. Griffes (1884–1920)—in the early *Roman Sketches* for piano that he wrote in a language and style derived from French impressionistic piano music of fifty years ago; in the later Sonata in which he struck out in a new language and style related to the "modern" tendencies of his time, producing a work that is impressive by the authoritative manipulation of the materials rather than effective as musical communication.

That creative power was as unmistakable in Aaron Copland's engaging *Music for the Theater* when it was first heard in 1925. And it remained so even in the unattractive, inaccessible works written in an austere, harshly dissonant "modern" idiom that came after *Music for the Theater*—notably the *Piano Variations* (1930). But one was glad to have it manifest itself again in the lovely and accessible ballet score *Billy the Kid* (1938), the first of a series of such ballet and film scores written in this new, simpler and more attractive idiom, which have continued to be more engaging than the occasional instrumental works. And the most recent dramatic score, the opera *The Tender Land*, seems to me the finest—Copland's largest and most richly filled-out canvas, so to speak. (Earlier I spoke of Copland's attempt, in a book he published in 1941, to persuade us that music like Schönberg's in Europe or his own *Piano Variations* here, when rightly heard and understood, was as natural and acceptable to our ears, as interesting to our minds, as people a hundred years ago found their music. In that connection it is interesting to note that in 1938 Copland had written the first of the ballet and film scores which Arthur Berger, in his excellent book on Copland, tells us represented his decision to stop writing esoteric abstract works for a small special public and write instead music that would interest the large general music public—a decision implying recognition that music like Schönberg's in Europe or Copland's *Piano Variations* here was *not* as natural and acceptable to our ears, as interesting to our minds, as people a hundred years ago found their music.)

In more recent instrumental music Harold Shapero's *Symphony for Classical Orchestra* has impressed me with the creative power I have been talking about. It is evocative of the past but stamped with the impress of Shapero's mind in the way some of Stravinsky's works are; and it is like Stravinsky's also in the assured mastery of the operation and the engaging result.

In opera the distinguished creative achievements other than Copland's *The Tender Land* have been Virgil Thomson's *Four Saints in Three Acts* and *The Mother of Us All*. Thomson, whom I don't find successful with autonomously organized instrumental pieces, is brilliantly successful with music organized around words—specifically the words of Gertrude Stein, which he uses in those two works. His music separates, differentiates, articulates the endless repetitions, gives them point, structure, climax, and achieves something unique, delightful, often very funny, sometimes very moving. Also very fine is Thomson's score for the ballet *Filling Station*.

But what about Menotti's operas? I have already indicated that the music is derivative in a profusion of styles ranging from contemporary down to Puccini and even lower; and I listened to *Amahl and the Night Visitors*, as I have in fact listened to Menotti's other operas, with incredulous amazement—finding it difficult to believe I was really hearing these sugary, trashy tunes, that they could even have occurred to anyone operating as a serious composer today, that he could not have been too embarrassed to let anyone else hear them, and that other people could have considered them worth publishing to the world. But a lot of people like Puccini and worse; and the other reason for Menotti's success—his success even with sophisticated and professional listeners—is his choice of dramatic subjects whose development powerfully engages the audience's interest and emotions—so powerfully, in fact, that the audience is misled into thinking its interest and emotions are being powerfully engaged by the music, whereas actually the most striking fact about *The Consul* was the expressive inadequacy of the mellifluous melodic idiom for the moments of dramatic climax that it expanded in the arias and ensembles.

And what about Gershwin's *Porgy and Bess?* Gershwin's career as a serious composer represented the fallacious idea that since he was an outstanding writer of distinctively American show tunes, he was the man to write the distinctively American symphony and opera, and those show tunes were the material to make it out of—which was like saying the Austrian symphony or opera had to be made by Johann Strauss out of his waltzes. If Johann Strauss had acted on this idea he would have produced works like Gershwin's Piano Concerto and *Porgy and Bess*, which are filled with character-

178

istic Gershwin show music that communicates exactly what it would communicate in a musical show. And *Porgy* represents the additional fallacy, that because the American Negro has contributed to the amalgam of Broadway show music, Broadway show tunes are the right musical medium for any drama about Negroes: we have, then, Negro life in Catfish Row expressed in tunes like *Summertime* and *Bess, You Is My Woman Now* that one might have heard sung by white singers in a Gershwin musical, and that don't acquire any meaning connected with Negroes in Catfish Row when they are sung by colored singers in *Porgy and Bess*. In addition we have these tunes alternating with even more glaringly incongruous material in styles borrowed from grand opera—like the recitative in which Catfish Row Negroes sing such facts as that they will have to get up at five o'clock the next morning.

Only in *An American in Paris* does Gershwin invent delightfully imaginative non-show-music material, in addition to the superb blues in the middle. In this piece he also is able to integrate his material in a coherent form; and it is for me his one success as a serious composer.

The fallacious thinking responsible for *Porgy and Bess* is responsible also for what has been called an "American folk opera"—Kurt Weill's *Down in the Valley*. Here it is folk songs that are the right musical medium for any play about rural folk; so that we have the rural characters of *Down in the Valley* singing their anguish and terror and other powerful emotions in expressively unrelated American folk melodies separated from their own texts. And as if this weren't enough, when the man about to be hanged thinks with desperate longing of his girl, or she thinks similarly of him, each breaks into what in actual style—including Robert Russell Bennett style of orchestration—is a leading tenor's or soprano's number in a Broadway musical.

A word, finally, about Charles Ives (1874-1954). The great to-do in recent years about the originality that showed itself in his use of this or that revolutionary procedure many years before Schönberg seems to me to be about what is unimportant: the important thing is what music Ives produced with whatever technique he used. In the Symphony No. 2, then, one hears occasional lovely writing, especially in the slow portions; but one hears it in a progression that rambles on, shifting from one thing to another in one tempo and another, with no integration and no cumulative effect. The best of Ives's music is fitful and eccentric in that way; but some of it is like the Symphony No. 3, which did not, when I heard it, register on my mind as a coherent and meaningful piece of musical thinking.

24

PERFORMANCE

There is a record of a rehearsal at the 1950 Prades Festival in which Casals stops to explain to the orchestra: "Every note is variety—this is what gives life—otherwise it's something dry. . . ." And it is fascinating to hear him achieve with the orchestra the enlivening inflection of melodic phrase and accompanying figuration that makes the Prades Festival performances of Bach so extraordinary.

The principle that Casals states to the orchestra he also illustrates in his own playing of the cello. The record of the rehearsal is included as a bonus in the volume of 1951 Perpignan Festival performances of chamber music of Beethoven (Columbia SL-169); and in the performance of the great *Archduke* Trio one hears an impressive demonstration of the exciting life that Casals creates in music with the bold inflections and distentions of his powerfully sustained tone in powerfully sustained phrasing.

String tone lends itself to sustained phrasing; not so piano tone, which begins to die out as soon as it is struck. And one remarkable feature of Schnabel's playing of the piano in the service of his playing of music was his ability to create continuity and tension from one note to the next, which made a phrase of melody not a mere succession of notes but something with the continuous life one hears in the phrase of Casals. This, and the ability to carry the tension beyond the phrase through the entire movement, can be heard in the famous performance of the concluding movement of Beethoven's Sonata Op. 111 on Angel COLH-63—the sustained progression from the spaciously meditative opening to the super-earthly end.

To speak of continuity and cohesive tension is to speak of what is outstanding in a Toscanini performance: once the progression begins it never sags, but keeps going with the un-failing continuity of impetus, tension and shape in the de-veloping form of sound that is as remarkable in the perform-ance of Ponchielli's *Dance of the Hours* on Victor LM-1834, as in the old performance of Beethoven's *Leonore* No. 1 Over-ture on Victor LCT-1041. The continuity of shape is achieved by the continuity and coherence in tempo and sonority that also are characteristic of a Toscanini performance—the coher-ence of the tempos that relate the successive sections in the finale of Beethoven's Ninth on Victor LM-6009 in a single coherent progression from one dazzling sublimity to the next.

Toscanini's delighted exclamation once, "It's like reading the score," as he listened to a recorded performance of his, expressed his basic principle that the shape of a work in living sound should be the one indicated by the composer's direc-tions in the printed score. But another observation of his—that Mozart could be boring if the conductor didn't know what to do between the *p* in the first measure and the *f* eight measures later—made it clear that realizing in sound what was on the printed page was not for him a matter just of pro-ducing the *p* here and the *f* eight measures later; and in the performance of Mozart's G minor on Victor LM-1789 one hears a great deal of enlivening inflection between the *p* and the *f*—as one hears also in Casals's and Schnabel's perform-ances. The two statements did however define the type of per-formance these musicians produced: the performance in which the inflections of tempo and sonority stay within the limits set by the composer's directions—whether the infrequent direc-tions of Mozart or the frequent ones of Debussy—and make precisely detailed the forms in sound which those directions outline roughly.

Nor was Toscanini's exclamation concerned only with shape: it expressed his basic principle that whatever is printed in the score must be heard distinctly in the performance. An enormous amount of effort at rehearsals went into balancing the instrumental sonorities to produce the clarity and transparency of texture, the distinctness of strands in that texture, that one hears in his performance—whether of Beethoven's Ninth or of Debussy's *Ibéria* on Victor LM-1833. Not only effort: to make them heard against the weight of strings and brass he doubled the woodwinds in Beethoven's Ninth; and to achieve similar clarity and distinctness he made many such changes in Debussy's scoring of *La Mer*. But there were instances when he had to accept failure: "I have tried everything," he said once sadly, pointing to the bassoon part in one of the tuttis of Beethoven's *Consecration of the House* Overture, "but I am afraid I will never hear these bassoons."

The good in art becomes the criterion by which one recognizes the bad; and that is true of performance, but with at least one qualification. The good performance is the one that realizes in living sound the form indicated by the composer's directions about tempo and sonority; but the performance that changes this shape with tempos and sonorities different from those the composer asks for is not necessarily bad. We accept it as valid if it is consistent with what we think is the expressive character of the work, and if in addition it has the other characteristics I have mentioned: if it is coherent in tempo and sonority, continuous in impetus, tension and shape. What is bad, then, in the performances in which Stokowski changes the composer's tempos and sonorities is that they distort the works to the point of sheer elephantiasis and give music by Bach or Mozart or Musorgsky the expressive effect of the love duet in Wagner's *Tristan und Isolde* or the Bacchanale in *Tannhäuser*. So with the distortions that Koussevitzky introduced into nineteenth-century music with his over-emphatic changes of tempo and sonority. But bad too, on the other hand, were Koussevitzky's performances of eighteenth-century music with no enlivening inflection at all, which revealed his lack of the knowledge of what to do between the *p* here and the *f* eight measures later—the smooth, silky performances of Mozart, for example, that someone characterized well as "a brilliant façade concealing the absence of thought."

There is, then, a distinction to be made between a performer's playing of his instrument and his playing of music. It is a distinction which doesn't occur to most of the people hearing the beautiful and exciting sounds produced by a Stokowski or a Koussevitzky, a Heifetz or a Horowitz, and which is difficult for them to understand when someone else makes it: to perform music is, after all, to produce the sounds; to produce beautiful sounds would seem to be to perform it well; and performances by great virtuosos would seem to be not good and bad but only different. It isn't easy for these people to understand that the dazzling beauty of Heifetz's tone represents masterly playing of the violin, but that his fussy, wailing inflection of this tone often produces a sentimentalizing and cheapening performance of the music he is playing. Or that Horowitz's infinite gradations of piano tone represent masterly manipulation of the piano, but that the unvarying mannered manipulation of melodic phrase employing these infinite gradations of tone is his one way of operating with every composer—whether Chopin or Schubert or Mozart or Scarlatti—and a way that is good for none.

The difference, then, with Toscanini, Casals, Schnabel, Szigeti, Cantelli, and only a very few others is that in addition to being great performers on their instruments (I say this with full awareness of Schnabel's occasional blurring of difficult passage-work and Szigeti's occasional wiry tone) they are great performers of music. And this is true also of singers like Flagstad, Steber, Bjoerling, and in earlier years Rethberg, Matzenauer, Schipa, Hempel, McCormack. In his recorded

184

performance of *O Paradiso!* Caruso, arriving at a high B flat, holds and expands it from *pp* to an overwhelming *ff*, then breaks off to take breath before completing the phrase; whereas Bjoerling, in his recorded performance, connects the expanded B flat with the next note as part of the continuous and beautifully shaped phrase: in the Caruso performance, then, one hears an exceptionally beautiful voice and a mastery in its manipulation; in the Bjoerling not only these but the art in musical phrasing that Caruso did not have. This vocal art in the service of beautiful musical art is what one hears in Flagstad's singing in *Dido and Aeneas*, Rethberg's singing of *Ave Maria* from *Otello*, Hempel's of *Deh vieni non tardar* from *Figaro*.

25

JAZZ

In addition to what the creative powers of a Griffes, a Copland, a Virgil Thomson have produced operating on one emotional level, there is what such powers have produced operating on another emotional level: the superb show music of Kern, Berlin, Gershwin, Rodgers, Porter, and others; the superb creative performances of jazz musicians like Louis Armstrong and Bix Beiderbecke. As against the well-oiled performances of written-out arrangements by large bands—whether in the smooth "sweet" style of Guy Lombardo or the vigorous "hot" style of Benny Goodman —the ones I call creative are the freely improvisatory "hot" performances by small groups of players. Recording has given permanent life to some of these performances and makes it possible to hear and discuss them as one does a piece by Haydn or Berlioz.

As a matter of fact when we listen to an early Armstrong cornet solo we hear something similar to what is so exciting in Haydn and Berlioz: the moment-to-moment working of a mind which we observe this time in the very process of creation, operating with an inventive exuberance that is controlled by a sense for coherent developing form.

In addition to the Armstrong performances with his Hot Five (1925) and Hot Seven (1927) on Columbia CL-851 and 852, there are the ones with Earl Hines at the piano (1928) on 853, and the ones with large commercial bands

186

(1928) on 854. They document his playing and singing from
the time when these operated in the framework and context
of the integrated performances of the Hot Five and Seven
that were still close to their New Orleans origins of group
improvisation, to the time when a big band merely provided
a plushy background for the solo entertainer who began with
a sensitively ornamented trumpet statement of a current song
hit, continued with an extravagantly free vocal treatment of
it, and carried this to its climax in a final spectacular trumpet
solo. And listening to the groups of performances together
we perceive how much better the Hot Fives and Sevens are,
as wholes, than the performances of the Earl Hines combination, brilliant and exciting though these are; and also how
much better Armstrong's own work is in those early performances, superb and beautiful though it is in later ones—
e.g. the 1928 *Muggles* and *West End Blues*, the 1929 *I Can't
Give You Anything but Love*. Within the framework and context
of the Hot Five and Seven performances Armstrong's solos,
no matter how impassioned, how fantastic, how breathtaking
in their virtuosity, remain under control and complete their
developing structure; but already in the performances with
Hines we hear the spectacular getting to be formless at times,
as in those series of ever higher high notes; and we hear this
carried to its occasionally incoherent extreme in the concluding exhibitions of trumpet virtuosity of the 1929 performances.

Armstrong did some of his finest creative playing with
singers—notably with Bessie Smith. Her performances on
the four Columbia records document the change in the
material she sang—from the authentic blues with which she
began as a Negro folk singer, to the popular songs and novelty
numbers of her later years as a vaudeville entertainer. They
also document the succession of jazz musicians who recorded
with her—from Clarence Williams, the pianist of her first
recording of *Down-Hearted Blues* in 1923, and Louis Armstrong, Joe Smith, Charlie Green and others of Fletcher
Henderson's band, to the group including Jack Teagarden,

Chu Berry and Buck Washington that played at her last recording session ten years later. But they document no change in the magnificent voice and style: the long phrases with their powerful momentums and tensions and wonderful inflections of rhythm and pitch that one hears at the beginning are heard all the way to the end, and exercise their effect in her every performance, no matter of what or with whom. Which doesn't keep us from preferring the performances of the best music with the best players; and for me these are the *Cold in Hand Blues*, *You've Been a Good Ole Wagon*, *Reckless Blues* and *St. Louis Blues* that Bessie recorded with Armstrong in 1925, and the *Baby Doll* and *Lost Your Head Blues* that she recorded with Joe Smith in 1926, which are outstanding among the excellent performances on Columbia CL-855 and 857. Smith does some beautifully sensitive trumpet-playing around her singing; and Armstrong produces on muted cornet a progression of delicate, florid and derisive comment that gets to be hilariously funny.

As for Beiderbecke, the one phrase of the late Otis Ferguson that has remained in my memory is his characterization of a Beiderbecke performance years ago: "as fresh and glistening as creation itself." It was more successful than my own attempts to describe what made the playing unique and, for some people, more exciting and moving than any other: "the unfailing continuity in the varied invention; the tensile strength of the continuous line of cornet sound, and at the same time its delicacy; the boldly soaring attack or rise to a high point, the sensitive fall away from this high point or at the end of a phrase." I find these terms inadequate; but I have no better ones now for what, in Beiderbecke's first phrase in *I'm Coming Virginia*, sends chills down my spine and brings tears to my eyes. This and other of his outstanding recorded performances—*Singin' the Blues*, *Clarinet Marmalade*, *Ostrich Walk*, *Riverboat Shuffle*—are on Columbia CL-845; and on 844 are the outstanding *Jazz Me Blues*, *Sorry*, *Since My Best Gal Turned Me Down*, *Thou Swell* and *Ol' Man River*—the last two being examples of his wonderfully sensitive "straight" playing of hit songs.

Recording gives continued life to these improvised performances—but only as long as the records continue in print; and a number of outstanding performances have had their lives ended, for the time being, by the discontinuance of the records. There was the Johnny Dodds *Wild Man Blues* on Brunswick 58004, with an Armstrong cornet solo more controlled and less extravagant than the one in the *Wild Man Blues* on Columbia CL-852. There was Jess Stacy's piano-playing in *The World Is Waiting for the Sunrise* on Decca 5133. There were the performances of the pianist Joe Sullivan, the cornetist Muggsy Spanier and the clarinetist Frank Teschmaker in several famous examples of the exciting Chicago ensemble style: the Chicago Rhythm Kings *There'll Be Some Changes Made* and *I've Found a New Baby* on Brunswick 58017; the Miff Mole *Shim-Me-Sha-Wabble* on Columbia CL-632, which had also the McKenzie and Condon Chicagoans *China Boy* and *Sugar*, and the Condon Footwarmers *Makin' Friends* featuring the superb trombonist Jack Teagarden. There were a number of the best—i.e. the early (1927 to 1931)—Duke Ellington performances on Brunswick 58002, in which the band was still small (ten or twelve men); the arranged ensembles and backgrounds were still quite simple in harmony and style, leaving plenty of room for the soloists to play with freedom and at length; and the playing of the entire band had the relaxed freedom and vitality of jazz performance.

Some of these early Ellington performances may now be on Columbia C3L. And as I write, Jess Stacy's playing in the *Blues in Israel* that was on Decca 5134 can be heard on English Parlophone PMC-1222; Victor LPM-1246 still offers some of the best performances of the pianist Fats Waller; LPM-1443 includes the superb performances with Louis Armstrong and Jack Teagarden at a 1948 concert in Town Hall. Also, Columbia C3L-22, with the performances of Mildred Bailey

—each made a delight by the exquisite inflection of the lovely small voice in phrasing whose subtle displacement of accents is controlled by a feeling for the shape of the phrase (as against the extravagant freedom with rhythm and notes in Billie Holiday's later singing that makes what is sung no longer recognizable as the phrases of the song)—offers with Bailey's singing the exciting playing of small groups that have Teddy Wilson, Mary Lou Williams, Billy Kyle and Ellis Larkin at the piano. And several performances recorded late in 1935—in particular *Some Day, Sweetheart* and *Willow Tree*— are made especially notable by the fresh and richly inventive playing Wilson was doing at that time. One cannot hear his marvelous playing in the Red Norvo *I Surrender, Dear* and *Blues in E flat* that were transferred to Epic LN-3128; but his incandescent performance in *What a Little Moonlight Can Do* can still be heard on Columbia CL-637, which has *Miss Brown to You, I Wished on the Moon* and others that Wilson recorded at that early time with the young Billie Holiday.

26

CRITICISM

The comments of Berlioz on *Selva opaca* from *William Tell* that I quoted in my discussion of Rossini occur in the long essay on *Tell* that Berlioz wrote for the *Gazette musicale de Paris* in 1834 and that is reprinted in Strunk's *Source Readings in Music History*. I consider this one essay well worth the price of the entire volume; but at the very least it is worth a visit to the library; for it is, as far as I know, the only article available in print here of the formal music criticism Berlioz wrote for French periodicals and newspapers, and I know no better introduction to the writing of the greatest of music critics. And remembering again how indiscriminately the word *great* is tossed about, I will establish what I mean when I apply it to Berlioz's criticism.

What I mean is much the same as what I meant when I applied it to Beethoven's music. Not only does one find in Berlioz's criticism the critical perception that is the absolute essential in such writing; not only does one find this perception formulating itself with literary brilliance and delightful gaiety and wit. In addition one finds—behind all the literary brilliance and gaiety—that perception dealing rigorously with the work of art before it; and with this integrity in relation to the material there is an intensity, a passion, a greatness of spirit in the operation that bring tears to my eyes whenever I read the writing.

These personal qualities appear most vividly of course in the personal writing—the *Memoirs*, the letters. Consider for example the letter—quoted by Turner in his book on Berlioz—in which Berlioz tells his father of his determination to become a composer:

> I have voluntarily embarked upon a magnificent career (one can give no other epithet to that of the arts) and not upon my destruction; because I believe that I shall succeed, yes, I believe it: it is not an occasion for modesty; to prove to you that I leave nothing to chance, I consider, I am convinced that I shall distinguish myself in music, everything points to it outwardly; and within me the voice of nature is stronger than the strictest objections of reason. I have everything imaginable in my favor, if you will support me: I begin young; I shall not need to give lessons like so many others to support myself; I have certain attainments and possess the foundations of others in a way that leads to a deeper development, and indeed I have experienced passions of sufficient strength not to be mistaken as to their true accents whenever it may be necessary to depict them or make them speak.
>
> If I am mercilessly condemned to die of hunger in the event of failure (and in truth I would not stop sooner), your reasonings and your disquietude would be better founded; but there is no question of that, and, fixing it at the lowest, I shall have one day two thousand francs income; but let us say fifteen hundred, I could live all the same on this sum; even with twelve hundred I should be content, supposing music brought me in nothing. In short, I want to make my name; I want to leave some trace of my existence on the earth; and so strong is this feeling, which indeed in itself is wholly noble, that I would prefer to be Gluck or Méhul, dead, than what I am in the prime of life. . . .
>
> Such is my way of thinking, such I am and nothing in the world can change me; you can withdraw all help from me or force me to leave Paris, but I don't believe it; you would not thus make me lose the best years of my life and break the charmed needle, being unable to prevent it from obeying the attraction of its pole.

Adieu, my dear father, re-read my letter and do not attribute it to a momentary state of exaltation, for I have never been more calm.

I embrace you tenderly, also mother and my sisters,

Your respectful and affectionate son,

H. Berlioz

I share Turner's doubt that one can read this without being moved, and especially moved if one knows what came of those confident hopes—if one has read Berlioz's own account in his *Memoirs* of the experiences that led him to write twenty years later:

> . . . I end . . . with profuse thanks to sacred Germany where the worship of art has kept itself pure; to you, generous England; to you, Russia, who saved me; to you, my good friends in France; to you, lofty hearts and minds of all the nations I have known. I was fortunate in knowing you; I have, and I will faithfully keep, the most precious memory of our relations. As for you, maniacs, stupid mastiffs and bulls, as for you my Guildensterns, my Rosencrantzes, my Iagos, my little Osrics, serpents and insects of every kind, "farewell my . . . friends"; I despise you, and I hope not to die before I have forgotten you.

The *Memoirs*, then, is something to read because it is a remarkable and superbly written personal document. But also, in the absence of English translations of published collections of Berlioz's formal critical writings, the *Memoirs* is valuable for the incidental observations on music one encounters in it.

The only collection of Berlioz's letters available in English, the *New Letters of Berlioz 1830-1868*, offers a poor selection (few of the personal letters that are so moving; many letters concerned with plans, negotiations and arrangements for publication and performance) poorly and inaccurately translated.

In addition to his formal music criticism, some of which he collected in the volume *A travers Chants*, Berlioz wrote feuilletons—imaginative, ironic, witty, and often very funny. Of

193

the two published collections, *Les Soirées de l'orchestre* and *Les Grotesques de la musique*, only the first was published here as *Evenings in the Orchestra* in a translation that was old-fashioned but that may turn out to be preferable to the new one by the translator of the *New Letters*.

For music criticism comparable with Berlioz's—the finest written in English, and some of the finest in any language—read the concert reviews and articles of Bernard Shaw. You may be surprised to hear that he did such writing; but the fact is you will do better to read what he said about a performance at Covent Garden in 1890 than what you will find in a newspaper about a performance at the Metropolitan today—or for that matter what Shaw himself said later about world events. He was not a great spirit; but the music criticism he wrote in his early thirties reveals a genial and attractive human being astonishingly different from the perversely unpleasant and silly world-figure of later years. And it reveals him, at that early period, using vast resources of literary brilliance, fun and wit in the service of a distinguished critical perception and taste in music that is an additional agreeable surprise to someone familiar only with the later Shaw who concerned himself almost exclusively with politics and sociology. In his method of operation as a critic, then, Shaw resembles Berlioz; and what makes him a great critic is an integrity like Berlioz's in relation to his material—the fact that behind all the brilliance and fun and wit the critical perception and taste deals rigorously with what is before it. And the result is a flow of comment on the daily events of those distant musical seasons that is still some of the most discerning, the most instructive, the most enjoyable you can read in any language.

You are not likely to be interested in the performance of Boito's *Mefistofele* that Shaw wrote about on May 29, 1889; but it provided the occasion for his observation that Gounod's *Faust* was "a true musical creation, whereas Boito has only

194

adapted the existing resources of orchestration and harmony very ably to his libretto"—which embodies an instructive distinction you will find useful when you listen to much of the new music written today. And relevant to some opera productions you may see today is Shaw's remark that "the house likes Boito's prologue, in spite of the empty stage and the two ragged holes in a cloth which realize Mr. Harris's modest conception of hell and heaven."

In no newspaper today are you likely to encounter the accurate perception and good sense of Shaw's comment after a performance of Brahms's *Requiem*. The audience's delusion that "Brahms is a great composer, and the performance of this masterpiece of his an infinitely solemn and important function" was, he says, "not confined to those who, having found by experience that good music bores them, have rashly concluded that all music that bores them must be good. It raged also among the learned musicians, who know what a *point d'orgue* is, and are delighted to be able to explain what is happening when Brahms sets a pedal pipe booming and a drum thumping the dominant of the key for ten minutes at a stretch, whilst the other instruments and the voices plough along through every practicable progression in or near the key, up hill from syncopation to syncopation, and down dale from suspension to suspension in an elaborately modernized manner that only makes the whole operation seem more desperately old-fashioned and empty." And adding that Brahms seems to have thought he could produce more remarkable effects than Beethoven by keeping his pedal-points going even longer than Beethoven's, Shaw observes that while the academics like this sort of thing the genuine musician dislikes nothing more than "an attempt to pass off the forms of music for music itself, especially those forms which have received a sort of consecration from their use by great composers in the past"—which neatly exposes Brahms's classicism for what it is.

Nor on the other hand will you find anything more perceptive on Verdi than what Shaw wrote after Verdi's death—his insistence, for example, that there was no evidence in a single measure of his last three operas that Verdi had heard a note of Wagner, but evidence instead that he had heard Mendelssohn and Beethoven, whose music "is the music of a Germany still under that Franco-Italian influence which made the music of Mozart so amazingly unlike the music of Bach. Of the later music that was consciously and resolutely German and German only . . . of the music of Schumann, Brahms and Wagner, there is not anywhere in Verdi the faintest trace. In German music the Italian loved what Italy gave. What Germany offered of her own music he entirely ignored." This is still the answer to those who even today will have it that the writing in Verdi's last operas represents the influence of Wagner.

Of the four volumes of Shaw's music criticism in the complete edition of his writings published in England only the first, *London Music in 1888-1889 as Heard by Corno di Bassetto*, was published here; but the three of *Music in London 1890-1894* can be found in libraries; and a paper-cover volume has just been published with a selection from all four.

The gaiety of Berlioz and Shaw is not in W. J. Turner: even his irony, however intense, is quiet. He writes with a poet's precision of statement, in the expression of a poet's insights. Those insights give us the illuminating statements about Mozart; they also enable him to make this astonishing observation after Toscanini's concerts in London in 1935—that as he had sat watching Toscanini he "was suddenly reminded of Berlioz's remark: 'Do you think I make music for my pleasure?' I am certain that it is not a pleasure for Toscanini to conduct, but rather that he suffers. It is because of his extreme musical sensibility and intense concentration. Here lies the essence of his superiority." Astounding, because it was written fifteen years before an afternoon on which Toscanini said: "Conducting is for me great suffering. When I am alone with the score I am very happy; when I am on the podium

196

I am always afraid. I am afraid the horn will be late, the clarinet will not play correct. . . ."

Turner, with the same dislike of Brahms the serious composer as Shaw's, expresses it in different terms. Explaining why he rates the Haydn Variations and the final passacaglia movement of the Fourth Symphony highest in Brahms's work, he says it is because in his variation-writing Brahms is not "being a poet (in the Aristotelian sense) or a great creator; he is merely being a musician"—that is, a craftsman. "I do not like Brahms when he goes forth to battle. . . . Brahms was much too earnest, and to be earnest is always to be ridiculous, since it is given only to the elect, the few supremely great—a Beethoven, for example—to be not earnest but serious. . . . But Brahms when he is being entirely natural and self-forgetful, when he is not at all obsessed by the tramp of Beethoven behind him . . . then he is a truly great and inspired musician."

Of the four collections of Turner's reviews and articles only the first, *Music and Life*, was published here and can be found in a few libraries. Of his other books the *Mozart* is still available; the *Beethoven* is in a few libraries; but the *Berlioz* was not published here.

In this country the writings of Philip Hale and H. T. Parker are worth investigating in the library; but the only newspaper music criticism worth reading in recent years was Virgil Thomson's; and the three collections of his reviews and articles —*The Musical Scene, The Art of Judging Music,* and *Music Right and Left*—contain numerous examples of the operation of a critical apparatus of perception and intellect that would make the writing a pleasure to read even without its additional delights of felicitous and witty statement. But I must add that with those pieces of distinguished criticism there are many pieces of irresponsible nonsense.

The difference between sense and nonsense with Thomson is most often the difference between the writing in which his

197

mind is in contact with the real facts that are before him—the facts that one recognizes in the music or performance he is discussing; and on the other hand the writing which deals with things one cannot discover in the music or performance—things which exist only in his head, and to which he applies ideas with no more basis in reality. When, in explanation of his opinion that "Horowitz's playing is monotonous and, more often than not, musically false," Thomson writes that Horowitz "never states a simple melody frankly. He teases it by accenting unimportant notes and diminishing his tonal volume on all the climactic ones. The only contrast to brio that he knows is the affettuoso style"—he describes what anyone can hear in the playing. So when he writes that "Mitropoulos has taken over the Philharmonic-Symphony concerts like an occupying army," refers to Mitropoulos's "Panzer division tactics," and amplifies this with the observations that "all is discipline, machine finish, tension and power" and "he makes every piece . . . sound nervous and violent." But I don't recognize in Yvonne Lefebure's piano-playing what Thomson describes in his statement that "her differentiations between time and accent also aid orchestral evocation, because melodic passages, as on the *bel canto* instruments, are played without downbeat stresses, the accentual pattern being rendered, as in real orchestral playing, by sharp pings, deep bell strokes, and articulations recalling those of harp, bow-heel, and the orchestra's percussion group." Nor do I recognize Toscanini's performances in Thomson's contention that they have meter but not rhythm, and still less in his mumbo-jumbo about the marriage of historical and literary with musical culture in the Great Tradition of Wagner, von Bülow, Nikisch and Beecham that is lacking in Toscanini's conducting.

Much of Thomson's writing is a spinning out of such fancy schematizing ideas about facts imagined or altered to fit; and much of this schematization is concerned with tradition. An article *Tradition Today*, for example, is about the conductors, dominantly exemplified for Thomson by Reiner and Monteux, who operate as the preservers of "the traditions of interpretation as these have been handed down," as against men like Stokowski and Koussevitzky who operate rather with "a highly personalized ability to hold attention"; about American conductors of the second type who "have the excuse of having passed their youth out of contact with a major musical tradition, of not having known the classics early enough to feel at home with them"; and about one of them, Leonard Bernstein, who "knows what American music is all about, but the western European repertory he is obliged to improvise. . . . That is why, I think, he goes into such chorybantic ecstasies in front of it. He needs to mime, for himself and others, a conviction that he does not have. He does no such act before American works of his own time. He takes them naturally, reads them with authority." And I might add that in conversation Thomson once ascribed a similar ignorance to Toscanini, contending that whereas Toscanini had learned the operatic traditions in the opera house, he had found himself, at fifty, having to deal with the symphonic repertory without knowledge of *its* traditions, and had solved the problem by doing a complete streamlining job on the music.

Actually Bernstein and Toscanini learned the classics as early, and in the same way, as Reiner and Monteux. If Toscanini began his career in the opera house it was because that is where a conductor usually begins in Europe: Muck, Mahler, Walter, Reiner all conducted opera before they conducted the symphonic repertory. And when Toscanini began to conduct this repertory—at thirty, not at fifty—it was with the knowledge of the music and of the traditions of its performance that he had acquired in his youth in the same way as those other conductors: from hearing it performed and studying the scores. The striking differences in Toscanini's performances of symphonic music, like those in his performances of opera, represented not his ignorance of tradition but the modification of it by his personal musical taste: what

199

Thomson called streamlining was actually a personal performing style which, in opera no less than in symphonic music,
tended toward plastic simplicity, economy and subtlety—
which, for example, tended to set a single subtly modified
tempo for the several sections of a movement. Toscanini
would have been open to criticism for this only if the tradition had had the authority Thomson mistakenly endows it
with: if, that is, it had gone back in a straight line to an
authoritative first performance. But actually the line had
begun with first performances that had represented nothing
more authoritative than the judgment and taste each conductor had applied to what he had found in the score; it had
continued with successive modifications of those performances
by later conductors in accordance with *their* judgments and
tastes; and there was nothing in all this that forbade further
modifications by Toscanini in accordance with *his* judgment
and taste.

The successive European performances were transferred to
this country by the succession of European conductors who
came here; and it was from them that American conductors,
including Bernstein, learned in their youth the symphonic
repertory and the traditions of its performance. It was, then,
not for lack of knowledge of these traditions that Bernstein
played Beethoven's *Eroica* badly; nor was it possession of this
knowledge that caused him to play a Mozart symphony
beautifully. And he went into the same chorybantic ecstasies
before a Copland piece as before the Mozart.

But such failures of Thomson and the defects responsible
for them are those of a man who also has produced some of
the finest music criticism written anywhere. And Tovey's observation about Schubert can be applied to Thomson: his
occasional weaknesses and inequalities do not make him a
critic of less than the highest rank.

Tovey's observation can also be applied to the occasional
weaknesses and inequalities of his own writing. These begin

with his limitations of sympathy and understanding, which represent the ideas on the history of music that he absorbed from his teacher Parry. But it was also from Parry that he learned his procedure of point-to-point analysis of music; and this procedure, applied to works of composers for whom he does have sympathy and understanding, gives us those excitingly illuminating descriptions of the courses of events in Haydn's symphonies and Mozart's concertos in *Essays in Musical Analysis*—each of which achieves the primary purpose of criticism as it is defined by E. M. Forster: "It considers the [individual work of art] in itself, as an entity, and tells us what it can about its life." Moreover, this examination and description of the life in particular works underlies Tovey's generalizations of a composer's practice, such as are found in the monumental essays on Schubert and Haydn in *The Main Stream of Music*.

With the extraordinary musical perception there is the understanding and knowledge of a mind that has ranged widely in territory outside of music; and there is also formulation of this perception and understanding in statements that are often epigrammatic in their concentration and clarification of sense and their impact and brilliance. But sometimes the mind ranges so far afield, or the formulation becomes so epigrammatic, that the thought is obscure and difficult to follow. It is mostly in the articles and lectures on general matters—*Normality and Freedom in Music, The Main Stream in Music, Stimulus and the Classics of Music*, and others—that one finds the elliptically allusive or epigrammatic obscurities, the embarrassing professorial humor that are additional weaknesses and inequalities in Tovey's writing. And these don't in the slightest degree lessen the magnitude of the powers and achievements he exhibits elsewhere—the powers and achievements of the great critic who is able to describe in such illuminating fashion the courses of events in particular works of Schubert and Haydn, and to derive from these observations of particular behavior the illuminating general statements

201

about each composer like this one about Schubert: "We are right in thinking that his maturest works in large instrumental forms are diffuse and inconsistent. . . . But when we find (as, for instance, in the first movement of the great C major Symphony) that some of the most obviously wrong digressions contain the profoundest, most beautiful, and most inevitable passages, then it is time to suspect that Schubert, like other great classics, is pressing his way toward new forms." Or this one about Haydn: "He is rightly believed to be on a level with Mozart as a master of form; but his form is described as 'regular and symmetrical.' And when you come to look at it, you find not only that all the rules of form as observed by both Mozart and Beethoven are frequently violated by Haydn, but that they are so seldom observed that it would be quite impossible to infer them from his mature practice at all. More recent writers have tried to show some recognition of this by saying that in Haydn's works we see the sonata forms 'in the making.' This only increases the confusion; for Haydn's most nearly regular works are his earlier ones, when he wrote on the lines of J. C. and C. P. E. Bach; whereas his freedom of form becomes manifest just about the time when he came to know Mozart. The mutual influence of Haydn and Mozart is one of the best-known wonders of musical history; and the paradox of it is that while its effect on Mozart was to concentrate his style and strengthen his symmetry, the effect on Haydn was to set him free, so that his large movements became as capricious in their extended course of events as his minuets had always been in the cast of their phrases."

Of the several other excellent books mentioned in earlier chapters Copland's *Music and Imagination*, containing his Charles Eliot Norton lectures at Harvard in 1951-52, includes a little of the fallacious ad hoc reasoning of the propagandist for contemporary music; but for the most part, in these lectures concerned with "the relation of the imaginative mind to the different aspects of the art of music," Copland is the critic—a critic operating with the special insight of the composer and a gift for felicitous statement. Concerning the enormous wealth of color combinations offered by the modern orchestra, for example, Copland remarks that it has been the undoing of the radio or movie orchestrator: "Where there is no true expressive purpose anything goes; in fact, everything goes, and it all goes into the same piece."

Dent's *Mozart's Operas* is a product of the unusual combination of scholarship which provides interesting information about Mozart's materials, problems and methods with each opera; esthetic perception which illuminates the final work of art; and a clear and graceful style which makes the writing a pleasure to read. And equally good is Dent's little Pelican book, *Opera*.

Sullivan's *Beethoven* and Toye's *Verdi* are two of the best books on individual composers; and others are Kirkpatrick's *Domenico Scarlatti*, Toye's *Rossini*, Walker's *Hugo Wolf*, Berger's *Aaron Copland*. And Wotton's *Hector Berlioz*, the one good book on Berlioz other than Turner's, is worth looking for in the library.

Finally, the three volumes of *Letters of Mozart and His Family*. They are interesting for the comments of Mozart and his father on the music of their contemporaries, and for the information they give us about the musical life of the period, which should correct some mistaken ideas about it that are still current. But their chief interest is in what they tell us about the personality and life of the most extraordinary musical genius we know of; and Mozart's own letters are fascinating and moving personal documents.

I should add that what the letters tell us about Mozart does not—as some would leap to conclude—reveal any additional meaning in the music that we wouldn't perceive without them: on the contrary, it is from the music that we learn of emotional and spiritual resources that we wouldn't know of from anything he said—resources which apparently only the artist was able to draw on, and which achieved explicit formulation only in his works of art. That is, Mozart's vivacity and love of fun are delightfully evident in the rush of absurdly mingled German and Italian in which, at the age of fourteen, he describes a performance of opera in Verona to his sister:

> . . . Oronte, il padre di Bradamanta, è un prencipe (fà il sign. afferi) un bravo cantante, un paritono, mà gezwungen, wen er in Falset hinauf, aber doch nicht so sehr, wie der Tibaldi zu Wien. Bradamante, figlia d' orionte, inamorata di Ruggiero mà (sie soll den Leone heyrathen, sie will ihm aber nicht), fà una povera Baronessa, che ha avuto una gran disgrazia, mà non sò che? Recita (unter einem fremden Nam, ich weiss aber den Namen nicht) ha una voce passabile, e la statura non sarebbe male, ma distona come il diavolo. Ruggiero un ricco principe, innamorato di Bradamanta, un Musico, canta un poco Manzolisch ed à una bellissima voce forte ed è già vecchio la cinquanta cinque anni ed à una leuffige gurgel. Leone, soll die Bradamanta heyrathen, reichissima est; ob er aber ausser dem Theatro reich ist, das weis ich nicht, fà una donna, la moglie di Afferri. à una bellissima voce, ma è tanto sussuro nell theatro, che non si sente niente. Irene fà una sorella di Lolli dell gran Violinisto, che abbiamo sentito a Vienna. à una schnoffelte voce, e canta sempre um ein viertil zu tardi, ò troppo à buon ora. . . .

But the letter tells us nothing that we can't hear—and nothing more than we do hear—when we listen to a musical embodiment of the vivacity and love of fun like the final rush of the Piano Concerto K.453. And from the letters we would know nothing of the sublimities we hear in the *Contessa, perdono* passage at the end of *Figaro*.

PART TWO

THE GREAT RECORDED
PERFORMANCES OF THE PAST

Replying to Toscanini's letter of resignation in 1954, David Sar-
noff wrote that Toscanini's "incomparable re-creations of the
great music of the past and present" had, happily, been "recorded
and preserved for us, and for posterity." What he failed to add was
that the recordings would be available to us and to posterity only if
they continued to be bought in quantities that RCA Victor considered sufficient to justify continuing production. And actually,
within a few years Victor had stopped producing some of Toscanini's
recordings, so that as I write these lines it is not possible to obtain the
records with his truly "incomparable" performances of Mozart's
Divertimento K.287, Tchaikovsky's *Manfred*, Berlioz's *Harold in
Italy*, Strauss's *Don Juan* and *Don Quixote*. One reason for the drop
in sales of Toscanini's recordings is the fact that the public buys the
recordings of the currently active performers it reads about, not of
the inactive performers it no longer reads about, not even inactive
performers as famous as Toscanini. Another reason is the advent of
stereo recording, which made Toscanini's recordings uninteresting
to those who care more about the latest in sound than about the
greatest in performance.

What happened in Toscanini's case has been happening ever since
the beginning of commercial recording. Always the companies have
talked about the phonograph's preserving performers' art for posterity; but always the recorded performances of yesterday have dis-
appeared from the catalogues, to be replaced by those of today; and
with each major change in recording technique—from acoustic to
electrical 78-rpm recording, from 78-rpm to long-playing micro-
groove, and most recently from mono LP to stereo—the recordings

made with the old technique have been replaced by recordings made with the new. And this chapter is concerned with some of the great recorded performances that have been lost in this way—performances which are worth hunting for in stores that sell old 78-rpm and LP records, and worth watching for among the occasional reissues.

What acoustic 78-rpm recording reproduced accurately was singing; and the records preserved some of the achievements in what has been called the golden age of singing—the age of Caruso, Melba, Tetrazzini, McCormack and their contemporaries. It must be noted that most of the singers in this period misused the music to show off their voices, instead of employing their voices in an effective presentation of the music; and what was recorded was performances like Caruso's of *Una furtiva lagrima*, in which the outpouring of vocal splendor burst the shape of the musical phrase, more often than performances like McCormack's of this aria, in which the beautiful voice was employed in a plastically coherent shaping of phrase. McCormack's famous performance of *Il mio tesoro* from *Don Giovanni* is on RCA Victor LM-2631; and additional beautiful performances of his, acoustically and electrically recorded, are on Angel COLH-123, unfortunately with added artificial resonance. (Caruso's voice, without electronic improvement, can be heard on Rococo 5244; Melba's on Angel COLH-125; Tetrazzini's, with added electronic gloss and glow, on COLH-136.)

Hempel not only had a soprano voice as lovely and a technique as spectacular as Melba's and Tetrazzini's, but was the great musician they were not. No one has equalled her sustained phrasing in the closing section of *Dite alla giovine* from *La Traviata* on Victor 89079, later on 15-1020, or her delivery of *Deh vieni non tardar* from *Figaro* on Victor 88450, which Victor should reissue. As for available records, the sound of her voice is more accurate on Scala 832 and 833 and imported Odeon E-83397 than on Odeon COLH-135, which has her HMV performances of arias from *The Magic Flute*, *The Seraglio*, *Ernani* and *La Traviata*.

Contemporary with Hempel at the Metropolitan were Destinn, whose superb dramatic soprano voice and earlier lyric soprano can be heard on Scala 804; the mezzo-soprano Matzenauer, whose extraordinary vocal and musical powers are revealed, on Collectors

206

Guild 611, in arias from *L'Africaine*, *Le Prophète*, *Don Carlo* and *Die Walküre*, among others; the tenor Slezak, whose remarkable voice and superb singing in an astonishing variety of styles can be heard, on Scala 844, in arias from *The Magic Flute*, *L'Africaine*, *William Tell*, *Carmen*, *Il Trovatore* and *Aida;* the tenor Urlus, whose beautiful and distinguished singing in a similar variety of styles is heard, on Rococo 5238, in arias from *The Magic Flute*, *William Tell*, *Carmen*, *Otello* and works of Wagner. And after Hempel there was, in Europe, Ivogün, whose exquisite soprano voice and enchanting style can be heard, on imported Odeon O-83395, in arias from *The Magic Flute*, *The Seraglio* and *The Barber of Seville*, among others.

A legendary singer of an earlier period is the soprano Lilli Lehmann, whose voice on Scala 826—though it no longer has luster or warmth—is steady and powerful, and whose florid singing in an aria from Handel's *Joshua*, and phrasing and style in arias from *The Seraglio* and *Don Giovanni*, are breathtaking. And another is the Russian lyric tenor Sobinov, whose beautiful and affecting performance of Lensky's last aria from *Eugene Onegin* is on Collectors Guild 0594, with similar performances of arias from *Don Pasquale*, *Lohengrin* and French and other Russian operas.

Though acoustic recording didn't reproduce the symphony orchestra well, Victor did achieve a remarkable approximation of the sound of the Boston Symphony conducted by Muck in the finale of Tchaikovsky's Fourth on 6050, and in the Marche Miniature from Tchaikovsky's Suite No. 1 and the Prelude to Act 3 of Wagner's *Lohengrin* on 547.

The advent of electrical recording in the mid-twenties brought the beginning of realistic reproduction of the orchestra; and in the fifteen or twenty years that followed, Victor recordings preserved the achievements of what might be called a golden age of orchestral performance in this country, in which the Philadelphia Orchestra playing under Stokowski, the Boston Symphony under Koussevitzky, the New York Philharmonic under Toscanini—each a group of exceptionally competent performers sensitized to the direction of a conductor extraordinarily equipped with the ear for orchestral precision and sonority and with the personal force and technical mastery to achieve them—produced their marvels of virtuoso execution and, in accordance with the particular conductor's taste, the Philadelphia Orchestra's tonal sumptuousness and splendor, the Boston Symphony's refinement and subtlety of orchestral color, the New York Philharmonic's radiance, transparency and sharpness of definition. And again it must be noted that the Toscanini performances offered orchestral virtuosity in the service of his unfailing sense for plastic proportion and coherence in the shaping of phrase and larger structure, whereas those of Koussevitzky and Stokowski offered orchestral sonorities that were among the wonders of the age, but with Koussevitzky's italicizing plastic distortions of nineteenth-century music, his playing of eighteenth-century music with no enlivening inflection at all, and Stokowski's playing of almost everything with the fever and luxuriance suitable for the Bacchanale from *Tannhäuser* or the second-act duet from *Tristan und Isolde*.

Two Koussevitzky-Boston Symphony performances that were not only examples of dazzling orchestral virtuosity but admirable statements of the music were those of Mendelssohn's *Italian* Symphony, reproduced more realistically by Victor DM-1259 than by the early M-294, and Prokofiev's *Classical Symphony*, reproduced more realistically by DM-1241 than by 7196/7. And two of the best Stokowski-Philadelphia Orchestra performances were the Dances from *Prince Igor* on M-499, and the Debussy *Fêtes* on 2034 of M-630.

As for Toscanini, the incandescent operation with the New York Philharmonic that he never duplicated with another orchestra was reproduced most realistically by the 1936 recordings they made at the end of his last Philharmonic season:

> Beethoven: Symphony No. 7, on M-317.
> Brahms: *Variations on a Theme of Haydn*, on M-355.
> Rossini: Overture to *Semiramide*, on M-408.
>   Overture to *L'Italiana in Algeri*, on 14161.
> Wagner: Prelude to *Lohengrin, Dawn and Siegfried's Rhine Journey* from *Die Götterdämmerung*, *Siegfried-Idyll*, on M-308.

But it could be heard even in the less realistically reproduced performances recorded in 1929:

> Haydn: Symphony No. 101 (*Clock*) and
> Mendelssohn: Scherzo from *A Midsummer Night's Dream*,
>   on M-57.

Mozart: Symphony K.385 (*Haffner*), on M-65.
Rossini: Overture to *The Barber of Seville*, on 7255.
Verdi: Preludes to Acts 1 and 3 of *La Traviata*, on 6994.

These were reissued on LP records—with sound that varied from excellent (*Lohengrin, Die Götterdämmerung*) to poor (Haydn, Mendelssohn)—as follows:

Beethoven Seventh, on Victor LCT-1013 and Camden CAL-352.
Brahms *Haydn Variations*, on LCT-1023.
Brahms *Haydn Variations*, Mozart *Haffner*, Mendelssohn *Scherzo*, Rossini *Barber*, on CAL-326.
Rossini *Semiramide*, Verdi *Traviata*, Wagner *Siegfried-Idyll*, on CAL-309.
Haydn *Clock*, Wagner *Lohengrin* and *Die Götterdämmerung*, on CAL-375.

In addition to documenting the incandescent operation of conductor and orchestra, these recordings document the Toscanini performing style of that period—relaxed, expansive, articulating and organizing and shaping the substance of a piece with much elasticity of tempo, and inflecting the phrase with much sharply outlined detail—as against the later style that was simpler, tauter and swifter, setting a tempo that was maintained with only slight modification, and giving the phrase only subtle inflection. Further documentation of the earlier style is provided by the performances Toscanini recorded with the BBC Symphony between 1937 and 1939:

Beethoven: Symphony No. 1, on M-507, later on LCT-1023.
Symphony No. 4, on M-676.
Symphony No. 6 (*Pastoral*), on M-417, later on LCT-1042.
Overture, *Leonore* No. 1, on 15945, later on LCT-1041.
Mozart: Overture to *The Magic Flute*, on 15190.
Rossini: Overture to *La Scala di Seta*, on 15191.
Weber-Berlioz: *Invitation to the Dance*, on 15192.

These are available on imported Odeon LP records as follows:

> Beethoven First, Mozart *Magic Flute*, on QJLP-106.
> Beethoven Fourth and *Leonore* No. 1, on QALP-10227.
> Beethoven Sixth, on ALP-1664 and QJLP-107.

And they are to be available here on Seraphim IC-6015.

Toscanini's earlier performing style is documented also by the performances he recorded with the NBC Symphony in its first years:

> Haydn: Symphony No. 88, on M-454, later on LCT-7.
> Mozart: Symphony in G minor (K.550), on M-631.
> Beethoven: Lento and Vivace from Quartet Op. 135, on M-590, later on LCT-1041.
> Symphony No. 5, on M-640, later on LCT-1041.
> Symphony No. 3 (*Eroica*), on M-765.
> Symphony No. 8, on M-908.
> Overture, *Leonore* No. 2, on HMV DA-1753/4.
> Overture, *Leonore* No. 3, on HMV DB-5703/4.
> Overture to *Egmont*, on HMV DB-5705.
> Rossini: Overture to *William Tell*, on M-605, later on LM-14.

And a towering example of Toscanini's earlier style is the Schubert Symphony No. 9 that he recorded with the Philadelphia Orchestra in 1941, which was not issued until 1963, and is still available on LD-2663. Toscanini's performance of this symphony realized its sustained tension, momentum and grandeur as no other has done; and the 1941 performance is the greatest of his statements of the work, reproduced with much of the beauty of its sound in the Academy of Music. (The other performances Toscanini recorded with the Philadelphia Orchestra in 1941-42—of Mendelssohn's *A Midsummer Night's Dream*, Tchaikovsky's *Pathétique*, Berlioz's *Queen Mab*, Debussy's *La Mer* and *Ibéria*—also are superior to those recorded later with the NBC Symphony, and are reproduced with beautiful sound; and they too should be issued by Victor.)

With the exception of this Schubert Ninth, and a few Verdi excerpts and 'pop' numbers with the NBC Symphony, the Toscanini performances on the Victor records available today date from 1944 and thereafter, and are in Toscanini's later simplified, swifter, tauter style. If one knows both the 1941 and the 1953 performances of the Schubert Ninth, or both the 1936 and the 1951 performances of Rossini's *Semiramide* Overture, one realizes that the early one is even greater than the later one; but if one knows only the later one, one cannot imagine anything greater; and what is true in these instances is true in all. The available records do not, then, have Toscanini's greatest performances; but they have great performances which one cannot imagine that Toscanini surpassed, and which one cannot hear equalled by any others—except the few that Cantelli recorded. And their greatness is evident even when they are defectively reproduced by the recording, as far too many of them are.

It would have been unthinkable that anyone should change what Toscanini produced at a concert; but when he produced the performance for a recording, Victor's supervisor of the recording could change its sound by his placing of the microphones and his other decisions affecting the acoustic characteristics of the hall. And the mistakes of a number of supervisors did imprint on wax or tape the shallow, coarse sound of the Sousa *Stars and Stripes Forever* on 11-9188, the compressed and lusterless sound of the Tchaikovsky *Pathétique* on M-1281 and LM-1037 and the Beethoven Ninth on LM-6009, the dim sound of the Mendelssohn *Midsummer Night's Dream* on M-1280 and LM-1221, the sound of the Beethoven *Missa Solemnis* on LM-6013 in which the chorus predominates over orchestra and soloists—instead of the facsimiles of the original spacious, lustrous, perfectly balanced sound that correct microphone placement would have achieved. Moreover, when it happened that a superb facsimile of the performance—of Beethoven's Eighth, of Musorgsky's *Pictures at an Exhibition*, of Bizet's *Carmen* Suite—*was* imprinted on the tape, and Toscanini had approved it, then a Victor music editor—assigned to make from this original the tape master used in the processing of the metal parts for the final disc records—could, and did, make the changes that resulted in the ear-piercing, raucous *Pictures at an Exhibition* on LM-1838, the harsh Eighth on LM-1757, the shallow, blowzily 'brilliant' *Carmen* Suite on LRM-7013. The worst of these editors went so far as to inflict on the clear, bright, solid Debussy

211

La Mer already issued on LM-1221 successive doses of 'enhancement' by echo-chamber resonance that produced the glossy, blurred and blowzy *La Mer* on LM-1833. And the transfer of 78-rpm recordings to LP provided this editor and others with the opportunity for various forms of electronic 'enhancement' that spoiled good recordings and made poor ones worse—an atrocious example being the 1964 version of the 1946 Tchaikovsky *Romeo and Juliet* on LM-7032, *Toscanini Concert Favorites*, in which the solid, bright, clear sound of the original 78-rpm recording is deprived of its solidity by a cut in bass, of its brightness by the treble-filter used to eliminate surface noise, and of its clarity by the addition of echo-chamber resonance.*

As I write, many of the recordings are being newly edited for reissue on lower-priced Victrola records to commemorate the hundredth anniversary of Toscanini's birth, arousing the hope that the new records will at last let music-lovers hear what he produced.

One should, then, acquire Toscanini's performances of the following works (the numbers I give are those of the hitherto available Victor records that are about to be replaced by the new Victrola records; and I add in parentheses the numbers of the Victrola records scheduled for release in 1967):

BEETHOVEN

Fidelio. NBC Symphony, with Bampton, Steber, Peerce, Janssen,

---

* One reason why the falsification continued and was carried to extremes was the record-reviewers' enthusiastic approval of it, exemplified by the following in *Harper's:* "You may well be amazed at what can now be done for recordings that are no more than four or five years old. Improved copying [of the original tape] is the basic difference. The joker is that, now, we can even 'improve' the original. A host of tricky techniques have been devised, not only to add reverberation (real or artificial) but also to alter balance, suppress hum and rumble, smooth out the frequency spectrum." Or by the review in *High Fidelity* which found that the improvement of the Toscanini recording of Debussy's *La Mer* with those tricky techniques gave it "the atmosphere of a concert hall", which was "a real improvement", adding only that electronic trickery couldn't give this recording the "clarity, brilliance and presence" of the recording of Musorgsky's *Pictures at an Exhibition*—this "clarity, brilliance and presence" being what the *High Fidelity* writer heard in the sound distorted and falsified by excessive peaking of treble: the ear-piercing trumpet sound at the beginning, the snarling sound of the brass in *Catacombs*, the harsh sound of the violins, the raucous sound of the full orchestra.

Belarsky and chorus directed by Wilhousky (derived principally from the 1944 NBC broadcasts), on LM-6025.

Missa Solemnis. NBC Symphony, with Shaw Chorale, Marshall, Merriman, Conley and Hines, on LM-6013.

Overtures.

> *For the Consecration of the House* (*Zur Weihe des Hauses*). NBC Symphony, on LM-9022 (originally on M-1287, and first transferred to LM-6).

> *Egmont.* NBC Symphony, on LM-1834.

> *Leonore* No. 3. NBC Symphony, on LM-6025 (*Fidelio*).

Septet. NBC Symphony, LM-1745 (withdrawn).

Symphonies. NBC Symphony, with Farrell, Merriman, Peerce, Scott, and Shaw Chorale in No. 9, on LM-6901. If individual symphonies are acquired, the *Eroica* on LM-2387 (from the 1953 broadcast) is reproduced with better sound that the one on LM-1042.

> (The new VIC-8000 will have the above-mentioned symphonies, overtures and Septet, with in addition the *Coriolan* and *Prometheus* Overtures and the Adagio and Scherzo of the Quartet Op. 135. VIC-8000 has already been released in England as VCM-1 and 2.)

BERLIOZ

Harold in Italy. NBC Symphony, with Carlton Cooley, viola (from the 1953 broadcast), on LM-1951 (withdrawn).

Rákóczy March from *The Damnation of Faust.* NBC Symphony (from the 1945 broadcast), on LM-6026.

The Roman Carnival Overture. NBC Symphony, on LM-1834 (VIC-1244).

Romeo and Juliet. NBC Symphony, with Swarthout, Garris, Moscona and chorus directed by Wilhousky (from the 1947 broadcasts), on LM-7034.

> (The *Queen Mab* Scherzo from this work will be on VIC-1267.)

BIZET

Suite from *Carmen.* NBC Symphony, on LM-6026 (VIC-1263).

BRAHMS

Symphonies.

No. 2. NBC Symphony, on LM-1731.

213

No. 3. NBC Symphony, on LM-1836.
No. 4. NBC Symphony, on LM-1713.
Variations on a Theme of Haydn. NBC Symphony, on LM-1725.

(The new VIC-6400 will have the above-mentioned works and a few others. It too has already been released in England as VCM-3.)

DEBUSSY

Ibéria (No. 2 of *Images* for orchestra). NBC Symphony, on LM-1833 (VIC-1246). The less bright, less clear, less spacious sound beginning at No. 48 in the second movement is that of a spliced-in passage from a 1948 performance that Toscanini preferred.
La Mer. NBC Symphony, on LM-1833 (VIC-1246).

DONIZETTI

Overture to *Don Pasquale.* NBC Symphony, on LM-6026.

DVOŘÁK

Symphony No. 9 (old No. 5) (*From the New World*). NBC Symphony, on LM-1778 (VIC-1249). Avoid the pseudo-stereo version on LME-2408.

FRANCK

Psyche and Eros from *Psyche.* NBC Symphony, on LM-1838 (VIC-1246). Its beautiful sound enables one to appreciate the distortion and falsification of the sound of Musorgsky's *Pictures* on the same record.

GLUCK

Act 2 of *Orfeo ed Euridice.* NBC Symphony, with Merriman, Gibson and Shaw Chorale (from the 1952 broadcast), on LM-1850 and LVT-1041 (withdrawn).

HAYDN

Symphony No. 101 (*Clock*). NBC Symphony, on LM-1038 (VIC-1262) (originally on DM-1368). The acoustic deficiencies of NBC's Studio 3A produced one of the most atrocious-sounding Toscanini recordings ever issued.

214

MENDELSSOHN

A Midsummer Night's Dream. NBC Symphony, with Phillips and women's chorus, on LM-1221 (withdrawn).

Octet. NBC Symphony (from the 1947 broadcast), on LM-1869 (withdrawn).

Symphony No. 4 (*Italian*). NBC Symphony (from the 1954 broadcast), on LM-1851.

MOZART

Concerto K.191 for Bassoon. NBC Symphony, with Leonard Sharrow, on LM-1030.

Divertimento K-287 for Horns and Strings. NBC Symphony, on DM-1355, LM-13 and LM-2001 (withdrawn).

Symphonies.

K.385 (*Haffner*). NBC Symphony, on LM-1038 (originally on M-1172). Another atrocious-sounding product of Studio 3A.

K.550 (G minor). NBC Symphony, on LM-1789 (not a transfer of the performance on M-631).

K.551 (known as *Jupiter*). NBC Symphony, on LM-1030 (originally on M-1080).

MUSORGSKY

Pictures at an Exhibition. NBC Symphony, on LM-1838 (VIC-1273). One can hear in the performance of Franck's *Psyche* on the same record the beautiful sound that is distorted and falsified in *Pictures.*

PROKOFIEV

Classical Symphony. NBC Symphony, on LM-9020. Toscanini plays the second movement with strict obedience to the *Larghetto* marked in the score—which is to say, too slowly for the proper flow and effect of the music.

RESPIGHI

Fountains of Rome and *Pines of Rome.* NBC Symphony, on LM-1768 (VIC-1244). Both are superbly reproduced; but in *Pines* there is a momentary break in the sustained note that begins the oboe solo in the *Janiculum* section, and a repeated cutting down of the crescendo in the final section that was one of Toscanini's most extraordinary achievements in orchestral performance.

ROSSINI

Overtures.

The Barber of Seville, La Cenerentola, La Gazza Ladra, Il Signor Bruschino. NBC Symphony, on LM-2040 (originally on M-1037).

Semiramide. NBC Symphony, on LM-2040 (originally on LRM-7054).

William Tell. NBC Symphony, on LM-1986 and LM-2040 (with poorer sound).

(*La Cenerentola, L'Italiana in Algeri, The Siege of Corinth,* on the new VIC-1248, and others on VIC-1274.)

Passo a sei from *William Tell.* NBC Symphony, on M-1037.

SCHUBERT

Symphonies.

No. 8 (*Unfinished*). NBC Symphony, on LM-9022 (originally on DM-1456 and LM-54).

No. 9. NBC Symphony, on LM-1835.

SCHUMANN

Manfred Overture. NBC Symphony, on LM-9022 (VIC-1249) (originally on M-1287, and first transferred to LM-6).

SMETANA

Die Moldau. NBC Symphony, on LM-2056 (VIC-1245) (originally on DM-1505 and LM-1118).

STRAUSS, RICHARD

Don Juan. NBC Symphony, on LM-1157 (withdrawn) and LM-7032 (poorer sound).

Don Quixote. NBC Symphony, with Frank Miller, cello, and Carlton Cooley, viola (from the 1953 broadcast), on LM-2026 (withdrawn).

Till Eulenspiegel. NBC Symphony, on LM-1891 (VIC-1267).

216

Tchaikovsky

Manfred. NBC Symphony, on DM-1372, LM-1037 and LVT-1024 (withdrawn).

Nutcracker Suite. NBC Symphony, on LM-1986 (VIC-1263).

Romeo and Juliet. NBC Symphony, on LM-7032 (bad sound) (VIC-1245) (originally on M-1178, and first transferred to LM-1178).

Symphony No. 6 (*Pathétique*). NBC Symphony, on LM-1036 (VIC-1268) (originally on M-1281).

Verdi

Choral Works.

Requiem. NBC Symphony, with Nelli, Barbieri, Di Stefano, Siepi, and Shaw Chorale (from 1951 broadcast), on LM-6018. This is a piecing together of parts of the performance and the dress rehearsal; and the tape used for the last section was one without the solo soprano's last "*Libera me*" seventeen bars from the end.

Te Deum from *Four Sacred Pieces.* NBC Symphony and Shaw Chorale (from 1954 broadcast), on LM-1849.

Operas. The opera specialists among record-reviewers have created the myth that Toscanini used, in his NBC performances of Verdi's operas, only the inexperienced and inferior singers who would submit to the tyranny of his "fast and rigid tempos" that "thwarted" singers' attempts to sing "expressively". Actually the singers he used were not inexperienced and inferior but some of the best available—Milanov, Albanese, Nelli, Merriman, Elmo, Peerce, Vinay, Warren, Valdengo—who sang expressively with him, as Destinn, Hempel, Homer, Matzenauer, Rethberg, De Luca and other famous singers of the past had done. And the beautifully, coherently plastic flow that one heard was created by a beat that was never anything but flexible in relation to the music, and was unyielding in relation to the singer only in compelling him to operate within that flow. As against the usual performances in which the orchestra plays perfunctorily in tempos that defer to the singers' every exhibitionistic extravagance, and which have no continuity, no coherence, no clarity of outline or texture, Toscanini's performances offer accurately and beautifully shaped vocal phrases that fit precisely into the accurate and beautiful orchestral contexts whose every detail is in active expressive re-

217

lation to what is being sung—all this in a progression that is clear, continuous and coherent. They constitute striking illustrations of W. J. Turner's analogy in explanation of the superiority of a Toscanini performance—the analogy of a poem printed clearly and correctly on good paper, as against the poem printed in smudged ink on blotting paper and with the punctuation all wrong. And all of them—the *La Traviata* with Albanese and Peerce, on LM-6003; the *Un Ballo in Maschera* with Nelli and Peerce, on LM-6112; the *Aida* with Nelli and Valdengo, on LM-6132; the *Otello* with Nelli, Vinay and Valdengo, on LM-6107; the *Falstaff* with Valdengo, Nelli, Elmo, Merriman and Stich-Randall, on LM-6111—produce the effect of revelation.

Collections. LM-6041, *Verdi and Toscanini*, has Act 4 of *Rigoletto* with Milanov, Peerce and Warren (from the Red Cross concert in 1944), the Overture to *I Vespri Siciliani* (from a 1942 broadcast), the Chorus of the Hebrew Slaves from *Nabucco*, the Trio from *I Lombardi* with Peerce, Della Chiesa and Moscona, the Overture and the aria *Quando le sere al placido* with Peerce (all from 1943 broadcasts), the *Hymn of the Nations* (from the OWI film), the *Ballabilli* from *Otello* (from a 1948 broadcast), and the Overture to *La Forza del Destino*. NBC Symphony.

(The new VIC-1248 is to have the Overtures to *I Vespri Siciliani* and *La Forza del Destino*, and the Preludes to Acts 1 and 3 of *La Traviata*, not previously transferred to LP from 18080.)

WAGNER

Duets from Act 1 of *Die Walküre* and Act 1 of *Die Götterdämmerung*. NBC Symphony, with Traubel and Melchior, on LM-2452.

Finale of *Die Götterdämmerung*. NBC Symphony, with Traubel, on LVT-1004.

Collections. LM-6020 has the Preludes to Acts 1 and 3 of *Lohengrin*, *Dawn and Siegfried's Rhine Journey* and *Siegfried's Death and Funeral Music* from *Die Götterdämmerung*, the Preludes to Acts 1 and 3 of *Die Meistersinger* (better sound on the first-issued LRM-7029), the Prelude and Finale from *Tristan und Isolde*, the Prelude and *Good Friday Spell* from *Parsifal* (better sound on the first-issued LM-15), and the *Siegfried-Idyll*. NBC Symphony.

(The new VIC-1247 is to have Preludes to Acts 1 and 3 of

218

Die Meistersinger, Preludes to Acts 1 and 3 of *Lohengrin* and the *Siegfried-Idyll,* now on LM-6020, and *A Faust Overture,* originally on M-1135 and first transferred to LRM-7023.)

(The new VIC-1278 will have the Prelude and Finale of *Tristan und Isolde* and the Prelude and *Good Friday Spell* from *Parsifal.*)

(The pieces on VIC-1247 and 1278 are among those in the VCM-4 already released in England, with in addition *Forest Murmurs* from *Siegfried,* the duets from *Die Walküre* and *Die Götterdämmerung, Dawn and Siegfried's Rhine Journey* and the Finale of *Die Götterdämmerung,* but not *Siegfried's Death and Funeral Music.*)

WEBER

Invitation to the Dance (orchestrated by Berlioz). NBC Symphony, on LM-2056.

Overtures to *Euryanthe, Der Freischütz* and *Oberon.* NBC Symphony, on LM-6026.

Toscanini Conducts Overtures, LM-7026, has performances with the NBC Symphony (all but two from broadcasts) of the Overtures to Mozart's *Don Giovanni, Figaro* and *The Magic Flute,* Gluck's *Iphigénie en Aulide,* Cherubini's *Anacreon* and *Medea,* Rossini's *The Siege of Corinth* and *L'Italiana in Algeri,* and others by Cimarosa and Brahms.

Among the most impressive, fascinating and moving demonstrations of Toscanini's powers were the performances in which he applied to light or 'pop' music the same taste in the molding of melodic phrase, the same feeling for continuity of impetus, tension and shape in a developing form in sound, as he did to a work of Haydn or Beethoven. He recorded a few of these performances in his first years with the NBC Symphony: of Paganini's *Moto Perpetuo* on M-590, Strauss's *Tritsch-Tratsch* Polka on 11-9188 and *Blue Danube Waltz* on 11-8580, the Overture to Thomas's *Mignon* on 11-8545, Waldteufel's *Skaters Waltz* on 11-8949, Sousa's *The Stars and Stripes Forever* on 11-9188 (not the relaxed 1943 performance, but one two years later that was tense and driving, as many—but not all—of Toscanini's performances were roughly from 1945 to 1947). And in 1952 he recorded the Overture to Hérold's *Zampa,* the *Dance of the Hours* from Ponchielli's *La Gioconda*, the Suite from Bizet's *Carmen*, the Prelude to Humperdinck's *Hänsel und Gretel*. The superb sound of the original tapes was heard in the *Dance of the Hours* on the first-issued LRM-7005, the slow introduction of the *Mignon* on LRM-7013, the *Hänsel und Gretel* on LRM-7014; but the Allegro of the *Mignon* was made thin and shallow, and the *Carmen* on LRM-7013 and *Zampa* on LRM-7014 were given a shallow, noisy, blowzy 'brilliance'.

The *Zampa*, with the same blowzy sound, and the *Dance of the Hours*, with added electronic gloss and softened, less solid plucked bass notes and tutti chords, are among the pieces on LM-1834, *Toscanini Plays Your Favorites*. The *Carmen*, with 'enhancement' removed, the *Mignon*, with excessive treble and bass boosts, and a marvelous Overture to von Suppé's *Poet and Peasant* (from a 1943 broadcast) are among the pieces on LM-6026, *Toscanini Omnibus*.

(The new VIC-1263 will have the *Dance of the Hours* and the *Carmen*.)

The electronically reprocessed and 'enhanced' sound leads me to advise against VCM- and VCS-7001, *Toscanini Plays Light Classics*, and LM-7032, *Toscanini Concert Favorites*.

In the late thirties Beecham recorded with his London Philharmonic a number of dynamically phrased and otherwise excellent performances of Mozart and Haydn symphonies:

Mozart

K.297 (*Paris*), on Columbia M-360.

K.338, on M-548, later transferred to LP on ML-4781 (with the performance of K.201 originally on M-333, whose ponderously slow tempos made it unacceptable).

K.385 (*Haffner*), on M-399, later on ML-4770.

K.425 (*Linz*), on M-387, later on ML-4770.

K.543, on M-456, later on ML-4674 (with the performance of K.550 in G minor originally on M-316, whose jaunty first movement was unacceptable).

K.551 (known as *Jupiter*), on M-194.

HAYDN

No. 93, on M-336.
No. 99, on M-264.
No. 104 (*London*), on M-409, later on ML-4771.

Beecham also recorded—with the Berlin Philharmonic and Lemnitz, Berger, Roswaenge and Hüsch—the excellent performance of Mozart's *The Magic Flute* on Victor M-541/2 that is available on imported Odeon 80471/3S, which reproduces it with slightly brighter and more cleanly defined sound than the much less expensive Turnabout 4111/3, but with the same lack of amplitude and solidity of bass.

The performances Beecham recorded with his Royal Philharmonic in his last years exhibited tendencies to tempos that made the music ponderous or static, to over-elaborated and exaggerated inflection of phrase, to excessive accentuation. Thus of the first six of Haydn's Salomon symphonies on Angel 36242/3/4, Nos. 95, 96 and 98 are effectively paced and sensitive; but Nos. 93, 94 (*Surprise*) and 97 are distorted by ponderous tempos, crude accentuation, insensitive, graceless phrasing, and general coarseness of execution and sonority. However the remaining six on Angel 36254/5/6 are done quite well, with only a few flaws—the impossibly slow tempo of the C minor section of the second movement of No. 103 (*Drum Roll*), the fussing with the Minuet of No. 104, the pedantic elimination from the Trio of the Minuet of No. 101 (*Clock*) Haydn's joke of keeping the accompaniment in the tonic while the melody goes into the dominant. And the performance of No. 100 (*Military*) is outstandingly fine, with a fluidity and a sensitiveness of inflection that contrast with the four-square character of the others. Avoid the stereo versions.

The later performances of Mozart symphonies also were inferior, except for the one of K.385 (*Haffner*) on Columbia ML-5001. But the performances of Beethoven's Mass in C, on Capitol G-7168, Dvořák's Symphonic Variations, on Columbia ML-4974, Berlioz's *Te Deum*, on Columbia ML-4897, Bizet's *Carmen* with De los Angeles and Gedda on Angel 3613, and Handel's *Solomon* (abridged, rearranged and reorchestrated by Beecham), on Angel 3546, are excellent.

Bruno Walter's best performances of the thirties were those of Mahler's *Das Lied von der Erde* with Thorborg, Kullman and the Vienna Philharmonic, on Columbia M-300, and of Haydn's Symphonies No. 86 with the London Symphony, on Victor M-576, No. 92 (*Oxford*) with the Paris Conservatory Concerts Orchestra, on M-682, and No. 100 (*Military*) with the Vienna Philharmonic, on M-472—the last two later on Camden 257. And his best post-war performances were those of Mahler's *Das Lied von der Erde* with Ferrier, Patzak (struggling with an old voice) and the Vienna Philharmonic, on London 4212, and Symphony No. 2 with the New York Philharmonic, Cundari, Forrester and the Westminster Choir, on Columbia M2L-256. The other post-war performances illustrated the observation by Toscanini that someone reported to me in Salzburg in 1937: "When Walter comes to something beautiful he melts"; and the melting over Mozart, Beethoven and Schubert in later years produced performances that were increasingly nerveless, soft and flabby.

As for Furtwängler, who had to an impressive degree what the twenty-year-old Bernard Shaw described so well as "that highest faculty of a conductor, which consists in the establishing of a magnetic influence under which an orchestra becomes as amenable to the *bâton* as a pianoforte to the fingers," I found it impossible to accept what Beethoven and Schubert were made to mean by the self-indulgent moment-to-moment vagaries and excesses which distorted shape and destroyed coherence in the works. In the amorphous music of Wagner, however, Furtwängler operated with a sense for continuity, and therefore with impressive effect; and the *Tristan und Isolde* with Flagstad and Suthaus, on Angel 3588, is for me the monument to his capacities as conductor and musician. Also, for the same reason, he provides Fischer-Dieskau's singing in Mahler's *Lieder eines fahrenden Gesellen* with a superb orchestral context, on Angel 35522.

One extraordinary performance of an orchestral work was recorded in the thirties by someone who was not a conductor—the pianist Edwin Fischer, whose performance of Haydn's Symphony No. 104 with a chamber orchestra, on Victor M-617, not only was superb in shape and expressive force, but offered the additional delights of incandescent ensemble performance by a small group of fine musicians.

I said earlier that Toscanini's performances on records were equalled only by the few recorded by Cantelli. His early death in 1956 deprived us of the one young conductor with technical and musical powers of the magnitude of Toscanini's, fanatical integrity and dedication like Toscanini's, a similar way of operating in relation to music that produced a similar result: a similar shaping of the work strictly on the lines laid out by the composer's directions about tempo and dynamics; a shaped progression with a similar steadiness, continuity and organic coherence, a similar clarity of outline, texture and structure, achieved with a similar precision of execution and sonority. But there were also important differences: as against the powerful tension in a Toscanini performance, one heard in Cantelli's performances serenity and youthful lyricism and grace; and in addition to this difference in general character and style there were differences in tempo, inflection of phrase, shaping of larger structure, which revealed Cantelli as someone with a mind and taste of his own. And though they were the performances of a young man, they didn't exhibit a trace of the immaturity which, inevitably, some critics claimed was detected by their discerning ears: the performances undoubtedly would change in time, but each as it was produced then emerged as something completely achieved and completely satisfying.

As I write, the only performances available are those of Mendelssohn's *Italian* and Schubert's *Unfinished* Symphonies with the Philharmonia Orchestra, reissued on Seraphim 60002, Mozart's Symphony K.201 and *Ein musikalischer Spass*, with the Philharmonia, on HMV XLP-30034 and QIM-6381 (Italy), and Brahms's Symphony No. 3, with the Philharmonia, on HMV XLP-30030. One hopes for further reissues of the following:

> Beethoven: Symphony No. 7, with the Philharmonia, on Angel 35620.
> Debussy: *Prélude à l'Après-midi d'un faune*, with the Philharmonia, on Angel 35525.
> *La Mer*, with the Philharmonia, on HMV-1228, QALP-10093 (Italy).

223

Nuages and *Fêtes*, with the Philharmonia, on
Angel 35525.
Haydn: Symphony No. 93, with the NBC Symphony, on
Victor DM-1323 and LM-1089.
Musorgsky: *Pictures at an Exhibition*, with the NBC Sym-
phony, on Victor LM-1719.
Tchaikovsky: *Romeo and Juliet*, with the Philharmonia, on
Victor LM-1719.
Symphony No. 5, with the La Scala
Orchestra, on Victor LHMV-1003.
Symphony No. 6 (*Pathétique*), with the
Philharmonia, on Victor LHMV-1047.
Wagner: *Siegfried-Idyll*, with the Philharmonia, on Victor
LHMV-13.

Another conductor who recorded only a few superb performances
before his premature death was Argenta. Still available on London
9192 is Rimsky-Korsakov's *Capriccio Espagnol* with the London Symphony; but the Berlioz *Symphonie Fantastique* with the Paris Conservatory Concerts Orchestra that was on London 9227 is available only
on imported Decca ADD-115 (the stereo version is available here on
London STS-15006); the Debussy *Images* with L'Orchestre de la
Suisse Romande that was on London LL-1735 is available only on
Decca LXT-5348; the Tchaikovsky Fourth with this orchestra that
was on London 9139 is available only on Decca LXT-5125; and the
Schubert *Unfinished* and Ninth that were on Omega 70 and 12 are
not available at all.

The pianist in whose performance of a Beethoven sonata one
heard—as in Toscanini's performance of a Beethoven symphony—a
clarifying articulation which seemed to reveal the structure and
expressive content of the work for the first time, was Schnabel. And
the force and authority of this new image of the work were such as to
establish Schnabel's performances of the sonatas and concertos, like
Toscanini's of the symphonies, as definitive—the ones by which
others were judged and, to this day, found less satisfying. There were
listeners for whom Schnabel's playing was an operation of intellect
without emotion; but actually, though the operation of a powerful
mind was evident, it was excess of emotion, not of intellect, that

224

produced the flaws in the performances—the occasional distention of phrase to the point of distortion, the occasional tempo too fast for clarity or accuracy, the occasional fortissimo beyond the limit of agreeable sound—these in addition to the occasional inaccurate execution of some of Beethoven's awkward passage work that Schnabel's fingers couldn't manage, though he was a superb pianist with a technique equal to the demands of most of the music he played.

I have heard no performances of Beethoven's late piano works that have realized their special expressive content as Schnabel's did, and specifically none that in this respect have even approximated his of the concluding variation movements of the Sonatas Op. 111, on Angel COLH-63, and Op. 109, on COLH-62, the concluding Arioso and Fugue of Op. 110, on COLH-63, the slow movement of Op. 106 (*Hammerklavier*), on COLH-61; none that have articulated and shaped the opening movements of Op. 101, on COLH-62, Op. 109 and Op. 110 as his did, and have given the first movement of Op. 111 the magnitude that his did. They are therefore the performances of these works to have, even with the finale of Op. 101 and the first movement of Op. 106 that Schnabel's fingers cannot execute accurately and clearly in the excessively fast tempos he plays them in. Regrettably the sound of Op. 111 is insufficiently bright and clear (this sonata was reproduced much better by Victor LCT-1109).

Nor has anyone equalled Schnabel's performances of Beethoven's earlier works—the Sonatas Op. 81a (*Les Adieux*), Op. 78 and Op. 90, on COLH-60, Op. 53 (*Waldstein*), Op. 54 and Op. 57 (*Appassionata*), on COLH-59. The Adagio of Op. 53 is an outstanding example of Schnabel's way of prolonging the time values of notes and rests in an intensifying enlargement of the musical shape for greater expressive force—the result in this instance being a spaciously, profoundly meditative and powerfully dramatic statement of the movement such as I have heard from no other pianist.

Still earlier are the Sonatas Op. 31 Nos. 2 and 3, on COLH-57 and 58, superbly performed except for Schnabel's over-emphatic treatment of the wistful finale of No. 2, and his inability to play the finale of No. 3 clearly in his fast tempo. (The sound is spoiled by added artificial resonance.) With the too infrequently played Op. 22 on COLH-55 is Op. 26, whose gracefully flowing first movement Schnabel attempts to give more expressive weight with his slow tempo and intensifying inflection, and which he makes pretentious and unattractive. With Op. 28 (*Pastoral*) on COLH-56 is Op. 27 No. 2 (known as *Moonlight*), whose customarily overstated opening movement Schnabel understates with wonderful effect, but whose finale he makes blurred and shapeless. And COLH-53 has Op. 10 No. 3, the first specimen of the Beethoven dramatic utterance in the sonata series.

I have heard no one achieve anything comparable with Schnabel's statement of Variation 20 of Beethoven's *Diabelli Variations*—to mention only one of the extraordinary things in the performance; and it is available on imported Pathé COLH-64. Available here on COLH-66 are the superb performances of the late Baga- telles Op. 126, the early ones Op. 33, the strange Fantasia Op. 77, and the little piece, *Für Elise*. And COLH-65 has the Variations Op. 35 (*Eroica*), whose manipulation of the two thematic fragments produces individual variations of lyric beauty and dramatic force that add up to a work impressively large-scale in structure and expressive content; together with the uninteresting Variations Op. 34, which holds attention with the way Schnabel plays it—the sensitive articulating and outlining of phrase, the enchanting grace.

As for the concertos, Schnabel's best performances were the first ones he recorded in the early thirties with English orchestras under Sargent: No. 1 on Victor M-158, No. 2 on M-295, No. 3 on M-194, No. 4 on M-156, No. 5 (*Emperor*) on M-155, all transferred to LP on Victor LCT-6700. Similar to these early performances of Nos. 4 and 5 were the ones a few years later with the Chicago Symphony under Stock, on M-930 and 939, of which No. 5 was later on LCT- 1015. After the war Schnabel recorded the performances of Nos. 2, 3, 4 and 5 with the Philharmonia under Dobrowen and Galliera that are, with the pre-war performance of No. 1, the only ones now available, on Angel GRE-4006 (also singly on COLH-1/5). If one listens to these performances of Nos. 3 and 4 after the pre-war performances, one hears losses in grace, suppleness, continuity of ten- sion and outline; but listened to by themselves they are beautiful per- formances. The post-war performances of Nos. 2 and 5 are un- changed, except for the less spaciously meditative slow movement of No. 2. The electronically reprocessed recorded sound is so poor that I advise acquiring the performances with the natural and more solid sound they have on German Electrola 60620/3 and 80845.

After the war Schnabel also recorded with Pierre Fournier superb performances of Beethoven's Cello Sonatas Op. 69, on Victor M-1231, Op. 102 No. 1, on DM-1370, and Op. 102 No. 2, on HMV DB-6829/31—all transferred later to LCT-1124.

As with late Beethoven, so with late Schubert: I have heard no performance of Schubert's posthumous Sonata in B flat that has realized its expressive content as Schnabel's does, on Angel COLH-33. Nor have I heard a performance comparable with his of the posthumous Sonata in A on Victor M-580, now on imported Pathé COLH-84. And in the performance of the Sonata Op. 53 on M-888, now on Angel COLH-83, though he treats the lyrical second movement with ponderous expressiveness that distorts the phrases, and exaggerates the lilt of the Scherzo, his articulation of the energetic first movement and the enchanting grace of his delivery of the finale are yet to be equalled in my experience.

The enchanting grace produces imcomparable performances of Schubert's smaller pieces—the *Moments musicaux* on Victor M-494, now on Angel COLH-308, together with the lovely *Andantino varié* and diffuse *Divertissement à l'hongroise* for piano four hands, which Schnabel plays with his son Karl Ulrich; the Impromptus on imported Odeon 80684—of which Op. 90 No. 1 is played with a turbulence that seems to me unsuitable.

And Schnabel's beautiful playing of the music and the piano makes the pre-war performance of Schubert's *Trout* Quintet with members of the Pro Arte Quartet on Victor M-312, now on Angel COLH-40, something to have.

Then there is Schnabel's playing of Mozart, unique in its subtle articulation and clear outlining of melodic phrase, its delicacy and suppleness and at the same time its cohesive tension and strength. I have heard nothing comparable with his delivery of the long progression of melody in the extraordinary Andante of the Piano Concerto K.467 in the performance on Victor M-486, now on Angel COLH-67, together with the performance of the Concerto K.595 originally on M-240. And the beautiful performance of the Concerto K. 459 on M-389 is now on imported Odeon 80829, also with K.595.

After the war Schnabel recorded performances of the Concertos K.466 and 491 with the Philharmonia under Susskind, which were available briefly on Victor LHMV-1012.

To the pre-war performance of the Sonata K.310—with an

227

excessively turbulent and rhythmically unsteady first movement—
Schnabel added, after the war, performances of the Sonatas K.332
and 570; and all three are available on imported Pathé COLH-305,
with the powerfully phrased performance of the Rondo K.511 that
is one of Mozart's most extraordinary pieces of writing.

And Angel COLH-42 has Schnabel's playing in the Piano
Quartet K.478 with members of the Pro Arte Quartet, originally
on Victor M-251.

Two outstanding piano performances of the late twenties that
one hopes will be reissued on LP were Backhaus's of Chopin's Etudes,
on Victor M-42, and Brahms's *Variations on a Theme of Paganini*, on
7419/20.

Gieseking's sparkling performances of Mozart's Concerto K.271,
on Columbia M-291, and Beethoven's Concerto No. 1, on M-308,
are two more that one hopes will be reissued on LP.

Rachmaninov's famous performance of Schumann's *Carnaval* on
Victor M-70 was transferred to LCT-12. And his excitingly en-
livening playing in the performance of Beethoven's Violin Sonata
Op. 30 No. 3 with Kreisler, on 8163/4, and their performance of
Schubert's Sonata Op. 162, on M-107, can be heard on LM-6099.

Lipatti left only a comparatively small number of recorded
performances:

> Bach's Partita No. 1 and two chorale preludes, Mozart's
> Sonata K.310, on Columbia ML-4633.
> Chopin's Concerto No. 1, on Seraphim 60007.
> Chopin's Sonata Op. 58, Barcarolle, Nocturne Op. 27
> No. 2, Mazurka Op. 50 No. 3, on Columbia ML-4721.
> Chopin's Waltzes, on ML-4522.
> Schumann's Concerto, with the Philharmonia under von
> Karajan, on ML-4525.

These enable one to hear the lyricism, grace, elegance and
verve, the unfailing taste and feeling for continuity in phrase
and large structure—to say nothing of the precision of execution
and the tonal beauty—that made the playing of this young artist
so distinguished. But Angel 3556 has his performances of the same
Bach partita, Mozart sonata and Chopin waltzes and two Schubert
Impromptus at his last public recital at the 1950 Besançon Festival,
where he was so ill and weak that he could barely climb the stairs

to the auditorium, but where, by an almost unimaginable effort of will, he not only managed to play with his precision, lyricism, elegance and verve, but—under the stimulation of the occasion— raised them to sheer incandescence.

The performances of the celebrated harpsichordist Landowska worth listening to are the ones she recorded in the thirties—of Bach's *Chromatic Fantasy and Fugue* and other pieces, on Angel COLH-71, Scarlatti sonatas, on COLH-73, and Handel suites, on COLH-304. Her post-war gigantesque pounding and distortion on Victor records —offered by her, and accepted by awed listeners, as divine revelation—I heard as unmitigated murder.

The greatest playing of music on the violin that I can remember is Szigeti's in the thirties and forties—its excitingly enlivening inflection of phrase with continuity of tension and outline from note to note, its further continuity of tension and shape from phrase to phrase in the larger structure. No other violinist has made of the violin's first entrance in Beethoven's Violin Concerto what Szigeti made of it—with his dynamic inflection of the very first phrases, his breathtaking crescendo of energy in the ascending rush of two-note figures to the conclusion of the passage; and no one has achieved anything like his similarly dynamic playing in the rest of the work, with the orchestra under Bruno Walter, on Columbia M-177. Szigeti himself didn't achieve its equal in the excellent performance with the New York Philharmonic under Walter, on MM-697, which was the one transferred to LP on ML-4012.

Nor has anyone equalled the performances Szigeti recorded with the London Philharmonic under Beecham: of Mendelssohn's Concerto, on M-190, later on ML-2217, Mozart's K.218, on M-224, and Prokofiev's No. 1, on M-244, both later on ML-4533.

The greatest realization I heard of Bach's Concerto in D minor was Szigeti's performance of the violin version with the New Friends of Music Orchestra under Stiedry, on M-418, later on ML-4286 (in his post-war performance with the Prades Festival Orchestra under Casals, on ML-4352, his tone was wiry and granular, his phrasing unimpressive). And I heard nothing like his tremendous performance of Bach's Chaconne, which is preserved by the recording of the six Sonatas and Partitas for unaccompanied violin on Bach Guild

229

627/9 (in the many dull pages of these works the only real expressive eloquence is that of Szigeti's playing).

Other superb Szigeti performances were those of Mozart's Divertimento K.287 (with an inadequate supporting group), on Columbia M-322, Handel's Sonata No. 4 (actually No. 13), on 17098/9, and Mozart's Sonata K.304, on 69005-D.

In addition, Vanguard recently has issued performances obtained from recordings of concerts. VRS-1109/12 has the Beethoven sonata series at the Library of Congress in the early forties, in which Arrau's wooden playing has a dampening effect on Szigeti much of the time, but not in the Sonata Op. 47 (*Kreutzer*), where Szigeti's own emotion of the moment is strong enough to produce incandescent playing. And on 1130/1, which has a Library of Congress concert of 1940, Szigeti is stimulated by the musically sensitive and alive playing of Bartók in superb performances of Beethoven's *Kreutzer* Sonata, Debussy's Sonata and two Bartók works. The performances come through in spite of the deficiencies in sound.

What one must pray for is the issuing of the sonata recital of Szigeti and Schnabel at the Frick Collection in the late forties, with its incomparable performances of Mozart's K.481 and Beethoven's Op. 96.

One of the high points of the performer's art in my experience occurred in Casals's pre-war performance of Beethoven's Cello Sonata Op. 102 No. 2 with Horszowski, on HMV DB*3914/6: in the slow movement, at the return of the opening section, Casals's inflection and timing of the cello's comments on the piano's statements, and at the end of this section his sustained delivery of the raptly meditative passage that paused before the concluding fugue, then his statement of the theme of the fugue. And the unique powerfully sustained tone and phrasing produced comparable performances of the Sonatas Op. 102 No. 1 with Horszowski, on Victor 14306/7, and Op. 69 with Schulhof, on Victor M-134.

In addition there were the famous performances of trios that Casals recorded with the violinist Thibaud and the pianist Cortot in the twenties, after the three had been playing together for their own pleasure almost twenty years. They were fascinating as the incandescent working together of three strikingly dissimilar individuals— Casals with his power of tone and phrasing, Thibaud with his grace and elegance, Cortot with his intimacy and warmth. Their performance of Beethoven's Trio Op. 97 (*Archduke*) on Victor M-92 is now on Angel COLH-29; those of Schubert's Op. 99, on M-11 and later on LCT-1141, and Haydn's Op. 73 No. 2, on 3045/6, are now on COLH-12. Casals also recorded with Cortot the performance of Beethoven's Variations on *Bei Männern* on Victor 1749/50.

In the Perpignan Festival performance of Beethoven's Trio Op. 97, on Columbia ML-4574, one heard the violinist Schneider and the pianist Istomin playing with less grace and more force than Thibaud and Cortot, and Casals again dominating with the power of his tone and phrasing. And the same was true of the Prades Festival performances of Schubert's Trios Op. 99 by Istomin, Schneider and Casals, on ML-4715, and Op. 100 by Horszowski, Schneider and Casals, on ML-4716.

Casals's performance of Beethoven's Sonata Op. 102 No. 1, on ML-4878, can stand comparison with his pre-war performance, but not those of Op. 102 No. 2, on ML-4876, and Op. 69, on ML-4878, though someone who doesn't know the pre-war performances will find these recent ones powerful and moving. Serkin, striving for power in his playing of the piano parts, achieves mere loudness and crudeness.

In the thirties the violinist Goldberg and the pianist Kraus recorded for English Parlophone the incandescent performances of Mozart sonatas that were issued here on LP on Decca DX-103, and the equally fine ones of Haydn trios, with the cellist Pini, that were issued on DX-104. And Decca 8505 had Kraus's excellent performance of Mozart's Concerto K.456.

Kraus's more recent playing has been medicre; but Goldberg had a distinguished performance of Bach's Concerto No. 2 on Decca 7507, and has equally fine performances of Mozart's Concertos K.216 and 218 on 9609.

The Busch-Serkin Trio's performance of Schubert's Trio Op. 100 on Victor M-374, later on Angel COLH-43, had Serkin's sensitive and beautiful playing of those early years. And Adolf Busch also led his Busch Chamber Players in their famous performance of Bach's *Brandenburg Concertos* on Columbia M-249 and 250, now on Angel COLC-13 and 14.

In the thirties the first recordings of the Budapest Quartet acquainted listeners with a tonal, musical and ensemble excellence beyond any previously heard here in quartet-playing:

MOZART

K.465, on Victor M-285.

K.499, on M-222.

K.590, M-348.

BEETHOVEN

Op. 18 No. 2, on M-601.

        No. 3, on M-289.

Op. 59 No. 2, on M-340.

Op. 74 (*Harp*), on M-467.

Op. 130, on M-157.

SCHUBERT

Op. 29, on M-225.

WOLF

Italian Serenade, on 4271.

After recording for Victor the superb performances of Haydn's Op. 54 No. 1 on M-869 and Mozart's K.458 (*Hunt*) on M-763, the group began to record for Columbia:

MOZART

K.421, on M-462, later on ML-4360.

K.387, on M-969, later on ML-4360.

Quintet K.406 (with Katims), on M-830, later on ML-4143.

Quintet K.515 (with Katims), on M-586, later on ML-4034.

Quintet K.516 (with Katims), on M-526, later on ML-4469.

Quintet K.593 (with Katims), on MM-708, later on ML-4143.

Quintet K.614 (with Katims), on ML-4469.

HAYDN

Op. 64 No. 5, on MM-853, later on ML-4216.

Op. 74 No. 3, on X-274, later on ML-4029.

Op. 76 No. 4 (*Sunrise*), on MM-864, later on ML-4216.

BEETHOVEN

Op. 18 No. 1, on M-444, later on ML-4005.
No. 4, on M-556, later on ML-4029.
No. 6, on MM-754, later on ML-4073
Op. 59 No. 3, on M-510.
Op. 95, on M-519, later on ML-4073.
Op. 127, on M-583.
Op. 131, on M-429, later on ML-4106.
Op. 132, on M-545, later on ML-4006.
Op. 135, on M-489.
Quintet Op. 29 (with Katims), on M-623.

SCHUBERT

Quintet Op. 114 (*Trout*) (with Horszowski), on MM-938, later on ML-4317.
Quintet Op. 163 (with Benar Heifetz), on M-497, later on ML-4437.

The later of these performances showed a deterioration of the first violin's tone, which increased in the performances of the fifties:

Beethoven: Quartets and *Great Fugue*, on SL-172/4 (ML-4576/87).
Mozart: Quartets K.387, 421, 428, 458, 464, 465, on SL-187 (ML-4726/8).
Schubert: Quartets Op. 29, Op. 161, *Death and the Maiden*, on SL-194 (ML-4831/3).
Haydn: Quartets Op. 76, on SL-203 (ML-4922/4).
Mozart: Quartets K.499, 575, 589, 590, on SL-228 (5007/8).
Quintets (with Trampler), on M3L-239 (5191/3).

If one listened to these performances after earlier ones—to the Mozart K.499 on ML-5007 after the one on Victor M-222, to the Mozart quintets with Trampler after the ones with Katims—one perceived their loss of the earlier sensitiveness, grace and life; but if one listened to them by themselves one heard superb and satisfying performances.

But in the still later performances of the sixties—the Beethoven quartets on M5L-277, the Mozart clarinet quintet on ML-5455 and piano quartets on ML-6083, the Schubert quintets on ML-5873 and 5936—the deterioration in the tone and intonation of the first violin, then in the tone of the cello, and even in the treatment of the music, reached the point where the playing was musically unsatisfying and unpleasant to listen to.

Already in the mid-forties the short-lived New Music Quartet was exhibiting an unprecedented technical, musical and ensemble incandescence in its performances. Unfortunately, with the Budapest Quartet recording the major quartet repertory for Columbia, the best that the New Music Quartet was allowed to do was the delightful Boccherini quartets on Columbia ML-5047 and the early Mozart quartets on ML-5003. And all that remains today is the few performances on Bartók records—including the pieces by Boccherini, Scarlatti and Tartini on 911, and the ones by Gibbons, Locke and Purcell on 913.

An outstanding European quartet, the Quartetto Italiano, which played with extraordinary refinement of tone, execution and style, recorded beautiful performances of Boccherini's Op. 6 No. 1 and Haydn's Op. 64 No. 6 on London LL-320, Boccherini's Op. 39 No. 3 and Op. 58 No. 3 on Angel 35062, Haydn's Op. 33 No. 3 (*Bird*) and Op. 76 No. 4 (*Sunrise*) on Angel 35297.

And the New York Quartet—Horszowski, piano, Schneider, violin, Katims, viola, Miller, cello—recorded a superb performance of Mozart's Quartet K.478 on Columbia ML-4627.

In the thirties the recordings of the Glyndebourne Festival performances of Mozart's operas offered not only the first performances of the entire works on records, but performances conducted by Fritz Busch with elegance, style, wit and, in the case of *Don Giovanni*, power that made them definitive—the ones by which others have been judged, and usually found to be inferior. The first release offered only the ensembles of *The Marriage of Figaro* in one volume; then the arias were issued in two additional volumes; and finally the combination of the three in Victor M-313/4/5 offered the succession of arias and ensembles without their dramatic context of recitative— a deficiency to regret and disregard, and not repeated in the *Così Fan Tutte* on Victor M-812/3/4 and the *Don Giovanni* on Victor M-423/4/5, which were recorded with their recitative.

The recent LP transfers that were available on imported Odeon

234

records have been issued here on much less expensive Turnabout records: the *Figaro* on Odeon 80833/5, on Turnabout 4114/6; the *Don Giovanni* on Odeon 80598/600, on Turnabout 4117/9; the *Così* on Odeon 80681/3, on Turnabout 4120/22. The Turnabout records produce exactly the same sound as the Odeon: agreeable and clear, but occasionally dim, in the *Figaro;* brighter and otherwise better in *Don Giovanni;* with heavy bass and peaked treble in the *Così.* The sound also comes off the Turnabout records with the same artificial echo, most obtrusive and disturbing in the *Così,* and with the same high-frequency distortion, slight in the *Don Giovanni* and *Così,* more frequent and pronounced in the *Figaro.*

There remain the singers, who follow in alphabetical order.

The exquisitely pure and clear soprano voice of Baillie is heard on imported Odeon HQM-1015 in Purcell's *Tell me Some Pitying Angel, With Verdure Clad* from Haydn's *The Creation, I Know that My Redeemer Liveth* from Handel's *Messiah,* and pieces from his *Samson* and *Judas Maccabaeus.*

Bjoerling's tenor voice stood out among all others in the way Caruso's had done—by its unique timbre, combined with extraordinary range and power; and it was used with a musical taste that Caruso didn't have. The unique silvery luster, the range and power, the musical taste are heard on the following records:

Rococo 31, which has arias from *Il Trovatore, Rigoletto* and *Un Ballo in Maschera* sung in Italian and Swedish, and the *Ingemisco* from the Verdi *Requiem,* recorded early in Bjoerling's career.

Angel COLH-148, with arias from *L'Elisir d'Amore, L'Africaine, Rigoletto* and *Carmen,* among others, recorded between 1936 and 1948.

Angel COLH-150, with arias from *Faust, Il Trovatore, Rigoletto* and *Aida,* among others, recorded in the same period.

Victor LM-6008, which has the performance of *Il Trovatore* with Milanov and Warren.

Victor LM-2003, with a 1955 recital in Carnegie Hall, at which Bjoerling is a little breathless in the arias from *Don Giovanni* and *Carmen* and a little too excited in Schubert's *Die Forelle,* but produces a brilliant performance of Strauss's *Cäcilie* and

235

ear-ravishing *mezza voce* singing in *Traum durch die Dämmerung* and Foster's *I Dream of Jeannie with the Light Brown Hair*.

Victor LM-2269, with 1958 performances of arias from *Martha*, *L'Elisir d'Amore*, *Prince Igor* and *Eugene Onegin* (the last two in Swedish) and excerpts from the complete recordings of *Aida*, *Rigoletto* and less consequential operas.

Victor LM-2784, with the amazingly beautiful singing Bjoerling did to the very last—the performances of the aria from *Eugene Onegin* and *Lohengrin's Narrative* (both in Swedish), among other things, at his last concert in Gothenburg, and of songs by Schubert, Strauss and others at a Carnegie Hall recital two years earlier.

One of the greatest impersonations in operatic history, Chaliapin's Boris Godunov, is brought to life again by the excerpts on Angel COLH-100—most powerfully by the final scene recorded at the performance in Covent Garden, London, on July 4, 1928.

Camden CAL-320 had some of the excerpts from Verdi operas recorded for Victor by the baritone De Luca, including *Povero Rigoletto* and *Cortigiani, vil razza dannata* from *Rigoletto*, which—for listeners accustomed to the bellowing in this scene—was made notable and exciting by the fact that every note was *sung*, and that the most intense expressiveness and dramatic force were achieved by singing done with a style and art I have heard from only a few singers. The beautiful voice wasn't damaged by the artificial echo added in some of the performances.

The sumptuous contralto voice of Ferrier is to be heard on the following records:

London 4212, which has Mahler's *Das Lied von der Erde* and three songs to texts of Rückert, conducted by Bruno Walter.

London 5103, with excerpts from the Glyndebourne Festival performance of Gluck's *Orfeo ed Euridice* conducted by Stiedry (not always well reproduced by the transfer from the 78-rpm records).

London 5258, with beautiful performances of Schubert's *An die Musik*, *Gretchen am Spinnrade*, *Die junge Nonne* and *Der Musensohn*, Schumann's *Widmung* and *Volksliedchen*, and arias from Handel's *Xerxes* and Gluck's *Orfeo* (the dubbed orchestral sound isn't always bright and clean).

236

London 5291, with arias from Purcell's *The Fairy Queen* and Handel's *Atalanta* and songs of Wolf and Jensen broadcast in Norway in 1949—the sound marred occasionally by defects in the tape of the broadcast.

Flagstad's very first Victor record, 8859, with the *Tristan* Finale she recorded in 1935, documented the singing which overwhelmed New York audiences that first season: not only the voice itself with its voluminous splendor all the way to the top, but the production and deployment of it that were no less phenomenal—the production seemingly as natural and casual as that of speech, the deployment which had it going effortlessly wherever it was called on to go in the long musical phrase, rising to a squarely attacked and securely held high note, and from this one to another and still another, before descending to complete the phrase, all as though it presented no difficulty and breath were not even involved. The record documented not only the naturalness and ease of the singing but its musical rightness—the unfailing perfection of the simply inflected phrases of those early years, as against the subtler inflection of the post-war years, done with subtler use of an aging voice that had to be treated with more caution.

Victor never reissued 8859, but did reissue some of the other prewar recordings:

Abscheulicher! from *Fidelio*, with the Philadelphia Orchestra under Ormandy, on 14972, transferred to Camden CAL-462, which is now available in England as Victrola 1208.

Duet from Act 2 of *Tristan und Isolde*, with Melchior (and with Brangäne's warning sung by Flagstad), Finale of *Tristan*, Finale of *Die Götterdämmerung*, with the San Francisco Opera Orchestra under McArthur, on M-644, of which the *Tristan* due is now on LM-2618.

Duet from Act 3 of *Lohengrin*, with Melchior and the San Francisco Opera Orchestra under McArthur, on M-897, now on LM-2618.

"At that time [1935] I took the high C's regularly," Flagstad said to Louis Biancoli in 1941, when she was no longer producing those breath-taking high C's of her first *Tristans*, and when her high range no longer had the voluminous splendor it had had. The

237

losses were increasingly evident in her post-war singing; but the middle and lower range retained its voluminous luster, the way of singing continued unchanged, and the deployment of the voice in the long, subtly inflected phrases is still some of the greatest, most affecting singing one can hear on records. I recommend

Purcell's *Dido and Aeneas*, conducted by Geraint Jones, on imported Odeon ALP-1026.

Tristan und Isolde, conducted by Furtwängler, on Angel 3588.

Wagner's Wesendonck songs, with the Vienna Philharmonic under Knappertsbusch, on London 5259.

Schubert's *Dem Unendlichen, Der Erlkönig* and *Ave Maria*, Schumann's *Der Nussbaum, Die Lotosblume, Erstes Grün, In der Fremde* and *Die Soldatenbraut*, on London 5262.

Arias of Bach and Handel, with crude orchestral contexts provided by Boult with the London Philharmonic, on London 5277.

The two singers who stand out in my recollection of the twenties are Chaliapin in performances of *Boris Godunov* and other operas, and Gerhardt in recitals of German *Lieder*. Her mezzo-soprano voice, though past its prime and a little tremulous, was still lovely; but what made her performances exciting and memorable experiences was the subtlety of her inflection of the voice as she deployed it with sensitiveness to the flow and shape and expressive content of the musical phrase. Of the performances she recorded at this time, Rococo 5245 offers a number of songs of Schubert—including *An die Musik, Gretchen am Spinnrade, Das Lied im Grünen* and eight songs from *Die Winterreise*—most of them with the marvelous piano accompaniments of Bos.

In 1932 Gerhardt, with Bos at the piano, recorded songs of Wolf for Volume 1 of HMV's Hugo Wolf Society; and these performances were reissued first on Rococo 5202, with an additional performance recorded in the mid-twenties, and three recorded, with Nikisch at the piano, in 1907. Later they were reissued on Angel COLH-142, which eliminated the 78-rpm surface noise reproduced by the Rococo record. The 1932 voice is a tremulous shadow of the beautiful voice of 1907, but a shadow which is still lovely much of the time, and still a medium with which the matured art can produce its subtleties and marvels of expressive phrasing.

238

And Rococo 5207 offered a number of other songs that Gerhardt recorded with Nikisch in 1907 and 1911, including Schubert's *Du bist die Ruh'* and *Der Tod und das Mädchen*, Schumann's *Mondnacht* and *Ich grolle nicht*, Wagner's *Schmerzen*, Strauss's *Ständchen* and *Wiegenlied*, and Wolf's *Verborgenheit*. In these one hears not only the loveliness of the young voice, but, astonishingly, the same wonderful inflection of voice and phrase as in the performances she recorded at fifty. The record also offers a later performance of *O del mio dolce ardor* from Gluck's *Paride ed Elena*, in which the delivery of the sustained phrases is something to marvel at.

No doubt there will be an LP record devoted to the singing of the bass Kipnis; and it should include, among his operatic performances, the superb *Il lacerato spirito* from *Simone Boccanegra* that was on Victor 8684, in addition to the songs of Wolf that he recorded for the Hugo Wolf Society, and some of the Brahms songs that were on Victor M-522 and M-751.

The great Isolde of the twenties and thirties, Leider, on Angel COLH-132, sings the first-act narrative from *Tristan und Isolde*, parts of the second-act duet with Melchior, and the final *Mild und leise*, to which Melchior adds *Wohin nun Tristan scheidet* from Act 2 and the marvelous *Wie sie selig* from Act 3. The record also offers Leider's superb performances of *Or sai chi l'onore* from *Don Giovanni* and *Abscheulicher!* from *Fidelio*.

The extraordinarily lovely soprano voice of Lemnitz, the Pamina in Beecham's *The Magic Flute*, is heard on Rococo 5203 in her finely drawn performances (in German) of arias from *Il Trovatore* and *Aida* and duets from *Orfeo ed Euridice* (with Klose) and Tchaikovsky's *The Sorceress* (with Roswaenge), in addition to excerpts from *Der Freischütz*, *Tannhäuser*, *Lohengrin* and *Arabella* (with Hüsch).

Angel COLO-112 has Lotte Lehmann's early performances of excerpts from *Der Freischütz*, *Fidelio*, *Tristan* and inferior works, in which one hears the distinctively luscious voice in its prime, the short-breathed singing that broke Beethoven's phrases even then, the suffusion of the singing with the personal warmth that achieved the miracle one used to witness in the opera house—of dull Elisabeth and pallid Elsa being transformed into radiant beings who touched one's heart. In the Finale of *Tristan* Lehmann is quietly impressive

239

at first, but loses impressiveness in an overexcited acceleration to the climax of the piece.

Sieglinde was another character whom Lehmann brought to exciting life, as one can hear in the performance of Act 1 of *Die Walküre* with Melchior, conducted by Walter, on Angel COLH-133. And her famous impersonation of the Marschallin in *Der Rosenkavalier* is documented in the performance of parts of this work with Olszewska, Schumann and Mayr, on Angel GRB-4001.

When Lehmann loaded onto a dramatic song like Schubert's *Der Doppelgänger* the personal emotion and expressive projection that worked those miracles in the opera house, they destroyed the shape of its phrases. But she did well with a quiet song like *An die Musik* or a vivacious one like Schumann's *An den Sonnenschein*, and was a sheer delight in a humorous one like Schumann's *Die Kartenlegerin*. And in later years the necessity of employing an aging voice with care and skill and restraint resulted not only in an improved quality of the high notes that had been constricted and shrill, but in a refinement and subtilization of style: expressive effect was no longer achieved directly by bursts of vehemence which threw the voice around without regard for the damage to the musical phrase; instead it was achieved by inflection of the voice in a phrase that had continuity and coherence. These inequalities were exhibited in the following:

> Songs of Mozart, Schubert, Schumann, Brahms and Wolf, on Victor M-292.
>
> Songs of Schubert, Schumann, Wolf, Brahms and others, on Victor M-419.
>
> Songs of Wolf, on Victor M-613.
>
> Schubert's *Die Winterreise*, on Victor M-692, Columbia M-466 and M-587.
>
> Schumann's *Dichterliebe*, with pallid accompaniments by Bruno Walter, on Columbia M-486, transferred to LP on ML-2183, then on ML-4788.
>
> Schubert's *Die schöne Müllerin*, on Columbia M-615, later on ML-5996, now available in Germany on CBS 72209.

Camden CAL-378, now available in England as CDN-1015, had, among others, several of the best of Lehmann's early Victor performances—Beethoven's *Ich liebe dich*, Schubert's *An die Musik* and *Der Erlkönig*, Brahms's *Botschaft*, Wolf's *In dem Schatten meiner Locken*, *Anakreon's Grab*, *Auf ein altes Bild* and *Auch kleine Dinge*.

Most of these are also on RCA 430.661, available in France. And RCA 430.529 has the early Victor performances of Mozart's *An Chloë* and *Die Verschweigung*, Schubert's *Im Abendroth* and four songs from *Die Winterreise*, Schumann's *Die Kartenlegerin*, *Alte Laute*, *Waldesgespräch* and *Frühlingsnacht*.

Columbia ML-5778, now available in Germany and France as CBS 72073 and in England as BRG-72073, had the later Columbia performances of Schubert's *Die junge Nonne* and *Der Doppelgänger* (its shape still destroyed by excessive vehemence), Schumann's *Aufträge* and *Der Nussbaum*, and songs of Beethoven, Brahms, Wolf and Strauss.

Melchior's best singing is heard in the excerpts from *Tristan und Isolde* on Angel COLH-132 and the performance of Act 1 of *Die Walküre* on COLH-133.

The bass voice of Pinza without the bloom of its early years, but with the dusky magnificence of its later years, is heard on Columbia ML-5239 in the Catalogue Aria (which he hams up) and Serenade from *Don Giovanni*, *Se vuol ballare* and *Aprite un po' quegl' occhi* from *Figaro*, and Mozart's concert aria *Mentre ti lascio*, *La calunnia* from *The Barber of Seville*, *Il lacerato spirito* from *Simone Boccanegra*, and *I Have Attained the Highest Power* from the Rimsky-Korsakov version of *Boris Godunov*. The voice is a little older in the performances, on Victor LM-1751, of the Catalogue Aria (which he hams up again), the Champagne Aria (which is rhythmically slovenly) and the Serenade from *Don Giovanni*, *Se vuol ballare* and *Non più andrai* from *Figaro*, Sarastro's arias from *The Magic Flute*, *Ella giammai m'amò* from *Don Carlo*, and arias from *Simone Boccanegra*, *Ernani*, *I Vespri Siciliani* and *Nabucco*.

The unique sumptuous and luscious soprano voice of Ponselle in its early years is heard—with her musical deficiencies in those years—in the performances transferred to LP on Scala 803. It was reproduced accurately on Victor LCT-10 only in the superb 1926 performances of arias from *La Vestale* originally on Victor 6605; but on the later CBL-100 these were among the performances spoiled by the fake brightness and gloss of electronic 'improve-

241

ment'—the two performances not spoiled in that way being the 1925 aria from *La Gioconda* and the final trio from *La Forza del Destino*.

One of the great examples of vocal art in my experience was Rethberg's performance of *Ave Maria* from *Otello* on Victor 7393— the simple, effortless emission of the exquisite voice in a sustained flow that articulated and shaped the phrases into a wonderfully beautiful statement of the piece. This and others—the performances of *L'amerò, sarò costante* from Mozart's *Il Re Pastore*, *Batti, batti* from *Don Giovanni*, *Roi de Thulé* from *Faust*, *Ma dall' arido stelo divulsa* from *Un Ballo in Maschera*—were on Camden CAL-335, but with fake electronic brightness, gloss and resonance. The ear-ravishing voice and art at an earlier stage, untouched by electronic manipulation, can be heard on Scala 834, which offers, among other performances of Meyerbeer excerpts, one by Rethberg of an aria from *L'Africaine* (in German).

It is preceded on this record by a performance of *O Paradiso!* from *L'Africaine* (in German), which enables one to hear the splendor of Roswaenge's tenor voice in its prime without the excessive echo-chamber resonance in which it is heard in this piece and others from *I Vespri Siciliani*, *Rigoletto*, *Otello* and *Die Meistersinger* on Telefunken HT-24.

The enchanting combination of unique light-tenor voice and incomparable elegance of style offered by the singing of Schipa can be heard, on Angel COLH-117, in arias from *Don Pasquale* and *L'Elisir d'Amore* that were originally on Victor 1282 and 6570, duets from *La Sonnambula* and *Don Pasquale*, with dal Monte, that were not issued here, and other pieces by Gluck, Scarlatti and Massenet. Regrettably they must be heard with added artificial resonance. Not yet reissued are the performances of Rossini and Verdi arias— the two from *The Barber of Seville* that were on Victor 1180; the *Parmi veder le lagrime* from *Rigoletto* and *Quando le sere al placido* from *Luisa Miller* that were on 7145; the *Parigi o cara* from *La Traviata* (spoiled by Galli-Curci's singing) that was on 1754. The acoustically recorded performances on Scala 805 and 847 exhibit the voice with a little more velvet, the style with occasional excesses in phrasing that improved taste eliminated in the later performances; and they are reproduced without artificial resonance (847 has, in addition to the earlier *Parmi veder le lagrime* and aria from *Lucia di Lammermoor*,

242

the electrically recorded aria from *L'Elisir d'Amore*). And Schipa's singing makes the performance of *Don Pasquale* on imported Odeon QALP-10121/3 (Italy) worth having.

Schorr's impersonation of Hans Sachs in *Die Meistersinger* is documented on Angel COLH-137 by most of the excerpts he recorded between 1927 and 1931 (originally on Victor 7319, 7425/6/7, 7680/1/2, 9285), which include some of the best passages in the work, enlivened by Schorr's sensitive use of his fine voice and Schumann's beautiful singing in the historic performance of the third-act quintet. Regrettably missing is the exquisite third-act duet, *Sieh' Evchen, dächt' ich doch*, of which Schorr and Rethberg recorded the beautiful performance that was on Victor 8195.

Angel COLH-130 and 131 have all but one of the performances of Schubert songs that Schumann recorded for HMV between 1927 and 1949. Victor M-497, 1764 in M-383, and 15737 had a number of these performances that enchanted one with Schumann's distinguished art in the use of her clear, silvery soprano voice—an art securely based on the perfect production and control of the voice that enabled her not only to toss it about delightfully in the lively songs but to spin it out in the wonderfully sustained phrases of *Nacht und Träume*, *Litanei* and *Nähe des Geliebten*. To these the Angel records add the ones Victor didn't issue, enabling one to hear for the first time, among other things, the sustained phrasing of *Du bist die Ruh'* and *Nachtviolen*. The performance of *Das Lied im Grünen* seems to me too mannered; and the voice doesn't have the power required by the climaxes of *Gretchen am Spinnrade;* but these are exceptions in a succession of marvel after marvel.

COLH-102 has a number of Strauss's songs and two by Wolf that Schumann recorded between 1927 and 1938, and additional songs by Wolf that she recorded in 1945 and 1946. In the later performances the voice has lost much of the bloom it still had in the earlier ones, making its characteristic edge even sharper; and its sound is further damaged by some of the transfers to LP; but luckily two of the most beautiful performances, of two of the most beautiful songs— *Und willst du deinen Liebsten sterben sehen* and *Wie glänzt der helle Mond*—are excellently reproduced.

COLH-154 has not only additional performances of the songs that Schumann sang here—some by Mozart, a few more by Strauss

—but the equally enchanting performances of arias from the operas of Mozart in which she sang in Europe: Cherubino's two arias, Zerlina's *Batti, batti* and Susanna's *Venite inginocchiatevi*, originally on Victor 1431 and 7076; *L'amerò, sarò costante* from *Il Re Pastore* and Susanna's *Deh vieni non tardar*, which were never issued here.

Schumann's singing in the duet that concludes the Presentation of the Rose is the greatest moment in the performance of parts of *Der Rosenkavalier* with Lehmann, Olszewska and Mayr, on Angel GRD-4001.

And the early performances on Rococo 6—of Zerlina's arias from *Don Giovanni* and the Jewel Song from *Faust* (in German, and with raucous orchestral accompaniments), among other things—enable one to hear Schumann's voice with the amplitude and bloom it had at the beginning, used with the flawless musical art that was hers already then.

Steber's Countess in the Metropolitan Opera *Figaro* of the early forties was one of the finest operatic characterizations in my experience; and the singing she did in this opera and later as Donna Anna in *Don Giovanni* and Fiordiligi in *Così Fan Tutte* was some of the greatest one heard at the Metropolitan. The performances she recorded in the forties for Victor—the Countess's arias on 11-8850; Zerlina's *Batti, batti* and Pamina's *Ach, ich fühl's* on 11-9114; Constanze's *Martern aller Arten*, Cherubino's *Non so più cosa son* and Susanna's *Deh vieni* on M-1157; Cherubino's *Voi che sapete* on 12-0526; the *Roi de Thulé* and Jewel Song from *Faust* on 11-9838; Micaela's aria and the aria from *Louise* on 12-0690—were never transferred to LP. Later she recorded the following for Columbia:

> Arias from *Ernani* and *La Traviata*, the Willow Song and *Ave Maria* from *Otello*, on MX-317 and 351, transferred to ML-2157, which had in addition arias from *La Forza del Destino* and *Don Carlo*.
>
> The two duets from *Otello*, with Vinay, and the Willow Song and *Ave Maria*, with the *Credo* (Guarrera), the duet *Tu?! Indietro!* (Vinay and Guarrera) and *Dio! mi potevi scagliar* (Vinay), on ML-4499.
>
> Constanze's *Traurigkeit ward mir zum Lose, Bester Jüngling* from *The Impresario*, Donna Elvira's *Mi tradi*, Donna

Anna's *Non mi dir*, Fiordiligi's *Per pietà*, Pamina's *Ach, ich fühl's*, on ML-4694.

The Metropolitan Opera *Così Fan Tutte* (in English), on SL-122.

Berlioz's *Les Nuits d'été*, on ML-4940, later on ML-5843.

Of these, the last two are still listed as available, and Steber can be heard also in Toscanini's performance of *Fidelio*.

No longer listed is Stand 101, which had Steber's superb performances of arias from *Idomeneo*, *The Seraglio*, *I Puritani* and *Ernani* at a recital in Carnegie Hall.

The unique voice and style of the mezzo-soprano Supervia can be heard in the excerpts from *Carmen* listed as available on Parlophone PMA-1024 (England), and the excerpts from Rossini operas listed as available on PMA-1025.

Teyte's exquisitely pure and bright soprano voice is heard, on Angel COLH-138, in *Le Spectre de la rose* and *L'Absence* from Berlioz's *Les Nuits d'été* and songs of Chausson, Duparc and Ravel.

Traubel's voice was at its peak, and deserved Toscanini's delighted exclamation, "*Che bella voce!*", in his 1941 performances of the Finale of *Die Gotterdämmerung*, on Victor LVT-1004, and the first-act duet from that work, on LM-2452; but in the first-act duet from *Die Walküre*, on the latter record, it was afflicted with tremolo. (Melchior sang with constriction and strain in both duets.)

Superb singing by the soprano Wildbrunn, whom I heard at the Vienna Opera in 1928-29, can be heard in the acoustically recorded performances (in German) of excerpts from *Un Ballo in Maschera*, *Don Giovanni*, *Fidelio* and the Wagner music-dramas, on Rococo 5220.

28

THE BEST RECORDED
PERFORMANCES OF TODAY

(March 1967)

This section is concerned with the recorded performances in the current catalogue by musicians who are active today.

The first thing to mention about it is that it is selective: it doesn't evaluate all the performances of all the works of all the composers, which one person couldn't even hear; but instead limits itself to the works discussed earlier in the book, and limits itself further to recommending the performance or performances of a work that I consider to be the best of the ones I have heard.

It is the best performance that I recommend, not the best or latest sound: I prefer the better performance, reproduced adequately, to the poorer one that is reproduced with more beautiful sound; the great Toscanini performance with the mono sound of his time, to an indistinguished one with the sound—mono or stereo—of today. In most instances I say nothing about the recorded sound, and one may assume that I consider it satisfactory. But a defect in the sound is something the reader should be informed of; and I therefore mention it.

Where both mono and stereo versions of a recording are available, in most instances I recommend the mono, because my ear has found the mono sound—though less spacious—to be a more accurate facsimile of the original, particularly in its greater solidity, its more clearly and strongly defined bass. But there is nothing to prevent anyone who prefers the spaciousness from acquiring the stereo version of a performance I recommend in mono.

246

RECORDED PERFORMANCES OF WORKS
LISTED UNDER NAMES OF COMPOSERS

ALBÉNIZ

Ibéria. Epic SC-6058 has de Larrocha's occasionally mannered but on the whole effective performances of the twelve pieces, in which the Spanish folk-style material is made fascinating by the harmonically sophisticated treatment that is done with mastery and taste.

BACH, CARL PHILIPP EMANUEL

Magnificat. Excellently performed on Bach Guild 552 by Prohaska with the Vienna Academy Chorus, State Opera Orchestra and soloists.

Symphonies Nos. 1 and 3. Acceptably performed on Bach Guild 504 by the Vienna Symphony under Günther.

BACH, JOHANN SEBASTIAN

Art of Fugue. Clearly and effectively performed on the organ by Walcha on Deutsche Grammophon ARC-3082/3.

Cantata No. 4, *Christ lag in Todesbanden.* Best performed on Deutsche Grammophon ARC-3063 by Fritz Lehmann with Fischer-Dieskau, Krebs and the Göttingen Bach Festival Orchestra.

Bach Guild 598 has a good performance by a Viennese group under Prohaska.

Capitol P-8535 has a good performance by the Wagner Chorale.

Chaconne (from Partita No. 2 for Unaccompanied Violin). In addition to Szigeti's performance (see in Chapter 27) there is the excellent performance of Grumiaux on Boston 202.

Chorale-Preludes for Organ. Deutsche Grammophon offers Walcha's excellent performances as follows:

The *Orgelbüchlein,* on ARC-3025/6, of which 3026 has most of the good pieces, including the great *O Mensch bewein' dein' Sünde gross* (BWV. 622), *Ich ruf' zu dir Herr Jesu Christ* (639) and *Wenn wir in höchsten Nöthen sein* (641).

A few of the *Miscellaneous Chorale-Preludes*, including *Herzlich tut mich verlangen* (BWV. 727) and *An Wasserflüssen Babylon* (653b), on ARC-3024 (with part of the *German Organ Mass* of the *Clavierübung*).

The *Eighteen Chorale-Preludes* and the *Schübler Chorale-Preludes*, on ARC-3027/9—the *Eighteen* including the great *Schmücke dich o liebe Seele* (BWV. 654), *Nun komm' der Heiden Heiland* (659), *Jesus Christus unser Heiland* (665) and *Komm' Gott Schöpfer heiliger Geist* (667).

Columbia ML-4601 has Schweitzer's two different performances of *O Mensch bewein' dein' Sünde gross* of the *Orgelbüchlein*, and his performances of *Ich ruf' zu dir Herr Jesu Christ* and *Gelobet seist du Jesu Christ* (BWV. 604) of the *Orgelbüchlein*, *Herzlich tut mich verlangen* of the *Miscellaneous*, and *Nun komm' der Heiden Heiland* and *Vor deinen Thron tret' ich* (668) of the *Eighteen*.

See also *German Organ Mass* under *Clavierübung*.

Chromatic Fantasy and Fugue. Excellently performed on the harpsichord by Valenti on Lyrichord 47 (with the Toccatas in C minor and D).

See also in Chapter 27: Landowska.

Clavierübung. The performance of the *Goldberg Variations* to acquire is Glenn Gould's on the piano on Columbia ML-5060. (Landowska's on Victor LM-1080 is something to avoid.)

The performances to acquire of the *Italian Concerto*, with its great slow movement, and the engaging Partita No. 1 are again Gould's on Columbia ML-5472—though a Gould perversity is the long decrescendo in the slow movement of the concerto instead of the crescendo implied by the build-up in the music.

For the Partita No. 1 see also in Chapter 27: Lipatti.

The organ pieces, under the title *German Organ Mass*, are performed by Walcha on Deutsche Grammophon ARC-3022/4. ARC-3022 has the great opening Prelude in E flat (BWV. 552) and—among several of the longer and more elaborate chorale-preludes—*Gott Vater in Ewigkeit* (669) and *Wir glauben All' in einen Gott* (680). ARC-3023 has *Aus tiefer Not schrei ich zu dir* (686) and *Gott heiliger Geist* (674); and it also has the boring four duets

248

for harpsichord. And ARC-3024 has the additional small-scale *Vater unser im Himmelreich* (683) and the concluding Fugue in E flat, impressive as a piece of fugal construction—with the group of *Miscellaneous Chorale-Preludes* mentioned earlier.

Concertos. The *Brandenburg Concertos* are excellently performed on Philips PHC-2-004 by Goldberg with the Netherlands Chamber Orchestra, and on Angel 3627 by Klemperer with the Philharmonia Orchestra. See also in Chapter 27: Busch Chamber Players.

The great Concerto in D minor for clavier or violin is performed superbly on the piano by Glenn Gould with an orchestra under Bernstein on Columbia ML-5211 (with Beethoven's Concerto No. 2). It is also performed effectively on the harpsichord by Malcolm with the Stuttgart Chamber Orchestra under Münchinger on London 9392, and by Anton Heiller with a Vienna State Opera orchestra under Caridis on Bach Guild 588. See also in Chapter 27: Szigeti.

The Violin Concertos in A minor and E are excellently performed by Grumiaux with the English Chamber Orchestra under Leppard on Philips 500-075, and by David Oistrakh with the Vienna Symphony on Deutsche Grammophon 18-820 (with the Concerto in D minor for two violins). And good performances by Suk with the Prague Symphony under Smetácek are on Crossroads 16-0037 (with the Concerto for two violins).

The Concerto in D minor for two violins is played well by David and Igor Oistrakh with the Royal Philharmonic under Goossens on Deutsche Grammophon 18-820 (with the Violin Concertos in A minor and E), and by Suk and Jásek with the Prague Symphony under Smetácek on Crossroads 16-0037 (with the Violin Concertos in A minor and E).

Fugues for Organ. Deutsche Grammophon offers Walcha's excellent performances as follows:

The great Toccata and Fugue in D minor (BWV. 565) and Toccata, Adagio and Fugue in C (564), with the Toccatas and Fugues in D minor (*Dorian*) (538) and F (540) on ARC-3204, which produces more clearly defined sound than the stereo record.

The great Fantasia and Fugue in G minor (BWV. 542) and

Passacaglia (and Fugue) in C minor (582), with the Fantasia and Fugue in C minor (537), on ARC-3205.

The powerful and affecting Prelude and Fugue in B minor (BWV. 544), with the Preludes and Fugues in E minor (548) and C (547), impressive as pieces of fugal construction, on ARC-3206.

The great Prelude and Fugue in A minor (BWV. 543), with the great opening Prelude and the concluding Fugue of the *Clavierübung* and the Preludes and Fugues in C minor (546) and G (541), on ARC-3207.

Karl Richter's excellent performances of the great Toccata and Fugue in D minor (BWV. 565) and Fantasia and Fugue in G minor (542) are on Deutsche Grammophon 138-907 (stereo, which is preferable to the mono version), with the Prelude and Fugue in D (532).

German Organ Mass. See *Clavierübung.*

Goldberg Variations. See *Clavierübung.*

Italian Concerto. See *Clavierübung.*

Kunst der Fuge. See *Art of Fugue.*

Mass in B Minor. Performed well on Victor LM-6157 by Shaw with the Shaw Chorale, Addison, Kopleff and other soloists.

Orgelbüchlein. See Chorale-Preludes for Organ.

Partita No. 1 for Clavier. See *Clavierübung.*

Passacaglia for Organ. Walcha's excellent performance is on Deutsche Grammophon ARC-3205 (with the Fantasia and Fugue in G minor).

St. Matthew Passion. Performed well on Angel 3599 by Klemperer with the Philharmonia Chorus and Orchestra, Schwarzkopf, Ludwig, Gedda, Pears and Fischer-Dieskau.

Suites for Orchestra. Performed well by Menuhin with the Bath Festival Chamber Orchestra on Capitol GBR-7252.

Toccatas for Clavier. The Toccatas in C minor and D are performed superbly on the harpsichord by Valenti on Lyrichord 47 (with the *Chromatic Fantasy and Fugue*).

Well-Tempered Clavier (*Das wohltemperirte Klavier*). Performed superbly much of the time but now and then with disturbing eccentricities and perversities of tempo and touch—by Gould on the piano on Columbia D3L-333. (Landowska's performance on Victor LM-6801 is something to avoid.)

Toccatas for Organ. See Fugues for Organ.

Collections. See in Chapter 27: Flagstad, and under MISCELLA-
NEOUS COLLECTIONS: Collegium Musicum, Schwarzkopf, Stader.

BEETHOVEN

An die ferne Geliebte. See Songs.

Bagatelles for Piano. Op. 119 and Op. 126 are remarkable examples
of Beethoven's late writing for the piano, with its introspective
remoteness and strangeness, its concentrated brevity, its abrupt
shifts of thought and style—especially remarkable because the reduced scale of the pieces makes for greater concentration and
abruptness. Schnabel's performances of Op. 126 and the engaging
early Op. 33 (see Schnabel) are the ones to acquire; and Matthews's performances of all three sets on Vanguard 1033 are good.

Concertos for Piano. In addition to Schnabel's definitive performances (see in Chapter 27) there are the performances of the great
pianists of today.

Gould's excitingly enlivening performance of No. 1 on Columbia ML-5298, deserves better than the crude and blaring orchestral context provided by Golschmann with a recording
orchestra. In the performance of No. 3 with an orchestra under
Bernstein, on ML-5418, Gould's slower than usual tempos produce a powerfully sculptured first movement, an excitingly
energetic finale. In the performance of No. 4 with the New York
Philharmonic under Bernstein, on ML-5662, Gould's constant
unusual manipulation of phrase gets to be wearying, and is at
times unconvincing; and his eccentricities and perversities—e.g.
arpeggiating what are written as solid chords, emphasizing an
Alberti bass over the melody it accompanies, fading out where
the music is building up—produce passages which I find impossible to hear as valid statement of the music. And in the performance of No. 5 (*Emperor*) with the American Symphony under
Stokowski, on ML-6288, in which the unprecedented shaping of the
piano's opening flourishes announces that Gould is re-examining
and rethinking every detail, the uncustomary results are much of
the time superbly impressive, but now and then eccentric, perverse
and impossible to go along with.

Cliburn's performances of No. 4, on Victor LM-2680, and No. 5,
on LM-2562, with the Chicago Symphony under Reiner, clearly

have also been freshly and completely thought out and achieved to the least accompaniment note; but as against Gould's eccentricity and perversity, Cliburn offers complete naturalness and rightness in the plastically coherent shaping he does with his unfailing sense for note-to-note continuity of tone, tension and outline in the developing phrase. Reiner, in No. 4, indulges in overemphatic and ponderous distention, which is made worse by the huge recorded sound in over-resonant space that requires drastic reduction of bass.

Fleisher offers another superbly conceived and achieved performance of No. 4 with the Cleveland Orchestra under Szell on Epic LC-3574 (with Mozart's Concerto K.503).

Rubinstein—in his performance of No. 5 with the Boston Symphony under Leinsdorf, on Victor LM-2733—plays not only with a new repose and continence, but with a correct style which his earlier playing of Beethoven didn't have—the result being a highly effective statement of the work. And LM-2947 has his similar playing in No. 3 with the same orchestra and conductor.

Concerto for Violin. Except for the beautiful writing in the development section of the first movement, at the solo violin's second entrance, this work would be regarded with less awe if Beethoven's name were not attached to it. There are excellent performances by Oistrakh with the French National Radio Orchestra under Cluytens on Angel 35780, and by Ricci with the London Philharmonic under Boult on Richmond 19034.

See also in Chapter 27: Szigeti, whose performance was the greatest of all.

Fidelio. Fricsay's pacing of the work, on Deutsche Grammophon 18-390/1, is not as right and effective throughout as Toscanini's (see in Chapter 27), but it may be preferred by some for its superior singers (Rysanek, Seefried, Häfliger, Fischer-Dieskau, Frick) and recorded sound.

See also in Chapter 27: Flagstad, Leider, Lotte Lehmann, and under MISCELLANEOUS COLLECTIONS: Evans, Farrell, Horne, Jurinac.

Missa Solemnis. In the performance on Deutsche Grammophon 39-208/9, von Karajan has the tenors sing *"Et incarnatus est"* almost inaudibly; more important, he doesn't impart to the hushed orchestral Prelude of the *Benedictus* the raptly mystical

252

character that makes it the greatest moment of the work in Toscanini's definitive performance (see in Chapter 27). Except for these details, the performance—with the Berlin Philharmonic, the Vienna Singverein, Janowitz, Ludwig, Wunderlich and Berry—is a good one.

Bernstein spoils a good performance with the New York Philharmonic, the Westminster Choir, Farrell, Smith, Richard Lewis and Borg, on Columbia M2L-270, by playing the Prelude of the *Benedictus* with a throbbing, heaving impassioned expressiveness.

Quartets. The marvelous new Guarneri Quartet has begun to record the performances that I expect will be the ones to acquire.

Meanwhile there are the Weller Quartet's excellent performances of Op. 74 (*Harp*) and Op. 95, reproduced by London 9431 without the spaciousness, clarity and brightness of sound now possible; and the Juilliard Quartet's excellent performance of Op. 132 on Victor LM-2765.

See also in Chapter 27: Budapest Quartet.

Septet for Strings and Winds. This is a piece I used to find uninteresting, until I heard it with the life imparted to it by the animation and phrasing of Toscanini's performances (see in Chapter 27), in which he used an increased number of strings to achieve proper balance with the winds.

Sonatas for Piano. In addition to Schnabel's definitive performances (see Schnabel in Chapter 27), there are Cliburn's beautiful performance of Op. 81a (*Les Adieux*) on Victor LM-2931 (with Mozart's Sonata K.330), and Richter-Haaser's performances of Opp. 110 and 111 on Angel 35749, which I would expect to be as good as those I heard in Carnegie Hall.

At every point in Gould's performances of Opp. 109, 110 and 111 on Columbia ML-5130, one hears his powerful musical intelligence operating attentively and independently, with results that are superbly impressive in Op. 110 and the finale of Op. 111, but impossible for me to hear as valid statements of the music in the finale of Op. 109 and the first-movement Allegro of Op. 111.

Haskil's performances of Op. 31 Nos. 2 and 3, on Philips World Series 9001, are very good.

Sonatas for Violin and Piano. The perceptive and beautifully integrated performance of Op. 96 by Grumiaux and Haskil that was on Epic LC-3381 is to be had on imported Philips A-00412-L

253

(Germany). The similar performances of the best-known Op. 47 (*Kreutzer*) and the fine Op. 30 No. 1 that were on LC-3458 are available on A-00430-L; the ones of Op. 12 No. 1, the engaging Op. 23, and Op. 24 (*Spring*), with its lovely opening, are on LC-3400 and A-00409-L; the ones of Op. 12 No. 3, the charming Op. 12 No. 2, and the fine Op. 30 No. 3 that were on LC-3488 are available on A-00400-L.

See also in Chapter 27: Szigeti, Rachmaninov, and under MISCELLANEOUS COLLECTIONS: Kulenkampf and Solti.

Sonatas for Cello and Piano. In the performances on Vanguard 1136/7 Janigro's excellent playing of the cello parts is admirably complemented by Demus's of the piano parts; but unfortunately the recording subordinates the piano that should be heard equally with the cello.

Du Pre and Bishop perform the Sonatas Op. 69 and Op. 102 No. 2, on Angel 36384, with a complete musical understanding that is astounding in such young players, an impressive mastery of their instruments, and a remarkable sense for ensemble operation which has them playing together as though with one mind.

See also in Chapter 27: Casals, Schnabel.

Songs. By now Deutsche Grammophon will have issued on 39-197 Fischer-Dieskau's performances of the cycle *An die ferne Geliebte* and a number of other songs.

See also in Chapter 27: Lotte Lehmann.

Symphonies. In addition to Toscanini's definitive performances (see in Chapter 27), there are von Karajan's with the Berlin Philharmonic, reproduced beautifully (though in over-resonant space) on Deutsche Grammophon 18-801/8, which offer a pacing and shaping of the works that much of the time is highly effective and satisfying, though not, for me, as effective and satisfying as Toscanini's, and not without occasional errors in musical judgment that result in ineffectiveness. For example, the rigorously maintained tempo in the second movement of the *Eroica* keeps the *fugato* episode from achieving the tremendous power Toscanini builds up with his distentions of the tempo for the entrances of the subject and for the climax; and in the first movement of the Ninth the similar rigorous steadiness keeps the beginning of the recapitulation from having the tremendous power Toscanini gives it with his volcanic distentions of tempo and sonority. In the Ninth,

254

moreover, the tenor solo is too fast for a march; the Minuet of the Eighth loses by its excessively slow tempo, the first movement of the *Pastoral* by its excessively fast one, the second movement of the Seventh by the slowing down of the alternating sections in major and therefore of the movement's basic rhythm that should continue unchanged in the basses, the finale of the Fifth by the slowed-down bassoon statement in the coda that breaks the momentum of the movement. The Toscanini performances are, then, still the ones for someone who wants the most effective statements of the works; and von Karajan's are the best of those reproduced with present-day sound.

An excellent performance of the Symphony No. 7—poised, steady, clear in texture, plastically coherent in shape—by Abbado with the Vienna Philharmonic is on London 9510.

See also in Chapter 27: Cantelli.

Trios. See in Chapter 27: Casals. (The Stern-Rose-Istomin performance of Op. 97 on Columbia ML-6219 is not good.)

Variations for Piano. In addition to Schnabel's definitive performances (see in Chapter 27), there are Matthews's performances of Opp. 34 and 35 and the fine *Thirty-Two Variations in C minor* on Vanguard 1032, which are good, and Richter-Haaser's effective performance of the *Diabelli Variations* on Seraphim 60027.

BELLINI

Norma. Callas's secure, beautiful and dramatically impressive singing in the early performance now available on imported Odeon QCX-10088/90 makes it preferable to the later performance on Angel 3615, in which her singing is unpleasantly shrill and wobbly, and to the performance on Victor LM-6166, in which Sutherland's singing exhibits its remarkable accuracy and style in florid passages, but also the unattractiveness of the lower range of her voice, and the little moans and little explosions of tone that are at times her way of phrasing melody.

I Puritani. Sutherland's singing in the performance on London 4373—notably her clear, steady, brilliant high notes in the climax of the great concluding ensemble of Act 1—is some of her best on records; but Callas's singing in the early performance on Angel 3502 also is exciting in the ensembles, and is lovelier and more moving in the lyrical passages.

255

La Sonnambula. Sutherland's mannered moaning in the performance on London 4365 is one reason for preferring the earlier performance with Callas on Angel 3568; and another is the better singing of the tenor Monti in the Angel performance.

Collections. Caballé—who sings *Casta diva* from *Norma* and *Col sorriso d'innocenza* from *Il Pirata* on Victor LM-2862 (with arias of Donizetti)—has an agreeable, but not in any way extraordinary, voice under a control which enables her to deploy it in a long phrase of recitative or melody, and in this to have it spin out one after another in a series of exquisite pianissimo high notes or project the series with power. This deployment of the voice—done with a sense for emerging shape of phrase, for style, for dramatic expressiveness—becomes impressive and even exciting; but it hasn't the expressive impact that the strangely beautiful voice and the emotional intensity of Callas gave to this music.

See also in Chapter 27: Schipa, Steber, and under MISCELLANEOUS COLLECTIONS: *The Age of Bel Canto*, Callas, Horne, Simionato, Sutherland, Tebaldi, Valletti.

BERG

Wozzeck. In addition to the superb performance conducted by Mitropoulos on Columbia SL-118, with Harrell, Farrell and the New York Philharmonic, there is now the effective performance conducted by Böhm on Deutsche Grammophon 18-991/2, with Fischer-Dieskau, Lear and the orchestra of the Berlin Opera.

BERLIOZ

Beatrice and Benedict. From the excellent performance conducted by Davis on Oiseau-Lyre OL-256/7, with Cantelo, Watts, the St. Anthony Singers and the London Symphony, one learns that the familiar overture has the outstanding pages—Beatrice's aria *Il me souvient le jour du départ* and the delightful finale—of this late work whose orchestral writing has some of the earlier fascinating liveliness and brilliance, but whose vocal writing hasn't the heart-piercing loveliness and expressive power of the great melodies of *Romeo and Juliet* and *The Damnation of Faust*.

Cléopâtre. Berlioz, while a student at the Paris Conservatoire, submitted this work in his third unsuccessful attempt to win the *Prix de Rome.* The orchestra's very first measures proclaim the fact that he is not fumbling with unschooled or unmatured powers, but is operating—most impressively in Cleopatra's invocation, "*Grands Pharoans,*" over the orchestra's powerful ostinato—with absolute assurance in a style that is completely individual and completely formed. In the performance on Columbia ML-5838, Tourel uses what remains of a once lovely voice with her distinguished musical powers, and is supported effectively by Bernstein and the New York Philharmonic.

The Damnation of Faust. The performance to acquire is the superb one conducted by Markevitch on Deutsche Grammophon 18-599/60, with Rubio, Verreau, Roux and the Lamoureux Orchestra, not the one conducted by Münch on Victor LM-6114.

L'Enfance du Christ. The performance to acquire is the excellent one conducted by Davis on Oiseau-Lyre 50201/2, with Pears, Morison, the St. Anthony Singers and the Goldsborough Orchestra.

Harold in Italy. I can recommend no performance other than Toscanini's (see in Chapter 27).

Les Nuits d'été. In addition to the great Steber performance (see in Chapter 27) there was the fine performance by De los Angeles with the Boston Symphony under Munch, on Victor LM-1907, and there is now, on Victor LM-2695, another great performance by Price with the Chicago Symphony under Reiner, flawed only by a couple of details of tempo.

Overtures. The *Roman Carnival* and *Corsair* Overtures and those to *Benvenuto Cellini* and *Beatrice and Benedict* are performed well by Munch with the Boston Symphony on Victor LM-2438 (with *Royal Hunt and Storm* from *The Trojans*).

See also in Chapter 27: Toscanini.

Requiem. One of Munch's better performances—with the Boston Symphony, the callow-sounding New England Conservatory Chorus, and Simoneau—is on Victor LD-6077.

Romeo and Juliet. I can recommend no performance other than Toscanini's (see in Chapter 27).

Royal Hunt and Storm. See *The Trojans.*

Symphonie fantastique. Davis's excellent performance with the London Symphony is on Philips 500-101.

The superb performance by van Otterloo with the Hague

Philharmonic that was on Epic LC-3005 is available on imported Philips 610-801-VL.

See also in Chapter 27: Argenta.

Te Deum. See in Chapter 27: Beecham.

The Trojans. The performance of Part 2, *The Trojans at Carthage,* conducted by Scherchen, on London DTL-93001/3, is no longer available. Avoid the performance of excerpts on Angel 3670.

Royal Hunt and Storm is performed well by Munch with the Boston Symphony on Victor LM-2438 (with Berlioz overtures).

BIZET

Carmen. Beecham's performance (see in Chapter 27) is the best. See also in Chapter 27: Bjoerling, Slezak, Supervia, Urlus.

For the orchestral suite see in Chapter 27: Toscanini.

BLOCH

Quintet for Piano and Strings. The excellent performance by Johana Harris and the Walden Quartet that was on MGM 3239 may be reissued.

BOCCHERINI

Quartets Op. 58 No. 5, Op. 64 Nos. 1 and 2. Superbly performed on Music Guild 123 by the Carmirelli Quartet, which also had excellent performances of Op. 39 No. 8 and Op. 44 No. 4 on London LL-1454 at one time.

See also in Chapter 27: New Music Quartet, Quartetto Italiano, and under MISCELLANEOUS COLLECTIONS: Virtuosi di Roma.

BRAHMS

Songs. I would expect Fischer-Dieskau's performances on Deutsche Grammophon 18-504 to be superb.

See also in Chapter 27: Lotte Lehmann, and under MISCEL-LANEOUS COLLECTIONS: De los Angeles, Ludwig, Schwarzkopf.

Symphonies. In addition to Toscanini's performances (see in Chapter 27) there are good performances of No. 2 by von Karajan with the Berlin Philharmonic on Deutsche Grammophon 18-925, and by Kertesz with the Vienna Philharmonic on London 9435.

See also in Chapter 27: Cantelli.

258

Variations on a Theme of Haydn for Orchestra. I can recommend no
performance other than Toscanini's (see in Chapter 27).

Variations for Piano. The Russian pianist Merzhanov's performance
of the *Variations on a Theme of Paganini* on Monitor 2013 is excellent,
except for a miscalculated tempo in Variation 10 of Book 1.

Fleisher's excellent performance of the *Variations on a Theme
of Handel* is on Epic LC-3331.

BRITTEN

Albert Herring. Parts of this opera offer brilliantly successful invention
for the dramatic situation; other parts only what the resourceful
craftsman was able to grind out to carry the words and action.
Britten himself conducts the excellent performance with Pears
in the title role on London 4378.

Serenade for Tenor, Horn and Strings. An excellent performance of this
attractive work by Lloyd, Stagliano and Boston Symphony
strings under Burgin is on Boston 205.

BULL

See under MISCELLANEOUS COLLECTIONS: Deller, Wolfe.

BYRD

Mass for Four Voices. Excellently performed on London 5795 by the
Choir of King's College under Willcocks's direction.

Collections. The pieces on Bach Guild 557, *William Byrd and His
Age*, are sung and played beautifully by the counter-tenor Deller
and the Wenzinger Consort of Viols of the Schola Cantorum
Basiliensis.

See also under MISCELLANEOUS COLLECTIONS: Deller Consort,
Welch Chorale, Wolfe.

CHABRIER

Collections. The *Suite pastorale, Marche joyeuse, Fête polonaise, España*
and less interesting *Danse slave* are played beautifully by L'Orchestre de la Suisse Romande under Ansermet, on London 9438,
in tempos that are insufficiently animated.

See also under MISCELLANEOUS COLLECTIONS: Philadelphia
Orchestra.

CHERUBINI

Medea. When this work created a sensation in New York some years
ago it was not merely with the unexpectedly impressive vocal
and orchestral writing, but with Farrell's singing of the title role.
Columbia ML-5325 offered a few passages with her beautiful
and expressively eloquent singing.

A La Scala performance of the entire work conducted by Serafin, on Mercury OL-3-104, has Callas singing not sensationally,
but impressively enough in her own way to carry a performance in
which the other roles are sung with insufficient dramatic force.
See also under MISCELLANEOUS COLLECTIONS: Callas.

Requiem Mass in C Minor. The lovely choral writing of this work
was another surprise when Toscanini broadcast the performance
with the NBC Symphony and Shaw Chorale that was on Victor
LM-2000.

Overtures. See in Chapter 27: Toscanini.

See also under MISCELLANEOUS COLLECTIONS: Callas, Farrell.

CHOPIN

Ballades. Ashkenazy's beautiful performances are on London 9422.

Barcarolle. See in Chapter 27: Lipatti.

Concerto No. 1. In addition to Lipatti's performance, which is the
finest (see in Chapter 27), there is the superb one of Harasiewicz
with the Vienna Symphony under Hollreiser that was on Epic
LC-3643 and is still available on imported Philips 698-021-CL
(Germany). And Rubinstein's performance with the New Symphony under Skrowaczewski, on Victor LM-2575, has the continence, the refinement and subtlety, the plastic coherence of his
recent playing.

Etudes. Ashkenazy's performances are on Bruno 14052-L; Harasiewicz's on imported Philips 698-068-CL (Germany).

Fantaisie. See below under Collections: Cliburn.

Impromptus. Horszowski's excellent performances were on Vox
PL-7870 (with the Concerto No. 1).

Mazurkas. Rubinstein's performances on Victor LM-6177 are some
of the finest he has ever recorded.

Nocturnes. A few are played beautifully by Harasiewicz on imported
Philips A-02340/1-L; but the tranquil opening pages of Op. 27

No. 2 and Op. 48 No. 1 are played *molto agitato*.

See also in Chapter 27: Lipatti, and below under Collections: Cliburn, Ashkenazy.

Polonaises. Performed well by Frankl on Vox VUX-2024.

See also below under Collections: Cliburn.

Preludes. The best performances are the ones by Gulda that were on London LL-755 and are now available on imported Decca LXT-2837.

Scherzos. Rubinstein's performances are on Victor LM-2368.

See also below under Collections: Ashkenazy, Cliburn.

Sonatas. As I write, Cliburn is about to record his superb performances of Opp. 35 and 58 for Victor. And the superb performance of Op. 35 by Harasiewicz that was on Epic LC-3633 is now available on imported Philips 698-011-CL (Germany) (with the Ballade Op. 47, Nocturnes Op. 15 No. 2 and Op. 27 No. 2, Etudes Op. 10 Nos. 1 and 12, and a few Mazurkas).

See also in Chapter 27: Lipatti.

Sonata Op. 65 for Cello and Piano. This seldom-heard, beautiful work is played with the required fluent ease, elegance and taste by Parisot with Mittman on Overtone 17 (with Schubert's *Arpeggione* Sonata), and by Starker with Sebök on Mercury 50320 (with Mendelssohn's less interesting Sonata Op. 58).

Waltzes. See, in Chapter 27, Lipatti, who played these pieces with subtleties of rhythm and inflection that are not heard in the excellent performances of Harasiewicz on World Series 9034 and Vàsàry on Deutsche Grammophon 19-485.

Collections. I have never heard from any other pianist a performance of the Polonaise Op. 53 as distinguished in conception and as beautifully executed as Cliburn's on Victor LM-2576—from first to last an operation of disciplined mastery which holds the lilt and grace and plasticity within the limits of a perfectly proportioned and coherent shape that is achieved down to the last accompaniment note with absolute accuracy of tonal values and timing. And he operates in the same way in the other pieces on the record: the Fantaisie, Ballade Op. 47, Nocturne Op. 62 No. 1, Scherzo Op. 39, Waltz Op. 64 No. 2, Etudes Op. 10 No. 3 and Op. 25 No. 11.

Ashkenazy's beautifully shaped and completely achieved performances of the Nocturne Op. 62 No. 1 and Scherzo Op. 54 are on London 9472 (with Debussy's *L'Isle joyeuse* and Ravel's *Gaspard de la nuit*).

COPLAND

Billy the Kid. The performance by Levine with the Ballet Theater Orchestra that was on Capitol P-8238 is now on Capitol HDR-21004, with the performance of *Rodeo* that was on P-8198 (also with performances of Bernstein's score for *Fancy Free* and bad ballet scores by William Schuman, Morton Gould and others).

The Tender Land. Copland himself conducts the performance of a large part of this fine work with the New York Philharmonic and good soloists on Columbia ML-6214.

CORELLI

Concerti Grossi Op. 6. I Musici's beautiful performances of Nos. 4, 7, 8 and 9 are on Epic LC-3264. See also under MISCELLANEOUS COLLECTIONS: I Musici, Virtuosi di Roma.

COUPERIN

Harpsichord Pieces. A number of engaging ones are played well by Anton Heiller on Bach Guild 619.

Pièces en concert. These charming pieces, originally for viola da gamba and figured bass, are played with grace and elegance by the cellist Fournier with the Festival Strings Lucerne under Baumgartner on Deutsche Grammophon 18-986 (with the Vivaldi Sonata in E minor).

Tenebrae Services (*Leçons de Ténèbres*). No. 1 was on Allegro 91, later on Concord 4005 and recently on Allegro LEG-9014 (Amram Record Sales), with tremendous expressive force from Cuenod's extraordinary singing. His voice is somewhat threadbare and rough in the later performance of all three on Westminster 9601.

DEBUSSY

Children's Corner for Piano. A good performance by Casadesus is on Columbia ML-4978 (with the uninteresting *Waldszenen* of Schumann).

Estampes (*Pagodes, Soirée dans Grenade, Jardins sous la pluie*) for Piano.

Exquisitely wrought performances by Sviatoslav Richter are on Deutsche Grammophon 18-849 (with fine performances of Chopin's Polonaise-Fantaisie Op. 61 and Etudes Op. 10 Nos. 1 and 12, but an erratically paced Ballade Op. 52, and Scriabin's uninteresting Sonata No. 5).

Etudes for Piano. These pieces, ostensibly exercising the hands in the playing of thirds, fourths, sixths and so on, exercise Debussy in the varieties of his fully developed style of writing for the piano; and some of the results—the Etudes concerned with thirds, octaves, eight fingers, chromatic steps—are as interesting pieces of music as the better-known ones with imaginative titles. Rosen's performances on Epic LC-3842 are first-rate.

Images for Orchestra (*Gigues, Ibéria, Rondes de printemps*). See in Chapter 27: Argenta, Toscanini.

Images for Piano (First Series: *Reflets dans l'eau, Hommage à Rameau, Mouvement;* Second Series: *Cloches à travers les feuilles, Et la lune descend sur le temple qui fut, Poissons d'or*). Gieseking, on Angel 35065, plays these pieces and *Estampes* in an excessively delicate style which doesn't attain the points of high sonority and splendor in some of them.

La Mer for Orchestra. See in Chapter 27: Toscanini, Cantelli.

L'Isle joyeuse. Ashkenazy's excellent performance is on London 9472 (with Chopin's Nocturne Op. 62 No. 1 and Scherzo Op. 54 and Ravel's *Gaspard de la nuit*).

Nocturnes for Orchestra. (*Nuages, Fêtes, Sirènes*). Performed well by Giulini with the Philharmonia Orchestra on Angel 35977 (with *La Mer*).

See also in Chapter 27: Cantelli.

Prélude à l'Après-midi d'un faune for Orchestra. Beecham's performance on Angel 35506 should be good.

See also in Chapter 27: Cantelli.

DELIUS

Brigg Fair and *The Walk to the Paradise Gardens*. Beautifully performed by Collins with London Symphony on London 9066.

DONIZETTI

Don Pasquale. Because of Oncina's unattractively hard, tight voice in

263

a part which needs a supple light tenor like Valletti's or Schipa's, I advise against the otherwise good performance on London 4260, and suggest instead the early performance with Valletti and Bruscantini on Cetra (Everest) 404 (mono; avoid the pseudo-stereo version) or the still earlier one with Schipa on imported Odeon QALP-10121/3 (Italy).

L'Elisir d'Amore. There are good performances on London 4321, with Gueden, Di Stefano, Corena, Capecchi and the chorus and orchestra of the Maggio Musicale Fiorentino under Molinari-Prandelli's direction; and on Seraphim 6001, with Carteri, Alva, Taddei, Panerai and the chorus and orchestra of La Scala under Serafin's direction.

La Favorita. In the performance on London 4322 Simionato's voice is clouded at times by strong vibrato, and Poggi's unattractive and quavering voice is even more damaging, but Bastianini and Hines are excellent, and the orchestra and chorus of the Maggio Musicale Fiorentino perform well under Erede's direction.

Lucia di Lammermoor. With Sutherland's mannerisms and the unattractiveness of the other singers' voices in the performance on London 4355, and with Callas's shrill, wobbly singing and Tagliavini's dessicated tenor voice in the performance on Angel 3601, the performance to acquire is the excellent early one with Callas and Di Stefano on imported Odeon QCX-10030/1 (Italy).

Lucrezia Borgia. This unfamiliar work has impressive dramatic writing which attains its highest point of affecting expressiveness in the concluding scene of Lucrezia and Gennaro; but the aria of the dying Gennaro that impressed me as the finest piece in the opera when I heard the concert performance with Caballé, is omitted in the performance on Victor LM-6176. Caballé's singing in this performance is described by what I say about her singing on LM-2862 (see under Bellini), to which I must add that the voice has even less tonal beauty on LM-6176. Kraus, Verrett and Flagello sing very well; and Perlea paces and shapes the work effectively.

Collections. For Caballé's performances of arias from *Roberto Devereux*, *Lucrezia Borgia* and *Maria di Rohan* on Victor LM-2862, see Collections under Bellini.

See also in Chapter 27: Bjoerling, Schipa, and under MISCEL-

LANEOUS COLLECTIONS: *The Age of Bel Canto*, Albanese, Evans, Horne, Sutherland.

DOWLAND

Songs or Ayres of foure parts with Tablature for the Lute so made, that all the parts together, or either of them severally, may be sung to the Lute, Orpherian, or Viol de gambo. Groups of these lovely pieces are sung beautifully by the Golden Age Singers with the lutenist Bream on Westminster 9602/3 and 9619.

A group from all four books and *The Musical Banquet*—including the especially fine *Flow My Tears, Weep You No More Sad Fountains, I Saw My Lady Weep, Flow Not So Fast Ye Fountains, In Darkness Let Me Dwell*—is sung superbly by the counter-tenor Oberlin with the lutenist Iadone, who adds two solo performances.

Lachrimae, or seaven Teares figured in seaven passionate Pavans, with divers other Pavans, Galiards, and Almands, set forth for the Lute, Viols, or Violons, in five parts. Played well, on Oiseau-Lyre 50163, by the Philomusica of London under Dart's direction.

See also under MISCELLANEOUS COLLECTIONS: Cuenod, Dowland.

DVOŘÁK

Quintet Op. 81 for Piano and Strings. Performed very beautifully by Curzon and the Vienna Philharmonic Quartet on London 9357. (Avoid the gigantesque performance on Vanguard 1148.)

Slavonic Dances. Performed well by Szell with the Cleveland Orchestra on Columbia M2L-326.

Symphonies. The engagingly melodious No. 8 (old No. 4) is performed best by Kubelik with the Berlin Philharmonic on Deutsche Grammophon 39-181.

Of No. 9 (*New World*) I can recommend no other performance than Toscanini's (see in Chapter 27), whose freedom from the traditional distortions makes the work "as fresh and glistening as creation itself".

FARNABY

See under MISCELLANEOUS COLLECTIONS: Deller.

FAURÉ

Requiem. Best performed, on Angel 35974, by Cluytens with the

Paris Conservatory Concerts Orchestra, the Brasseur Chorus, De los Angeles and Fischer-Dieskau.

FRANCK

Prelude, Chorale and Fugue for Piano. Cortot's performance is on imported Pathé COLH-69 (with a poor performance of Schumann's *Etudes symphoniques*).

Psyche. See in Chapter 27: Toscanini.

Sonata for Violin and Piano. Stern's phrasing is for the most part straightforward and unaffected, Zakin's excessively mannered, in their performance on Columbia ML-5470.

Variations symphoniques for Piano and Orchestra. Gieseking's fine performance with the Philharmonia under von Karajan is on Columbia ML-4536 (with Mozart's Concerto K.488).

GABRIELI, GIOVANNI

Processional and Ceremonial Music. The beautiful pieces for double chorus supported by instrumental groups on Bach Guild 581 are excellently performed by the chorus and orchestra of the 1957 Gabrieli Festival in Venice under Appia's direction.

Additional beautiful examples of this writing on Bach Guild 611 are performed by the chorus of the Gabrieli Festival under Gillesberger's direction this time, and with a group of brilliant-sounding modern brass instruments instead of the combination of old and modern instruments in the earlier performances.

See also under MISCELLANEOUS COLLECTIONS: Collegium Musicum.

GERSHWIN

An American in Paris. I have no better performance to recommend in place of Toscanini's, on Victor LM-9020 (with Prokofiev's *Classical Symphony*), whose opening section is too fast and unyielding for the leisurely saunter it should be, but whose blues section is paced and shaped with plasticity, grace and verve that are very exciting.

GESUALDO

Columbia ML-5234 and 5341 had groups of this composer's madrigals and sacred pieces—whose daring and strange harmonic progressions make them some of the most remarkable, powerful and moving music that has come down to us—sung well by a small group under Craft's direction. Available now is Columbia KL-5718, with additional vocal pieces sung under his direction, two instrumental pieces—one played by Biggs on the organ, the other by Rosenstiel on the harpsichord—and Stravinsky's *Monumentum pro Gesualdo*, his masterly instrumental reworking of three madrigals, performed by an orchestra under his direction.

See also under MISCELLANEOUS COLLECTIONS: Collegium Musicum, Deller Consort.

GIBBONS

A number of beautiful anthems and madrigals (including *The Silver Swan*) are on Deutsche Grammophon ARC-3053 (with *The Cries of London*, which I care less for)—sung beautifully by the Deller Consort. And the record also has several instrumental Fantasies, played well by the Consort of Viols of the Schola Cantorum Basiliensis.

See also under MISCELLANEOUS COLLECTIONS: Cuenod, Deller Consort.

GLUCK

Orfeo ed Euridice. For the French *Orphée et Eurydice* of 1774, Gluck not only revised the Italian *Orfeo* of 1762 but transposed much of it so that the role of Orpheus, originally sung by a castrato, could be sung by a tenor. For a revival in 1859 Berlioz was commissioned to make the changes in key in the French version that would enable a contralto to sing Orpheus; and his version is the one the public has heard since then. It is the one performed in Italian on Victor LM-6169, with singing by Verrett and Moffo that has insufficient dramatic impact.

Two performances of the 1774 French version are available— the one on Angel 3569 with the finer orchestral playing and choral singing; the one on Epic SC-6019 with the more beautiful singing by Simoneau, Danco and Alarie.

And Bach Guild 686/7 has a performance of the original Italian version of 1762, with in addition the three pieces Gluck inserted in Act 2 in the French version: the Dance of the Furies, the flute solo in the Dance of the Blessed Spirits, and *E quest' asilo* for soprano and chorus. The most striking difference in this 1762 version is in the orchestration of *Che puro ciel*—the charming flute figures around the oboe's melody, which Gluck, for no imaginable reason, removed in the French version. In the performance conducted effectively by Mackerras—with the Vienna Academy Chorus and a State Opera orchestra—Forrester and Steffek sing well, but Stich-Randall's voice is unattractive.

See also in Chapter 27: Toscanini, Ferrier, Gerhardt, Lemnitz, Schipa, and under MISCELLANEOUS COLLECTIONS: Berganza, Farrell, Horne, Schwarzkopf.

GRIFFES

Poem for Flute and Orchestra. See under MISCELLANEOUS COLLEC-TIONS: Philadelphia Orchestra.

Roman Sketches and Sonata for Piano. Excellent performances by Hambro are on Lyrichord 105.

The White Peacock. See *Roman Sketches*.

HANDEL

Acis and Galatea. Performed well, on Oiseau-Lyre 50179/80, by Boult with Sutherland, Pears, Galliver, Brannigan, the St. Anthony Singers and the Philomusica of London.

Alexander's Feast. Performed well, on Bach Guild 666/7, by Deller with Sheppard, Worthley, Bevan and the Oriana Choir and Orchestra.

Alcina. The work offers a profusion of arias, most of them very fine in their varied styles, but in a context of boring recitative. Sutherland carries her moaning to an extreme of mannered miniature crooning that makes her singing unbearable except in the arias in fast tempo in which she is compelled to sing out in full voice with an accuracy and style in the florid passages that are breathtaking. But there is superb singing by Sciutti, Berganza, Sinclair, Freni, Alva and Flagello, in a sensitive and spirited orchestral context that Bonynge provides with the London Symphony, and with Malcolm's richly inventive harpsichord accompaniment of the recitative.

L'Allegro ed il Penseroso. Milton's poems stimulate Handel's musical

268

imagination to a flow of superb invention, which Willcocks paces and shapes well in the performance on Oiseau-Lyre 50195/6 that has expecially lovely singing by Delman, Harwood and Watts, good singing also by Morison, Pears and Alan, and good contributions by the St. Anthony Singers and the London Philomusica.

Chandos Anthems. Passages of Handel's fine writing for chorus and his beautiful melodic writing for solo voices are offered by Nos. 4 and 6 on Vanguard SRV-227, and Nos. 2 and 3 on SRV-228. Alfred Mann sets good tempos; and life is imparted to the music by the excellent singing of Boatwright, Bressler, Held and the Collegium Musicum of Rutgers University, and the excellent playing of Raimondi and Krilov, among others.

Concerti Grossi Op. 6. Best performed by Menuhin with his Bath Festival Orchestra on Angel 3647. (I advise against the performance conducted by Schneider on Victor LM-6172.)

Concerto No. 3 for Oboe. See under MISCELLANEOUS COLLECTIONS: Philadelphia Orchestra.

Dettingen Te Deum. Epic LC-3540 had an excellent performance of this fine work in the original English by the Choir of the Netherlands Bach Society and soloists under van der Horst's direction.

Available now are the excellent performance in German, on Angel 36194, by the South German Madrigal Choir and soloists under Gönnenwein's direction; and a moderately good performance in English, on Nonesuch H-1003, by the Telemann Society Chorus and Orchestra and soloists under Schulze's direction.

Israel in Egypt. Best performed, on Decca DX-178, by Waldman with the Musica Aeterna Orchestra and Chorus, Addison, Kopleff, McCollum and Natale.

Julius Caesar. The most beautiful of the excerpts on London 5876 are sung by Sutherland, and for the most part with an unattractive voice and her annoyingly mannered style. But some good pieces are sung beautifully by Horne and the others.

An English catalogue still lists Deutsche Grammophon 18-637, with excellent singing of the excerpts by Fischer-Dieskau and Seefried.

Messiah. The performance on Philips 500-125/7 is not the first to use a small chorus and orchestra like those of Handel's day, and a chorus and orchestra as fine as the London Symphony Choir and Orchestra, with soloists as good as Harper, Watts, Wakefield, and

Shirley-Quick. And though it *is* the first to observe the conventions of Handelian performance—e.g. the double-dotting, the ornamentation of vocal parts—that is not what makes the performance so notable. What does, is the conducting of Davis, which keeps the music wonderfully alive and expressive with his tempos and inflection of phrase.

Angel 3705 offers another excellent performance which uses the small forces and observes the conventions of Handel's day—this one conducted effectively by Mackerras, with the Ambrosian Singers, the English Chamber Orchestra, Harwood, Baker, Tear, Herincx and an additional counter-tenor, Esswood. I find the timbre of Esswood's voice unattractive, and for this reason alone would choose Davis's performance; but in addition I find certain more animated tempos of Davis's more effective than Mackerras's, and prefer his choices of text.

The enlivening inflection of the orchestral playing in Davis's performance is not heard in Shaw's performance on Victor LM-6175, which is therefore bland and pedestrian.

Ode for St. Cecilia's Day. In the performance on Columbia ML-5606, the youthful Rutgers University Chorus sounds a little callow in the imposing choruses; but there is excellent singing of the beautiful arias by Addison and McCollum; and Bernstein conducts the New York Philharmonic effectively.

Royal Fireworks Music. The brilliant wind sonorities of the original become wearying; and one is grateful for the string sounds of the Harty arrangement that is played beautifully by the Amsterdam Concertgebouw Orchestra under van Beinum on Richmond 19101 (with the Harty *Water Music* Suite).

Samson. Most impressive in this work is the writing for Samson, which communicates a personal magnitude that Peerce's agreeable-sounding and expressive singing doesn't achieve, in the performance (with cuts) conducted by Abravanel, on Bach Guild 648/50, with the Utah Symphony, the youthful-sounding University of Utah Symphonic Chorale, Curtin and other soloists.

Semele. The performance of this superb work on Oiseau-Lyre 50098/100 has excellent singing by Vyvyan and Herbert with the New Symphony under the effective direction of Anthony Lewis.

Solomon. See in Chapter 27: Beecham.

Sonatas Op. 1 for Solo Instrument and Figured Bass. All fifteen are played well on the violin by Olevsky, on Westminster 9064/6, with continuo by the harpsichordist Valenti and cellist Martin Ormandy.

Suites for Harpsichord. Nos 1, 5, 7 and 8 of the First Book, on Bach Guild 593, and No. 6, on 592, are fine pieces; Nos. 2, 3 and 4 are less interesting. All are played superbly—with enlivening rhythm, inflection and variety of tone—by Anton Heiller.

See also in Chapter 27: Landowska.

Water Music (Complete). The entire assemblage of pieces turns out to include others as lovely and engaging as the ones Harty made familiar in his suite. It is best performed by Menuhin with his Bath Festival Orchestra on Angel 36173; but Boulez also conducts the less good Hague Philharmonic effectively in a performance on Nonesuch H-1127.

Collections. Seraphim 60028 has the lovely *Where'er You Walk* from *Semele* and arias from *Acis and Galatea*, *Alexander's Feast*, *Judas Maccabaeus*, *Joshua*, *Samson* and *Jephtha* which include three of Handel's greatest pieces—the recitative *Deeper and Deeper Still* and aria *Waft Her Angels* from *Jephtha* and the aria *Total Eclipse* from *Samson*. And Richard Lewis's beautiful tenor voice, his long-breathed, supple and expressive phrasing, his remarkably clear diction make his performances with the London Symphony under Sargent outstanding.

See also in Chapter 27: Baillie, Ferrier, Flagstad, Lilli Lehmann, and under MISCELLANEOUS COLLECTIONS: Berganza, Evans, Stader, Tebaldi.

HAYDN

Andante and Variations in F minor for Piano. Demus's performance on Deutsche Grammophon 19-206 should be good.

Concerto Op. 21 for Harpsichord. Performed well by Erna Heiller with a Vienna State Opera orchestra under Litschauer, on Vanguard 454 (with Concerto for trumpet).

An excellent performance on the piano by Devetzi with the Moscow Chamber Orchestra of Barshai is on Angel 36238 (with Mozart's Concerto K.414).

The Creation. Markevitch conducts an excellent performance, on Deutsche Grammophon 18489/90, with the Berlin Philharmonic, the Choir of St. Hedwig's Cathedral, Seefried, Holm and Borg.

See also in Chapter 27: Baillie, and under MISCELLANEOUS COL-
LECTIONS: Stader.

The Seasons. Nonesuch 3009 has a performance conducted effectively
by Goehr, with the orchestra and chorus of the North German
Radio, Stich-Randall and other good soloists.

Masses. The *Missa Sancta Caeciliae* is performed well by Jochum, on
Deutsche Grammophon 18-545/6, with the chorus and orchestra
of the Bavarian Radio, Stader, Höffgen, Holm and Greindl.

The *Missa Solemnis* in D minor (*Nelson Mass*) is best performed,
on Vanguard 470, by the Vienna Academy Chamber Choir, a
Vienna State Opera orchestra and a good solo group that includes Stich-Randall and Dermota, under Rossi's direction.

The *Missa in tempore belli* (*Paukenmesse*) is performed well, on
Deutsche Grammophon 18-882, by the chorus and orchestra of
the Bavarian Radio and a solo group that includes Morison and
Marjorie Thomas, under Kubelik's direction.

The *Theresienmesse* is performed superbly, on Argo RG-500, by
the Choir of St. John's College, Cambridge, with Spoorenberg,
Greevy, Mitchison, Krause and the Academy of St. Martin-in-
the-Fields, under Guest's direction.

Quartets. The extraordinary freedom of tempo and the enlivening
inflection of the Schneider Quartet's performances point up the
unpredictable and fascinating course of Haydn's lively and inventive mind as no other performances have done; and they are,
therefore, the ones to acquire, on the Haydn Society records.

9083/5 have Op. 17, of which No. 6 delights one with the
method that achieves outstanding movements in the others.

9086/8 have Op. 20, of which Nos. 4 and 5 are among the outstanding examples of the genre.

9017 and 9021 have Op. 33, of which the best-known No. 3
(*Bird*) is one of Haydn's masterpieces in the genre; No. 5, with its
extraordinary Largo, its real Haydn scherzo, its beautiful variation finale, and No. 6, with its highly elaborated first movement
and impassioned Andante, are superb works; No. 2 is very fine;
and Nos. 1 and 4 have fine individual movements. The Schneider
Quartet plays the first movement of No. 3 more slowly than I have
ever heard it played, and less effectively than in the usual faster
tempo.

9089/91 have Op. 50, of which Nos. 1 and 2 are not very interesting, but the other four are superb.

9053, 9058 and 9065 have Op. 76, of which all six are fine works, with especially notable examples of the Haydn method and its results: the fast movements of No. 1; the first movement, Andante and Minuet of No. 2; the first movement of No. 4 (*Sunrise*); the first movement of No. 5.

9095 has Op. 77, of which No. 2 carries to incandescence the method that delights one in No. 1.

In addition, 9015 has Op. 33 No. 3, Op. 76 No. 2 and Op. 50 No. 6.

The Budapest Quartet's performances of Op. 76, on Columbia SL-203, exhibit refinement and smoothness, as against the Schneider's more detailed, more energetic, more sharply rhythmed, and therefore more enlivening inflection.

In Op. 54 the Haydn operation rises to incandescence; and the Allegri Quartet's performances on Westminster 19094 are good, except for a tempo too fast for the proper articulation and effect of the first movement of No. 2.

The Juilliard Quartet paces and shapes Op. 54 No. 2 effectively, on Epic LC-3931, but not Nos. 1 and 3; and the group's tone is not agreeable to the ear.

The Haydn operation is not incandescent in Op. 55, but it is enjoyable; and the Allegri Quartet's performances on Westminster 19084 are effective.

Of Op. 71, Nos. 2 and 3 are engaging, No. 1 less interesting; of Op. 74, all are delightful; and the Griller Quartet, on Vanguard 1041/2, plays them competently, though without the Schneider Quartet's excitingly enlivening rhythm and phrasing.

See also in Chapter 27: Budapest Quartet, Quartetto Italiano.

Sonatas for Piano. Gould electrified one's mind and held it fascinated with the sharply incisive shaping and continuous tension of the object in sound that he made of Peters No. 3 on Columbia ML-5274 (with Mozart's Sonata K.330 and Fantasia and Fugue K.394).

Balsam's blander and less effective performances of a number of pieces are on Oiseau-Lyre 273/5.

Symphonies. In addition to the Beecham performances (see in Chapter 27) there are the following:

273

Nos. 88 and 104 (*London*), performed well by Klemperer with the New Philharmonia on Angel 36346.

Nos. 88 and 98 (corrected text), excellently performed—with the animation and enlivening inflection that are lacking in Goberman's performance of the corrected text of No. 98 (which will be reissued on an Odyssey record)—by Jochum with the Berlin Philharmonic on Deutsche Grammophon 18-823.

Nos. 94 (*Surprise*) and 99, performed well by Krips with the Vienna Philharmonic on London 9222.

Nos. 94 and 101 (*Clock*), performed well by Karl Richter with the Berlin Philharmonic on Deutsche Grammophon 18-782. (Richter, regrettably, eliminates Haydn's little joke at the beginning of the Trio of the Minuet, correcting the incorrect harmony that Haydn carefully wrote in.)

Nos. 95 and 101, the first paced and shaped effectively, the second—especially the Andante—paced too slowly, by Reiner in his performances with a recording orchestra on Victor 2742. (Reiner also eliminates Haydn's little joke in No. 101.)

No. 96, performed well (but not from the corrected text, which, among other things, restores trumpets and kettledrums in the Andante) by the Prague Chamber Orchestra on Crossroads 16-0021.

No. 96 (corrected text), performed with more enlivening inflection than No. 98 by Goberman with a Vienna State Opera orchestra (to be reissued on an Odyssey record).

No. 100 (*Military*), performed acceptably by van Beinum with the London Philharmonic on Richmond 19096.

Nos. 100 and 102, performed in matter-of-fact fashion by Klemperer with the New Philharmonia, on Angel 36364.

No. 104 (*London*), performed well by Bernstein with the New York Philharmonic on Columbia ML-5349 (with Mendelssohn's *Italian* Symphony).

See also in Chapter 27: Toscanini, Beecham, Walter, Cantelli. Trios. See in Chapter 27: Casals, Goldberg.

HINDEMITH

The Four Temperaments. The performance on Epic LC-3356—by Goldberg with the Netherlands Chamber Orchestra and Fleisher as solo pianist—should be good.

Janáček

Slavonic Mass. Superbly performed, on Deutsche Grammophon 18-954, by Kubelik with the Bavarian Radio Orchestra and Chorus, Bedrich Janáček, organist, and Lear, Rössl-Majdan, Häfliger and Crass, who are superior to the soloists in Bernstein's effective performance with the New York Philharmonic and the Westminster Choir on Columbia ML-6137.

Lassus

The fine Masses *In Die Tribulationes* and *Bell' Amfitrit' Altera* are sung very beautifully by the Prague Madrigal Choir under Venhoda's direction on Bach Guild 651.

See also under MISCELLANEOUS COLLECTIONS: Collegium Musicum, Welch Chorale.

Mahler

Das Lied von der Erde. The noteworthy feature of Kletzki's performance with the Philharmonia on Angel 3607 is Fischer-Dieskau's singing of the songs usually sung by a contralto, which makes them sound as though they were intended to be sung only by him. I therefore prefer this performance—even with the unattractive tenor voice of Dickie—to any other, and specifically to the one excellently conducted by Klemperer on Angel 3704, with the superb singing of Ludwig and Wunderlich and the beautiful playing of the Philharmonia and New Philharmonia. I prefer it also to Bernstein's whipped-up and italicized performance with the Vienna Philharmonic on London 36005, in which Fischer-Dieskau's singing includes not only new subtleties but occasional new overemphasis and excessive vehemence.

Songs. The *Lieder eines fahrenden Gesellen* are sung best by Fischer-Dieskau, on Angel 35522, with the orchestral parts performed superbly by Furtwängler with the Philharmonia.

Four of the Rückert songs, including the great *Ich bin der Welt abhanden gekommen*, are sung marvelously by Fischer-Dieskau with the Berlin Philharmonic under Böhm on Deutsche Grammophon 18-879 (with the excessively lugubrious *Kindertotenlieder*).

Songs to poems of *Des Knaben Wunderhorn* are sung well, on Vanguard 1113, by Forrester and Rehfuss with the Vienna

275

Festival Orchestra under Prohaska. And some are sung superbly by Poell, on Vanguard 478, but others less well by Sydney, with a Vienna State Opera orchestra under Prohaska.

See also in Chapter 27: Ferrier, and under MISCELLANEOUS COLLECTIONS: Ludwig.

Symphonies. No. 1 is performed well by Solti with the London Symphony on London 9401, and by Ancerl with the Czech Philharmonic on Crossroads 16-0011.

No. 2 (*Resurrection*) is performed well, on Angel 3634, by Klemperer with the Philharmonia, Schwarzkopf and Rössl-Majdan. See also in Chapter 27: Walter.

No. 3 is performed well, on Columbia M2L-275, by Bernstein with the New York Philharmonic, the Schola Cantorum, the Boys' Choir of the Church of the Transfiguration, and Lipton.

No. 4 is performed well by Solti with the Amsterdam Concertgebouw Orchestra on London 9286. But there was on Epic LC-3304 a much finer performance by van Otterloo with the Hague Philharmonic that is still available on imported Philips GL-5811 (England).

MENDELSSOHN

Concerto for Violin. Performed well by Stern with the Philadelphia Orchestra under Ormandy on Columbia ML-5379 (with the Tchaikovsky Concerto).

Epic LC-3173 had a beautiful performance by Grumiaux with the Vienna Symphony under Moralt which is still available on imported Philips GBL-5582 (England) and 695015-KL (Germany). (Grumiaux's later performance on Epic LC-3762 was mannered and turbulent.)

See also in Chapter 27: Szigeti.

A Midsummer Night's Dream (Incidental Music). Kubelik's performance with the orchestra and chorus of the Bavarian Radio, on Deutsche Grammophon 18-959, is the only good one since Toscanini's (see in Chapter 27).

Octet for Strings. Columbia ML-6248 has an outstanding performance by Laredo, Schneider, Steinhardt and Dalley, violins, Tree and Rhodes, violas, and Parnas and Soyer, cellos (with Mozart's Concertone K.190).

See also in Chapter 27: Toscanini.

Symphonies. An excellent performance of No. 3 (*Scotch*) by Maag with the London Symphony is on London 9252.

For performances of No. 4 (*Italian*) see in Chapter 27: Cantelli, Toscanini, Koussevitzky.

MONTEVERDI

L'Incoronazione di Poppea. Angel 3644 has an abridged version of an excellent Glyndebourne Festival performance conducted by Pritchard, with admirable singing by Laszlo, Lewis and the others except Bible, whose voice is almost all tremolo.

Lagrime d'Amante al Sepolcro dell'Amata. See under MISCELLANEOUS COLLECTIONS: Collegium Musicum, Deller Consort.

Lamento d'Ariana. See under MISCELLANEOUS COLLECTIONS: Deller Consort, Netherlands Chamber Choir.

Madrigals. The *Madrigali Amorosi* from the Eighth Book of Madrigals are sung beautifully by the Deller Consort on Bach Guild 579.

A few of these are among the pieces that Boulanger recorded with a small vocal and instrumental ensemble in 1937, and that are now on Angel COLH-20, and another group of pieces which she performs with a vocal and instrumental ensemble on Decca 9627.

Masses. The two *Masses for Four Voices* published in 1641 and 1651 are sung well by the Choir of St. John's College, Cambridge, under Guest on Argo 494 (with two small pieces, *Laudate Pueri* and *Ut Queant Laxis*).

Vespers of 1610 (*Vespro della Beata Vergine*) and *Magnificat*. Performed beautifully on Oiseau-Lyre 50021/2 by Anthony Lewis with the London Singers, soloists headed by Ritchie, and an instrumental group.

A second *Magnificat* for the *Vespers*, a simpler one for six voices and organ continuo, is sung well by the Choir of the Carmelite Priory under Malcolm on Oiseau-Lyre 263 (with the *Mass for Four Voices* published in 1651).

MORLEY

Bach Guild 577, *The English Madrigal School, Volume 3*, has a number of lovely pieces, sung beautifully by the Deller Consort.

See also under MISCELLANEOUS COLLECTIONS: Cuenod, Deller, Deller Consort.

Mozart

Adagio and Fugue K.546. Performed well by Fricsay with the Berlin Radio Symphony on Deutsche Grammophon 19-398 (with Masonic Funeral Music K.477 and Haydn's *Te Deum*).

Concerto for Bassoon K.191. See in Chapter 17: Toscanini.

Concerto for Clarinet K.622. De Peyer's performance with the London Symphony under Maag, on London 9247, offers the most beautiful clarinet tone and phrasing I have heard in this work.

Concertos for Horn K.412, 417, 447 and 495. There is beautiful melodic writing in all four; but what makes K.447 the most impressive is the development section of the first movement, with its startling and dramatic shifts of key. Dennis Brain's performances, on Angel 35092, are astounding in their extraordinarily supple sustained tone and subtly detailed phrasing; and von Karajan provides them with beautifully sensitive contexts with the Philharmonia Orchestra.

Concertos for Piano. The performances on Epic SC-6054 and 6056 offer undistinguished piano-playing by Kraus and pedestrian playing by the Vienna Festival Orchestra under Simon.

Ashkenazy's superb performance on K.271 with the London Symphony under Kertesz is on London 9501, with his similar performance of K.246, a moderately engaging lesser work.

In the performance of K.271 on Vanguard VSD-71154 (stereo, which is preferable to mono in this instance), Brendel's playing admirably combines sensitiveness with strength and cohesive tension in the first movement, but is slack in parts of the Andantino, and doesn't have the verve the final Presto calls for. The reverse side has a good performance of K.449, an engaging work of lesser stature. Janigro provides excellent contexts with his Solisti di Zagreb. See also in Chapter 27: Gieseking.

Turnabout 4027 has good performances of K.450 and K.413, a minor work, by Frankl with the Württemberg Chamber Orchestra under Färber.

Vanguard 1080 had an excellent performance of K.453 by Gulda with an orchestra under Angerer.

Heliodor H-25042 has good performances of K.459 and 595 by Haskil with the Berlin Philharmonic and Bavarian State Orches-

278

tras under Fricsay. See also in Chapter 27: Schnabel.

RCA Victor LM-2635 has an effective performance of K.466 by Rubinstein with an orchestra under Wallenstein. See also Schnabel.

For K.467 see Schnabel.

The slow movement of K.488 calls for something more powerful than Gieseking's finely chiseled playing on Columbia ML-4536 (with Franck's *Variations symphoniques*); nevertheless it is a beautiful performance, with beautiful playing by the Philharmonia under von Karajan.

I have never heard K.491 played with the powerful sculpturing of phrase, the energy in runs and figurations, the sustained tension and momentum of Gould's performance with the CBC Symphony under Susskind on Columbia ML-5739.

The powerful K.491 elicits from Gieseking something bigger and stronger than his usual delicate miniature style in Mozart, on Angel 35501. The beautiful playing of the Philharmonia under von Karajan is reproduced with sharpness of string sound that necessitates reduction of treble.

For K.491 see also Schnabel.

Fleisher's excellent performance of K.503 with the Cleveland Orchestra under Szell is on Epic LC-3574 (with Betehoven's Concerto No. 4).

Concertos for Violin. The excellent performances of K.216 and 219 by Grumiaux with the London Symphony that were on Philips 500-012 are still available on imported Philips A-02224-L (England and Germany).

The excellent performances of K.216 and 218 by Grumiaux with the Vienna Symphony under Paumgartner that were on Epic LC-3060 are still available on imported Philips A-00199-L (Germany).

Another performance of K.218 by Grumiaux with the London Symphony under Davis is on imported Philips AL-3440 (England) or A-02253-L (Germany) (with K.207).

The excellence of the performance of K.219 on Pickwick 4013 (with Bach's Concerto No. 1) is not only in Milstein's luminous tone and unaffected phrasing but in the wonderfully enlivened orchestral context that Blech creates around his playing with the superb orchestra.

See also in Chapter 27: Goldberg, Szigeti.

Concertos for Miscellaneous Instruments. Columbia ML-4564 had a Perpignan Festival performance of the Sinfonie Concertante K.364 for violin and viola with fine playing by Stern and Primrose and orchestral playing excitingly enlivened by Casals's conducting.

Philips 500-130 has a superb performance of K.364 by Grumiaux and Pelliccia with the London Symphony under Davis.

Crossroads 16-0015 has a good performance of K.364 by Suk and Skampa with the Czech Philharmonic under Rdeel.

The Concertone K.190 for two violins and oboe is excellently performed, on Columbia ML-6248 (with Mendelssohn's Octet for strings), by Laredo, Tree and Arner with the Marlboro Festival Orchestra under Schneider.

Contredanses and German Dances. The engaging K.534, 600, 602, 605, 606 and 609—performed well by Litschauer with a Vienna State Opera orchestra on Vanguard 426—include wonderful details.

Additional engaging pieces in this genre—K.267, 462, 501 and 567—and a couple of marches are performed well by Boskovsky with the Vienna Mozart Ensemble on London 9412.

Divertimentos. A fine performance of K.334 for strings and horns by Prohaska with a chamber orchestra from the Vienna State Opera is on Vanguard 441.

The best of recent performances of K.563 for string trio is that of the Trio Italiano d'Archi on Deutsche Grammophon 39-150.

Masonic Funeral Music K.477. This series of musical gestures of solemnity, grief and resignation, with occasional dramatic events provided by startling modulations, is performed well by Fricsay with the Berlin Radio Symphony on Deutsche Grammophon 19-398 (with Adagio and Fugue K.546 and Haydn's *Te Deum*).

Masses. Deutsche Grammophon 18-631 offers an excellent performance of the Mass K.317 (*Coronation*) in which Markevitch conducts the Lamoureux Orchestra, the Brasseur Choir, and Stader, Dominguez, Häfliger and Roux.

Angel 36205 has an effective performance of the *Mass in C minor* K.427 in which Gönnenwein conducts the Southwest German Chamber Orchestra, the South German Madrigal Choir

280

and soloists among whom the soprano Mathis is outstanding in the beauty of her voice and phrasing.

A Musical Joke K.522. See in Chapter 27: Cantelli.

Operas. the 1935 Glyndebourne Festival performance of *Così Fan Tutte* (see in Chapter 27: Glyndebourne Festival) is the best currently available performance, and the one to acquire.

The exquisitely sung performance of *Così* that was on Angel 3522—with Schwarzkopf, Merriman, Simoneau, Panerai, Bruscantini and the Philharmonia Orchestra, conducted by von Karajan—is available on imported Columbia FLX-484/6 (France).

The *Così* on Columbia SL-122, paced and phrased well by Stiedry, has the moments of grandeur achieved by Steber's singing; but these are offset by Tucker's cold voice and tight singing in music that calls for a lyric tenor's warmth and ease, by the ear-jarring English words, and by the cold, veiled recorded sound.

In addition to the 1936 Glyndebourne Festival performance there is one other currently available performance on *Don Giovanni* that is superb—the one on Angel 3605, conducted by Giulini, with Wächter, Taddei, Alva, Sutherland, Schwarzkopf, Sciutti and the Philharmonia Orchestra and Chorus. (The one conducted by Klemperer on Angel 3700 I advise against.)

The best currently available performance of *Die Entführung aus dem Serail* is the one on Deutsche Grammophon 18-184/5, conducted by Fricsay, with Stader, Streich, Häfliger, Vantin, Greindl and the RIAS Symphony and Chorus.

The performance of *Idomeneo* conducted by Pritchard on Angel 3574 has the cuts—chiefly in recitative—made in the Glyndebourne Festival stage production, outstanding singing by Jurinac and Simoneau, and good singing also by Udovick and Lewis.

A good performance of *The Impresario* is on Period 532.

In addition to the 1937 Beecham performance (see in Chapter 27) there is one other currently available performance that is excellent—the one on Deutsche Grammophon 18-267/9, conducted by Fricsay, with Stader, Streich, Häfliger, Fischer-Dieskau, Greindl, the RIAS Symphony and Chamber Choir, and the Berlin Motet Choir.

In addition to the 1934 Glyndebourne Festival performance of

281

The Marriage of Figaro there is one other currently available performance that is excellent—the one on Victor LM-6408, paced well by Leinsdorf, with Tozzi, London, Della Casa, Peters, Elias and the Vienna State Opera Orchestra and Chorus.

The performance of *Figaro* that was on Epic SC-6022, and is still available on imported Philips GL-5777/9 (England) and A-00357/9-L (Germany), is paced more slowly than usual by Böhm—the result being a loss of animation and brilliance, but also certain gains: the exceptional clarity of the orchestral detail that is so rich in this work; the increased power of the Count's third-act aria; the increased effectiveness of the sublime *Contessa perdono* passage at the end. Except for Berry's Figaro—unattractive and unvarying in vocal color, and unenlivening in phrasing—the singing is first-rate, with Jurinac and Schöffler outstanding as the Countess and Count, and Streich an excellent Susanna.

London 5782 has Berganza's superb performances of Fiordiligi's arias and Dorabella's *E Amore un ladroncello* from *Così*, Cherubino's arias from *Figaro*, an aria from *La Clemenza di Tito* and the concert aria *Non temer*, with the London Symphony under Pritchard.

Epic LC-3262 had Simoneau's ear-ravishing performances of Ottavio's two arias from *Don Giovanni, Un' aura amorosa* from *Così*, an aria from *Titus* and the concert aria *Non temer*.

See also in Chapter 27: Hempel, Ivogün, Leider, Lilli Lehmann, Lotte Lehmann, Pinza, Rethberg, Schumann, Slezak, Steber, Urlus, Wildbrunn, and under MISCELLANEOUS COLLECTIONS: Albanese, Evans, Ghiaurov, Horne, Jurinac, Schwarzkopf, Sutherland, Valletti.

Davis's performances of the overtures with the Royal Philharmonic, on Seraphim 60037, are excellent, except for the Allegro of the Overture to *The Magic Flute*, which sounds insufficiently animated to someone acquainted with Toscanini's performance.

Piano Music (Complete). The Angel records acquaint us with a number of pieces which most of us have never heard—the earliest interesting chiefly for what they reveal about Mozart's initial talent and its development, some later ones interesting only as exercises of his exquisite craftsmanship; and others achieving impressive effect as works of art. Gieseking's playing is finely chiseled and sensitive but often without sufficient force; and in music in slow tempo it often lacks sustained tension. Some of the unfamiliar pieces, however, are played with the force and tension that are lacking in the familiar ones.

Angel 35068 offers several of the earliest pieces; the Variations K.180 on a theme of Salieri, in which one hears the operation of matured powers; and three late works: the fine Sonata K.570, and the unfamiliar Adagio K.356 for harmonica and Rondo K.616, both with remarkable modulations.

Angel 35069 has the best-known Sonata K.331, with its impressive minuet movement, the Sonata K.282, with its unusual Adagio opening movement, the Suite K.399, with interesting and attractive Mozartian transformations of Handelian styles in its Allemande and Courante; the Minuet K.355, a small but fine late piece; the Fantasy K.397 in D minor, whose Adagio is a miniature example of declamatory vocal style; and the Variations K.265 on *Ah vous dirai-je maman*, with two impressive slow variations.

Angel 35070 offers the powerful Sonata K.310; the Sonata K.280, an excellent display piece; and several first-rate unfamiliar pieces: the Variations K.179 on a minuet of J. C. Fischer, the Adagio K.540, and the Variations K.54, a late work with a wonderful variation in minor mode.

Angel 35071 has the powerful Fantasy K.475 and Sonata K.457; the Sonata K.333, with its fine opening movement; and the unfamiliar Variations K.353 on *La Belle Françoise*, a good work in which the slow variation is outstanding.

Angel 35072 offers the Sonatas K.279 and 311, of which the finales are good; and two unfamiliar pieces: the Fantasy and Fugue K.394, which I find uninteresting, and the Variations K.513 on *Ein Weib ist ein herrliches Ding*, of which Variation 6 in minor mode, the slow No. 7 and the elaborate No. 8 are outstanding.

Angel 35073 has the extraordinary Sonata K.533, remarkable in the large scale and contrapuntal elaboration of the Allegro, the startling harmonic progressions that achieve the utmost in expressive intensity in the Andante; and several less impressive pieces: the Rondo K.494, which Mozart published with K.533 as a concluding movement, the Sonata K.284, the sonata movement K.312, and the Fugue K.401.

Angel 35074 has two of Mozart's most remarkable pieces, the Rondo K.511 and Gigue K.574—the first unique in the chromaticism and expressive intensity of the exquisitely contoured principal melody and its recurring variations; the other equally so in its rhythmic intricacy. With these are the uninteresting Sonata K.281 and two engaging unfamiliar pieces, the Sonata K.547a and Variations K.398.

Angel 35075 offers the fine Variations K.455 on *Unser dummer Pöbel meint;* the equally good Variations K.264, with one of Mozart's wonderful syncopated and chromatic variations in minor and an extraordinary Adagio; the engaging Sonata K.283, with its superb finale; and the Sonata K.576, with some of Mozart's most developed, most complex writing for the piano.

Angel 35076 has the magnificent Fantasy K.396; the fine Sonata K.332, with another superb finale; the engaging "small sonata for beginners," K.545; and two unfamiliar pieces: the Variations K.354, of which Nos. 4, 8 and 10 are outstanding, and the Variations K.460, with good writing in the later pages.

Angel 35077 offers the fine Sonatas K.330 and 309; and three unfamiliar pieces: the Variations K.352, of which Nos. 4, 5 and 7 are outstanding; the Rondo K.485, entirely and interestingly unusual in its procedures; and the Capriccio K.395, a strange piece unlike any other by Mozart, reminiscent of Bach, and implying a larger scale than its actual small one.

Of the unfamiliar pieces on Angel 35078 the sonata movement K.400 is charming, the sonata movement and Minuet K.498a are good, and the Minuets and Trios K.315a are uninteresting. And the better-known German Dances K.509, which I found pleasantly inconsequential in their orchestral versions, are less attractive as arranged for piano.

Quartets. The superb Guarneri Quartet, which will no doubt record the six quartets dedicated to Haydn, offers meanwhile, on Victor LM-2888, beautiful performances of the later K.589 and 590 which are flawed by the cellist's mannered statement of the second subject in the first movement of K.589, and his slide in the slow movement of K.590.

K.387 and 464, of the six dedicated to Haydn, are performed, on Deutsche Grammophon 18-909, with admirable musical understanding by the Amadeus Quartet, whose first violin, unfortunately, has a somewhat coarse tone.

K.421 and 465 are also performed well by the Amadeus Quartet —except for the hurrying of the Andante of K.421—on Deutsche Grammophon 39-190; and the first violin's flawed tone is less obtrusive.

K.499 and 589 are performed by the Vienna Philharmonic Quartet, on London 9298, with phrasing as sensitive as the Budapest Quartet's, and with greater animation and more beautiful tone.

See also in Chapter 27: Budapest Quartet.

Quartets for Miscellaneous Groups. The performance of the Quartet K.370 for oboe and strings by the Soloists of the Berlin Philharmonic, on Deutsche Grammophon 18-996 (with the Quintet K.581 for clarinet and strings), has superbly phrased playing of the oboe part.

London 9061 offers good performances of the Quartets K.478 and 493 for piano and strings by Curzon and members of the Amadeus Quartet. See also in Chapter 27: Schnabel.

Quintets. See in Chapter 27: Budapest Quartet.

Quintets for Miscellaneous Groups. A good performance of the Quintet K.452 for piano and winds by members of the Vienna Octet is on London 9181 (with the Trio K.498 for clarinet, viola and piano).

The performance of the Quintet K.452 on London 9494 (with Beethoven's Quintet Op. 16) is made exciting by Ashkenazy's playing with the excellent London Wind Soloists.

The performance of the Quintet K.581 for clarinet and strings by de Peyer and members of the Melos Ensemble, on Angel 36241 (with the Trio K.498 for clarinet, viola and piano), is made notable by the ear-ravishing tone that de Peyer inflects so sensitively.

Requiem. London 4517 has an excellent performance conducted by Kertesz, with the Vienna Philharmonic and State Opera Chorus, Ameling, Horne, Benelli and Franc.

Rondo K. 511 for Piano. See in Chapter 27: Schnabel.

Serenades. The engaging *Serenata Notturna* K.239 is performed beautifully by Festival Strings Lucerne under Baumgartner on

285

Deutsche Grammophon 19-480 (with the unfamiliar and astonishingly good Divertimenti K.136, 137 and 138).

Klemperer's collaboration with the London Wind Quintet and Ensemble produces an unbelievably wonderful performance of the Serenade K.361 for thirteen winds on Angel 36247. I say "collaboration" because I am sure he must have dealt with the outstanding wind-players and musicians, up to a point, as equals, conferring with them about the tempos, which are well chosen, and about the phrasing, which is marvelous. But it is he who does for the performance what only a conductor can do for so large a performing group: establish the instrumental balances that result in the extraordinary clarity of the textures in which the individual lines are marvelously distinct and yet related; adjust the phraseological inflection of each line to bring it into relation with that of the others, producing in this way the marvelous working together in the performance.

The Serenade K.375 for winds is performed well by the London Wind Soloists on London 9347 (with the Divertimenti K.166 and 213).

The Serenade K.388 for winds is performed well by the London Wind Soloists on London 9348 (with the Divertimenti K.186 and 253).

Sonatas for Piano. Cliburn's beautiful performance of K.330 is on Victor 2931 (with Beethoven's Sonata Op. 81a).

Gould's electrifying performance of K.330 was on Columbia ML-5274 (with Haydn's Sonata, Peters No. 3).

See also in Chapter 27: Schnabel, Lipatti.

Sonata K.448 for Two Pianos. London 9411 has an excellent performance by Ashkenazy and Frager.

A quietly sensitive performance by Badura-Skoda and Demus is on Westminster 18044 (with the Sonatas K.358 and 381 for piano four hands).

Sonatas for Piano and Violin. Good performances of K.301 and 304 by Grumiaux and Tucker are on Boston 202 (with Bach's *Chaconne* for unaccompanied violin).

The performances of K.454 and 526 by Grumiaux and Haskil on Epic LC-3299 are very fine; but Haskil's playing lacks the verve and sparkle required by the brilliant Allegros of K.526.

Haskil plays with less energy than Grumiaux in the fine performances of K.301, 304, 378 and the less interesting K.376 that were on Epic LC-3602 and are still available on imported Philips L-00432-L (Germany).

See also in Chapter 27: Goldberg, and under MISCELLANEOUS COLLECTIONS: Kulenkampf and Solti.

Songs. Not all that Schwarzkopf sings exquisitely with Gieseking on Angel 35270 are as good as *Unglückliche Liebe, Abendempfindung, Der Zauberer, Das Veilchen, Das Lied der Trennung* and *An Chloë*. But one of the most delightful is the ironically humorous *Die Alte*, which is effectively pointed up by Schwarzkopf's dramatized performance.

Symphonies. Davis's excellent performances of K.200 and 504 (*Prague*) with the English Chamber Orchestra are on Oiseau-Lyre 266.

K.201 and 551 (*Jupiter*) are performed well by Fricsay with the Vienna Symphony on Deutsche Grammophon 18-709. See also in Chapter 27: Cantelli, Toscanini.

Epic LC-3215 had excellent performances of K.297 (*Paris*) and 200 by Paumgartner with the Camerata Academica of the Salzburg Mozarteum. See also in Chapter 27: Beecham.

For K.338 see Beecham.

A good performance of K.385 (*Haffner*) by Krips with the Israel Philharmonic is on London 9220 (with K.551). See also in Chapter 27: Toscanini, Beecham.

Davis's excellent performances of K.425 (*Linz*) and 319 with the English Chamber Orchestra are on Oiseau-Lyre 50218.

Kertesz's excellent performances of K.543 and 319 with the Vienna Philharmonic are on London 9354.

Böhm conducts good performances of K.543 and 425 (*Linz*), on Deutsche Grammophon 39-160, which have very beautiful playing by the Berlin Philharmonic.

Giulini's excellent performances of K.550 in G minor and K.551 (*Jupiter*) with the New Philharmonia are on London 9479. See also Toscanini.

Trio K.498 for Clarinet, Viola and Piano. Performed beautifully by de Peyer and members of the Melos Ensemble on Angel 36241 (with the Quintet K.581 for clarinet and strings).

287

Musorgsky

Boris Godunov. The only recording of Musorgsky's own work was Victor LM-6063, which had parts of the 1956 Metropolitan Opera performance (in disturbingly poor English) conducted by Mitropoulos, with Tozzi as Boris.

Pictures at an Exhibition. The only good performance of the original work for piano is Sviatoslav Richter's poorly recorded one on Columbia ML-5600; and even in this one the rushing of the *Promenades* conveys a running from picture to picture instead of a leisurely sauntering.

For the orchestral version see in Chapter 27: Toscanini, Cantelli.

Songs. Vishnevskaya's voice is not beautiful, but is a good instrument for her effective expressive singing in the powerful songs she does, on Philips 500-082, with orchestrated accompaniments: *Cradle Song, The Magpie, Night, Little Star, The Ragamuffin, On the Dnieper.* And Rostropovich's vivid playing of the piano part combines with her singing in a tremendous performance of *Songs and Dances of Death.*

The Nursery and *Songs and Dances of Death* are sung well by Davrath on Vanguard 1068.

Capitol P-8310 had a beautiful performance of the *Sunless* cycle by Kurenko.

See also under MISCELLANEOUS COLLECTIONS: Seefried, Ghiaurov.

Pachelbel

Two Toccatas in C and F, a Fugue in C, and four Chorale-Preludes for organ are on Overtone 8 (with works by Walther). One's ear is delighted first by the extraordinarily beautiful and clearly reproduced sound of the Holtkamp organ in Yale's Battell Chapel; then one notes the fine use of the instrument and the sensitive treatment of the music by Noss; and then the quality of the unfamiliar seventeenth-century music itself: the fugue very engaging, the Chorale-Preludes *Jesus Christus unser Heiland* and *Wie schön leuchtet der Morgenstern* simple but strong, the more involved *Warum betrübst du dich mein Herz* very beautiful, the majestic second part of *Ein' feste Burg* very imposing.

288

PALESTRINA

Missa Papae Marcelli. The beautiful performance of this famous and lovely piece by the Netherlands Chamber Choir under De Nobel that was on Epic LC-3045 is available on imported Philips A-00272-L (Germany).

Motets *Stabat Mater, Hodie Beata Virgo* and *Senex Puerum Portebat; Magnificat* and *Litaniae de Beata Virgine.* Sung well by the Choir of King's College, Cambridge, under Willcocks on Argo 398.

The Song of Songs. These twenty-one motets, to texts from *The Song of Solomon,* which are sung superbly by the Prague Madrigal Choir under Venhoda, seem to me the most beautiful and moving music by Palestrina that I have heard.

See also under MISCELLANEOUS COLLECTIONS: Collegium Musicum, Welch Chorale.

PROKOFIEV

Classical Symphony. See in Chapter 27: Toscanini, Koussevitzky.

Concerto No. 3 for Piano. Prokofiev's own performance on **Angel** COLH-34 (with solo pieces) is straightforward, strong, sharply rhythmed and outlined, brilliant. With bass restored and with an 8-kc cut-off the sound is remarkably good.

   In his superb performance with the Chicago Symphony under Hendl, on Victor LM-2507, Cliburn sets deliberate tempos for the middle movement and the beginning of the finale that he makes effective with his unfailing sense for continuity and shape.

Concerto No. 1 for Violin. A superb performance by Oistrakh with the London Symphony under von Matacic is on Angel 35243.

The Prodigal Son. Vox PL-9310 had an excellent performance of the entire ballet score by Barzin with the New York City Ballet Orchestra, recorded in an excessively live studio.

Quartet Op. 92. Capitol P-8151 had the Hollywood Quartet's performance of this work, which has a beautifully lyrical slow movement and a superb finale.

Scythian Suite. The superb performance by Markevitch with the National Orchestra of the French Radio that was on Angel 35361 is available on imported Columbia FCX-541 (France).

Symphony No. 5. Performed well by Ansermet with L'Orchestre de la Suisse Romande on London 9406, and by Oistrakh with the Moscow Philharmonic-Symphony on Melodiya Angel 40003.

Purcell

Fantasias for Strings. See below in Collections.

Ode for St. Cecilia's Day. This fine piece, characteristic in the boldness of its harmonic progressions and in the florid vocal writing that Purcell makes so exciting, is performed admirably on Bach Guild 559 by Tippett with the Ambrosian Singers, the Kalmar Chamber Orchestra and excellent soloists.

Operas. In addition to the great performance of *Dido and Aeneas* with Flagstad's overwhelming singing (see in Chapter 27), there is the excellent performance conducted by Anthony Lewis, on Oiseau-Lyre 50216, with impressive singing by Baker and good singing by most of the other soloists and the St. Anthony Singers, and good playing by the English Chamber Orchestra.

Another good performance of *Dido and Aeneas* is the one conducted by Deller on Bach Guild 664, with Mary Thomas and and other English soloists and the Oriana Concert Choir and Orchestra.

The performance of *Dido and Aeneas* conducted by Barbirolli on Angel 36359, with De los Angeles, I advise against.

Oiseau-Lyre 50139/41 has an excellent performance of *The Fairy Queen*, conducted by Anthony Lewis, with soloists headed by Morison and Vyvyan, the St. Anthony Singers, and the Boyd Neel Orchestra.

Allegro 9003 has excerpts from *The Fairy Queen*, excellently performed by Curtin and other soloists and the Cambridge Festival Orchestra and Chorus under Pinkham.

Oiseau-Lyre 50176/7 and 60008/9 (stereo, which is better in this instance) have a good performance of *King Arthur*, conducted by Anthony Lewis, with some good singing by Morison among others, but some that is not agreeable to the ear, and with a good chorus and orchestra.

Oiseau-Lyre 294 has a good performance of *The Indian Queen*, conducted by Mackerras, with Cantelo, Brown, Partridge, Keyte, Tear, the St. Anthony Singers and the English Chamber Orchestra.

Pavan and Chacony in G minor. See in Chapter 27: New Music Quartet.

Trio Sonatas. Nos. 1, 2, 4, 7, 8, 9 (the *Golden Sonata*) and 10 are performed well on Dover 5224 by the violinists Ciompi and Torkanovsky with cello and harpsichord continuo by Koutzen and Chessid.

Vocal Music. Three fine pieces—*Here Let My Life* from the Cantata *If Ever I More Riches Did Desire; Since from My Dear Astrea's Sight* from *Dioclesian;* and *Oh! Let me Weep* from *The Fairy Queen*—are the best things on Bach Guild 547 (with music of Jenkins and Locke), and are sung beautifully by Alfred Deller with Gustav Leonhardt, harpsichord, and a "consort of viols".

Several other pieces are performed well by Oberlin and the other musicians of the New York Pro Musica Antiqua on Counterpoint 519.

See also in Chapter 27: Baillie, Ferrier.

Collections. The vocal pieces on Bach Guild 570/1, *Homage to Henry Purcell*, include lovely examples of simple melody like *Fairest Isle* and *I Attempt from Love's Sickness to Fly;* the beautiful duet *Close Thine Eyes;* and magnificent examples of Purcell's powerfully expressive florid writing like *I Love and I Must* and *Tell Me Some Pitying Angel*. The instrumental ones include the superb *Fantasia upon One Note in Five Parts* and Pavan for three violins and viola de gamba (the one played by the New Music Quartet on Bartók 913); the fine Sonata in G minor for violin and harpsichord, and the *Golden Sonata*. Of the performers, Deller is impressive with his extraordinary inflection of a counter-tenor voice of peculiar and unattractive timbre; but I have no reservation about the beautiful and expressive singing of Cantelo and Bevan, and the brilliant harpsichord-playing of Malcolm.

A group of fine instrumental pieces—several of the Fantasias for four or five strings, including the outstanding one *Upon One Note,* the Pavan No. 4 in G minor, and the Trio Sonatas in G minor and C—are performed well by Menuhin and members of the Bath Festival Orchestra on Angel 36270.

RAMEAU

Concerts en sextuor. This is the best-known arrangement for strings of the charming and lovely *Pièces de clavecin en concert,* and is performed well by the Paillard Chamber Orchestra on Musical Heritage 567.

The original *Pièces de clavecin en concert* is performed well on Nonesuch H-1063 by Veyron-Lacroix, harpsichord, with Rampal, flute, and Neilz, cello.

Harpsichord Pieces. I like the delicate quality and moderate size of the sound of the Dowd harpsichord on which Fuller produces the sensitive and enlivening performances on Cambridge 601/3.

A number of attractive pieces are performed well by Anton Heiller, except for an occasional lack of rhythmic steadiness and clarity, on Bach Guild 614.

Operas. The excerpts performed well on Decca 9683 by singers and an instrumental group under Boulanger include music that is lovely and impressive.

Respighi

Fountains of Rome and *Pines of Rome*. See in Chapter 27: Toscanini.

Old Dances and Airs for Lute. Vanguard 466 has excellent performances of all three suites by Litschauer with a Vienna State Opera orchestra.

Rimsky-Korsakov

Capriccio Espagnol. Argenta's superb performance with the London Symphony is on London 9192.

Suite from *Le Coq d'or*. Ansermet's performance with L'Orchestre de la Suisse Romande on Richmond 19055 should be good.

See under MISCELLANEOUS COLLECTIONS: Tourel.

Rossini

The Barber of Seville. Angel 3638 has an outstanding performance conducted by Gui, with Bruscantini, De los Angeles and Alva.

In the performance on Angel 3559 Callas's high notes are shrill and tremulous, but her voice exerts its usual compulsion with the strange and beautiful timbre of its lower range, and her singing does so with its assurance and style, its powerful continuity of subtle expressive inflection of phrase. And the others in the excellent cast that includes Gobbi and Alva sing, under Galliera's direction, with the refinement and subtlety of phrasing and style that Galliera achieves also in the playing of the Philharmonia.

La Cenerentola. Gui's conducting makes the 1953 Glyndebourne Festival performance—which Victor offered briefly on LHMV-

600, and which is now available on imported Odeon QALP-
10066/8 (Italy)—one of the most extraordinary examples of the
combined operation of operatic performance ever put on records.
It is he who is responsible not only for the style of the singers—
Gabarain, Oncina, Bruscantini and Wallace—but for the orchestra's sharp-witted phrasing, the clarity of the ensemble of voices
and orchestra, the sustained tension and exciting cumulative
effect of the concerted numbers, and possibly the remarkable
accompanying of the recitative by Balkwill.

Le Comte Ory. The similarly superb Glyndebourne Festival performance conducted by Gui that was on Angel 3565 is available on
imported Odeon QALP-10200/1 (Italy). Unfortunately the
bloom is gone from Oncina's voice and it has a strong wobble
in the high notes one fears he won't manage; but the rest of the
singing is good.

L'Italiana in Algeri. Angel 3529 offers a superb performance of this
delightful work, conducted by Giulini, with an excellent cast in
which Simionato and Valletti are outstanding in the beauty and
style of their singing.

Except for the singing of Berganza the performance on London
4375 is inferior.

William Tell. The performance on Cetra (Everest) 420 (avoid the
pseudo-stereo version) has occasional hard and tight singing by
the tenor Filippeschi but excellent singing by Carteri, Taddei,
Corena and others in the performance with the orchestra and
chorus of Turin Radio under Rossi. The sound is poor.

Arias. London 5514 has Berganza's fine performances of arias from
The Barber of Seville, *La Cenerentola*, *L'Italiana in Algeri* and *Semiram-
ide*, and *Fac ut portem* from the *Stabat Mater*, with the London
Symphony under Gibson.

Tourel's fine performances of arias from *The Barber of Seville*,
La Cenerentola, *L'Italiana in Algeri* and *Semiramide*, originally on
Columbia 78-rpm M-691, were transferred to ML-2024.

See also in Chapter 27: Ivogün, Pinza, Schipa, Slezak, Supervia, Urlus, and under MISCELLANEOUS COLLECTIONS: *The Age
of Bel Canto*, Callas, Horne, Simionato, Sutherland, Tebaldi,
Valletti.

Overtures. See in Chapter 27: Toscanini.

Stabat Mater. The later sections of this work are very beautiful, and

293

are sung superbly by Stader, Radev, Häfliger and Borg in the performance with the Choir of St. Hedwig's Cathedral and the Berlin Radio Chorus and Orchestra conducted by Fricsay, on Heliodor H-25032.

Sonatas for Strings. Of these charming works of Rossini's teens in which it is astonishing to hear the operatic style of his maturity, Nos. 1 to 4 are performed excellently by I Solisti di Zagreb on Vanguard 488. Treble and bass must be reduced.

See also under MISCELLANEOUS COLLECTIONS: Virtuosi di Roma.

SCARLATTI

Valenti's early performances of the sonatas on Westminster 18328/-9/30 are his best, which surpass most others in their verve and their pointing up of the detail of the delightful pieces. One wishes he had used a more delicate-toned harpsichord; but the volume can be reduced.

A number of delightful performances by Sgrizzi are on Nonesuch H-1094.

The excellent performances by Malcolm on a lovely-toned harpsichord that were on London LL-963 are still available on imported Decca LXT-2918

See also in Chapter 27: Landowska.

SCHEIDT

Tabalatura Nova. One's pleasure from the excerpts of this unfamiliar seventeenth-century work on Overtone 3 is increased by the fine playing of Noss and the beautiful sound of the Holtkamp organ in Yale's Battell Chapel.

SCHUBERT

Duets for Piano. The infrequently heard and beautiful Fantasie Op. 103 and the engaging Rondo Op. 107 and *Marches caracteristiques* Op. 121 are among the pieces performed well by Badura-Skoda and Demus on Deutsche Grammophon 39-107.

The engaging Grand Duo Op. 140—thought by some to be an arrangement of the lost Gastein Symphony—is performed superbly by Gold and Fizdale on Columbia ML-5717; but they occasionally push expressive inflection of phrase and crescendos

294

of intensity further than the expressive content and the scale of this lyrical work warrant.

See also in Chapter 27: Schnabel.

Impromptus for Piano. See Schnabel.

Masses. The early, small-scale Mass in G, with lovely lyrical writing that expresses what Tovey calls Schubert's "fragrant piety", is sung beautifully by the Shaw Chorale with undistinguished soloists on Victor LM-1784.

In striking contrast to the lyrical writing in much of Schubert's Mass in A flat is the somber, powerfully expressive passage beginning with "*Et incarnatus est*" in the *Credo*. Deutsche Grammophon 39-108 has a good performance conducted by Raitzinger, with the Regensburg Cathedral Chorus, the Bavarian Radio Symphony, Stader, Höffgen, Häfliger and Uhde.

The Mass in E flat, written in the last year of Schubert's life, and with impressively forceful and dramatic passages as well as lovely lyrical ones, is performed well on Decca 9422 by the Musica Aeterna Chorus and Orchestra and soloists under Waldman.

Moments musicaux for Piano. See Schnabel.

Octet Op. 166 for Strings and Winds. Performed beautifully by the Vienna Octet on London 9110.

Quartets. The Quartetto Italiano, the European group of the caliber of the Guarneri Quartet here, offers, on Philips 500-139, a performance of the *Death and the Maiden* Quartet that is outstanding in ensemble excellence and musical effectiveness.

See also in Chapter 27: Budapest Quartet.

Quintet Op. 163 for Strings. The best available performance is the one by Stern, Schneider, Katims, Casals and Tortelier on Columbia ML-4714.

See also Budapest Quartet.

Quintet Op. 114 (*Trout*) for Piano and Strings. Deutsche Grammophon 19-488 has a fine performance by members of the Koeckert Quartet with a remarkable young pianist named Eschenbach.

Period 730 has a good performance by Galimir, Tuttle, Vargas and Levine with Nádás.

See also Schnabel, Budapest Quartet.

Die schöne Müllerin. See Songs.

Schwanengesang. See Songs.

Sonatas for Piano. Vanguard 1157 has Brendel's excellent performances of the great posthumous Sonata in C minor, the uncompleted Sonata in C, and the German Dances Op. 33.

London 9500 has Ashkenazy's masterly and beautiful performances of the fine Sonata Op. 143, the Sonata Op. 120, which is better known but of slighter stature, the Waltzes Op. 18, and the Hungarian Melody.

For other sonatas see Schnabel.

Sonatas for Violin and Piano. Op. 162 is performed well by Oistrakh and Oborin on Dover 5245 (with Beethoven's Sonata Op. 24 and Tartini's *Devil's Trill* Sonata). See also in Chapter 27: Rachmaninov.

Sonata for Cello and Piano (*Arpeggione*). Performed well by Parisot and Mittman on Overtone 17 (with Chopin's Sonata Op. 65).

Songs. In Fischer-Dieskau's performance of *Die schöne Müllerin* with Moore, on Angel 3628, one hears the deployment of the superb voice with a sensitivity to the musical flow and to the sense of the words that makes his the most distinguished and affecting *Lieder*-singing of today.

Wondering why Fischer-Dieskau had recorded another performance of *Die Winterreise* on Deutsche Grammophon 19-201/2 so soon after the one on Angel 3640, I heard the reason in the very first piano chords from Demus, which though quiet had an incisiveness of attack and tone that contrasted with the muffled playing of Moore on the Angel record. And it became clear that Demus's marvelous playing stimulated Fischer-Dieskau to greater expressiveness—and even to occasional excessive vehemence. Inexplicably the recording makes the piano barely audible behind the voice. See also in Chapter 27: Lotte Lehmann, Gerhardt.

Angel 36127 has Fischer-Dieskau's performances with Moore of the last songs of Schubert grouped under the title *Schwanengesang*, which include *Der Doppelgänger*, *Liebesbotschaft*, *In der Ferne*, *Abschied*, *Ihr Bild*, *Fischermädchen* and *Die Stadt*.

The unfamiliar songs on which Fischer-Dieskau lavishes his voice and art on Angel 35656 are uninteresting.

Angel 35624 has Fischer-Dieskau's performances with Moore of familiar songs which include *Im Abendroth*, *Geheimes*, *Nachtviolen*, *Liebesbotschaft* and *Abschied*, and unfamiliar ones which include the impressive *Totengräber's Heimweh* and the engaging *Der Einsame*.

Angel 35699 has Fischer-Dieskau's performances with Moore of *An die Musik, An Sylvia, Die Taubenpost, Frühlingsglaube, Die Sterne*, and a few songs that I care less for.

Deutsche Grammophon 18-715 has Fischer-Dieskau's performances with Demus of a number of Schubert settings of texts on subjects of Greek antiquity, of which the ones I find effective, in addition to the familiar *An die Leier*, are *Lied eines Schiffers an die Dioskuren, Aus Heliopolis* and *Freiwilliges Versenken*.

Angel 36341 has Fischer-Dieskau's performances with Moore of familiar and unfamiliar songs: *Du bist die Ruh', Der Jüngling an der Quelle, Fischerweise, Des Fischers Liebesglück, An die Laute* and *Die Forelle*, among others, a few of which are uninteresting.

Angel 36342 has Fischer-Dieskau's performances with Moore of *Das Lied im Grünen, Litanei, Der Tod und das Mädchen, Auf dem Wasser zu singen* and *Das Heimweh*, among others.

See also in Chapter 27: Bjoerling, Ferrier, Flagstad, Gerhardt, Lotte Lehmann, Schumann, and under MISCELLANEOUS COLLECTIONS: De los Angeles, Ludwig, Schwarzkopf, Seefried.

Symphonies. In addition to Toscanini's and Cantelli's performances (see in Chapter 27), there are good performances of the *Unfinished* Symphony on London 9382, and of the Symphony No. 9 on 9381, by Kertesz with the Vienna Philharmonic.

Trios. In addition to the Cortot-Thibaud-Casals and Istomin-Schneider-Casals performances of Op. 99 (see in Chapter 27), there is the excellent one by Istomin, Stern and Rose on Columbia ML-6116; and I would expect the one by the Trio de Trieste on Deutsche Grammophon 18-583 to be very good.

The Trio de Trieste performance of Op. 100 on Deutsche Grammophon 39-106 is superb. See also in Chapter 27: Casals, Busch-Serkin Trio.

Die Winterreise. See Songs.

SCHUMANN

Carnaval. Novaes's excellent performance is on Vox 11160 (with *Papillons*).

Another excellent performance by Casadesus was on Columbia ML-5146 (with the Fantasia Op. 17).

See also in Chapter 27: Rachmaninov.

Concerto for Piano. In addition to Lipatti's performance (see in Chapter 27) there is Cliburn's fine one with the Chicago Symphony under Reiner on Victor LM-2455.

Davidsbündlertänze. Excellently performed by Rosen on Epic LC-3869 (with a less good performance of *Carnaval*).

Dichterliebe. See Songs.

Etudes symphoniques. Ashkenazy's playing, on London 9471 (with the Fantasia Op. 17), is now quietly lyrical—and especially beautiful in the additional variations that are customarily omitted—and now impassioned, occasionally to the point of turbulent.

There was an excellent performance by Casadesus on Columbia ML-5642 (with *Papillons*).

Fantasia Op. 17. Ashkenazy's playing in the opening movement, on London 9471 (with *Etudes symphoniques*)—now impassioned again to the point of turbulent, and now lingeringly introspective—makes one aware of the movement's episodic character, yet manages to avoid discontinuity except at a couple of long pauses, where the continuity that his physical appearance would preserve in the concert hall is destroyed on the record.

The superb performance by Curzon that was on London LL-1009 (with *Kinderszenen*) is available on imported Decca LXT-2933.

Fantasiestücke Op. 12. Rubinstein's performance on Victor LM-2669 (with *Carnaval*) suffers from occasional flamboyance.

Kinderszenen (Childhood Scenes). The beautiful performance by Curzon that was on London LL-1009 (with the Fantasia Op. 17) is available on imported Decca LXT-2933.

Papillons. Novaes's fine, though mannered, performance is on Vox 11160 (with *Carnaval*).

There was an excellent performance by Casadesus on Columbia ML-5642 (with *Etudes symphoniques*).

Songs. Fischer-Dieskau and Demus operate marvelously together in the *Dichterliebe* cycle, on Deutsche Grammophon 39-109; but the singer's occasional excessive vehemence makes this performance less attractive than the one by these two artists that was on Decca 9930 and is available on imported Deutsche Grammophon 18-370.

Angel 36266 has Fischer-Dieskau's performance with Moore of the *Liederkreis* Op. 39, which includes several fine songs: *In der*

Fremde, Waldesgespräch, Mondnacht, Auf einer Burg, another *In der Fremde,* and *Zwielicht.*

Of the Schumann settings of Heine poems that Fischer-Dieskau sings with Demus on Deutsche Grammophon 39-110, only *Du bist wie eine Blume, Die Lotosblume* and *Die beiden Grenadiere* are familiar; and of the unfamiliar ones I find only *Der Hans und die Grete* impressive.

See also in Chapter 27: Ferrier, Flagstad, Gerhardt, Lotte Lehmann, and under MISCELLANEOUS COLLECTIONS: Schwarzkopf.

SHAPERO

Symphony for Classical Orchestra. An excellent performance conducted by Bernstein was on Columbia ML-4889.

SMETANA

The Bartered Bride. Angel 3642 has an excellent performance conducted by Kempe, with Lorengar, Wunderlich, Mercker, Frick, the RIAS Chamber Chorus and the Bamberg Symphony.

See under MISCELLANEOUS COLLECTIONS: Jurinac.

The Moldau. See in Chapter 27: Toscanini.

STRAUSS

Orchestral Works. In addition to Toscanini's performances of *Don Juan, Till Eulenspiegel* and *Don Quixote,* (see in Chapter 27), there is an excellent performance of *Don Quixote* by Szell with the Cleveland Orchestra and Fournier on Epic LC-3786.

Songs. Angel 35600 has Fischer-Dieskau's performances with Moore of *Traum durch die Dämmerung, Ständchen, Freundliche Vision, Ruhe meine Seele, Zueignung,* and several less familiar songs, of which the best is *Wozu noch Mädchen.*

Victor LM-2749 has good performances by Della Casa of *Ständchen, Zueignung, Die Nacht, Der Stern, Ach Lieb' ich muss nun scheiden,* and others that I find uninteresting.

See also in Chapter 27: Bjoerling, Gerhardt, Lotte Lehmann, Schumann, and under MISCELLANEOUS COLLECTIONS: Ludwig, Schwarzkopf, Seefried.

STRAVINSKY

Apollo (Apollon musagète). Stravinsky imparts to the performance on

Columbia ML-5215 (with *Orpheus*) the clarity, power and co-hesive tension that make his performances of his works the best.

Le Baiser de la fée. Stravinsky's performance with a recording or-chestra on Columbia ML-6203 is excellent; but even better was the performance with the finer Cleveland Orchestra on ML-5102.

Danses concertantes. As against the animation, lightness and grace of the performance conducted by Stravinsky that was on Victor LVT-1029, the one by Davis with the English Chamber Or-chestra on Oiseau-Lyre 50219 is ponderous and overemphatic; and this fault is heard also in the Davis performances of the engaging *Dumbarton Oaks Concerto* and Concerto in D for strings.

Jeu de cartes. Stravinsky's performance with the Cleveland Orchestra is on Columbia ML-6049 (with the Tchaikovsky-Stravinsky *Bluebird* Pas de deux).

Munch conducts a brilliant performance by the Boston Sym-phony on Victor LM-2567.

Davis's performance with the London Symphony on Philips 500-113 is unusual not only in the rather deliberate tempo of the first deal but in the detail that is beautifully fashioned by the conductor and beautifully realized by the orchestra.

Oedipus Rex. The performance conducted by Stravinsky that was on Columbia ML-4644 had better soloists, chorus and orchestra than the one he conducts on Columbia ML-6472, which is more powerful than the otherwise good one conducted by Davis on Angel 35778.

L'Oiseau de feu. The entire score of the original ballet is performed by Stravinsky with a recording orchestra on Columbia ML-5728, and on D3L-305 (with *Petrushka* and *Le Sacre du printemps*).

Orpheus. Stravinsky's performance with the Chicago Symphony is on Columbia ML-6046 (with *Apollo*).

Petrushka. Stravinsky's performance of the entire score with a re-cording orchestra is on Columbia ML-5732, and on D3L-305 (with *L'Oiseau de feu* and *Le Sacre du printemps*).

Pulcinella. Stravinsky's performance of the entire score, not just the usual instrumental suite, with a recording orchestra on Columbia ML-6281 is excellent; but even better was the performance with the finer Cleveland Orchestra on ML-4830.

The Rake's Progress. The performance Stravinsky conducts on Columbia M3L-310—with Young, Reardon, Raskin, Sarfaty,

300

the Sadlers Wells Opera Chorus and the Royal Philharmonic—
is excellent; but the Metropolitan Opera performance he conducted on SL-125 had one point of enormous superiority in the
more unctuously evil Shadow of Harrell, to say nothing of the
splendor of his voice.

Le Sacre du printemps. Stravinsky's performance with a recording
orchestra is on Columbia ML-5719, and on D3L-305 (with
L'Oiseau de feu and *Petrushka*).

Symphony in Three Movements. Stravinsky's performance with a recording orchestra is on Columbia ML-5731.

Symphony of Psalms. Stravinsky imparts only slightly less power and
tension to the first and last movements in the new performance
with the CBC Symphony and Festival Singers of Toronto on
Columbia ML-5948, than in the old performance on ML-4129;
and the slightly lessened power is compensated for by the greater
spaciousness and vividness of the recorded sound.

TALLIS

The 40-part Motet *Spem in Alium*—sung well by the Choir of King's
College, Cambridge, and the Cambridge Musical Society under
Willcocks's direction—is the most extraordinary of several beauti-
ful and affecting pieces of vocal polyphony on Argo 436, *Tudor
Church Music* Record 1.

Lamentations of Jeremiah and several other fine pieces are sung by the
Choir of King's College under Willcocks's direction on Argo
479, *Tudor Church Music* Record 2.

See under MISCELLANEOUS COLLECTIONS: Deller Consort, Wolfe.

TCHAIKOVSKY

Ballets. The entire beautiful score of *The Nutcracker* is performed
most effectively by Irving with the New York City Ballet Orchestra on Kapp 5007.

For the *Nutcracker Suite* see in Chapter 27: Toscanini.

The beautiful score of *The Sleeping Beauty* is paced most effectively, and cut least, in Ansermet's performance with L'Orchestre
de la Suisse Romande on London 7301.

The score of *Swan Lake* is performed, with some cuts, by Ansermet with L'Orchestre de la Suisse Romande on London 7201.

301

Concerto No. 2 for Piano. The finest performance of this work—
infrequently heard, but far superior to the popular No. 1 in substance and structure—is Nikolayeva's with the shabby-sounding
State Orchestra of the USSR under Anosov, which was on Classic
3008 and is now available on imported Chant du Monde
LDX-P-8085 (France).

World Series 9007 has a sensitive performance by Magaloff
with the London Symphony under Davis.

Columbia ML-6155 has Graffman's performance—effectively
straightforward, but without the sensitiveness and elegance that
much of the music calls for—with the Philadelphia Orchestra
under Ormandy.

Concerto for Violin. Performed well by Stern with the Philadelphia
Orchestra under Ormandy on Columbia ML-5379 (with Mendelssohn's Concerto).

Operas. With no modern recording of the superb *The Queen of
Spades* available, Ultraphone 141/3 offers a 1942 performance by
soloists, chorus and orchestra of Moscow's Bolshoi Theater, paced
well by Samosud, sung well, and reproduced with sound that is
clear and agreeable, though with an edge of high-frequency distortion.

See in Chapter 27: Bjoerling, Sobinov, and under MISCELLANE-
OUS COLLECTIONS: Albanese, Farrell, Jurinac, Tourel.

Orchestral Music. In addition to Toscanini's performance of *Manfred*, there is the effective one by Markevitch with the London
Symphony on Philips 500-110.

In addition to Toscanini's and Cantelli's performances of
Romeo and Juilet there is Giulini's with the Philharmonia on Angel
35980, with the equally fine performance of *Francesca da Rimini*.

Suites for Orchestra. The Divertimento in No. 1 and the Theme
and Variations in No. 3 are outstanding examples of the superb
orchestral invention in some of the movements of these works.
They could be paced more effectively than they are by Dorati,
in his performances of the four suites on Mercury OL-3-118; but
I can't imagine them being played more beautifully than they
are by the New Philharmonia.

The Theme and Variations from No. 3 is performed well by
Kempe with the Vienna Philharmonic on Angel 35975.

Symphonies. London 9426 has an excellent performance of No. 1—

in which one is amazed by occasional writing that could be the superb orchestral invention of Tchaikovsky's maturity—by Maazel with the Vienna Philharmonic.

London 9427 has an excellent performance of the similarly amazing No. 2 by Maazel with the Vienna Philharmonic.

London 9428 has an excellent performance of No. 3—even more amazing than the first two—by Maazel with the Vienna Philharmonic.

Deutsche Grammophon 18-789 has Maazel's superb performance of No. 4 with the Berlin Philharmonic. See also in Chapter 27: Argenta.

Angel 36141 has Klemperer's excellent performance of No. 5 with the Philharmonia.

In addition to Toscanini's and Cantelli's performances of No. 6 (*Pathétique*), there is Maazel's effectively straightforward performance with the Vienna Philharmonic on London 9409.

Trio. Admirably performed by Rubinstein, Heifetz and Piatigorsky on Victor LM-1120.

THOMSON

Four Saints in Three Acts. Victor LM-2756 has the 1947 recording of an abridged version (made by Thomson), with Thomson conducting the excellent soloists (some from the cast of the historic 1934 stage production), chorus and orchestra in a clear and sharp-witted performance that is well reproduced.

VERDI

Operas. In addition to Toscanini's performances (see in Chapter 27), there are the following:

The *Aida* on Victor LM-6158, which is worth having for the beauty, expressiveness and musical sensitiveness and taste of Price's and Vickers's singing.

The excellent *Falstaff* on Victor LM-6163, conducted by Solti, with Evans, Ligabue, Simionato, Freni and Elias.

The excellent *Falstaff* that was on Angel 3552 and is now available on imported Columbia 33CX-1410/2 (England) and C-90524/6 (Germany), conducted by von Karajan, with Gobbi, Panerai, Alva, Schwarzkopf, Merriman, Barbieri, Moffo and the Philharmonia.

The *La Traviata* on Cetra (Everest) 425 (avoid the pseudo-stereo version), which is worth having for the dramatically compelling singing of Callas, especially her subtly inflected quiet singing, in which her voice has the beauty it loses in her vehement singing.

There are no performances other than Toscanini's that I can recommend of *Un Ballo in Maschera* and *Otello*. And I advise against the *Falstaff* conducted by Bernstein on Columbia M3L-350.

As for the operas not performed by Toscanini, London 4432 offers an excellent performance conducted by Solti—with Tebaldi, Bumbry, Bergonzi, Fischer-Dieskau, Ghiaurov and Talvela—of *Don Carlo*, which has many pages that are among the incandescent achievements of Verdi's matured powers: all the superb writing in the scene that begins with Philip's *Ella giammai m'amò;* before that the second-act duets of Carlo and Elisabeth, then Philip and Rodrigo, which have vocal writing as flexible and free-ranging in phraseology, and supporting orchestral writing as imaginatively resourceful, as one hears in *Otello;* and the tremendous introduction of the last act, leading to Elisabeth's *Tu che le vanità*, whose grandeur is something heard nowhere else in Verdi.

There is superb writing also in *La Forza del Destino;* and the performance on London 4408, conducted effectively by Molinari-Prandelli, has beautiful singing by Tebaldi, Simionato, Bastianini, Siepi and Corena that makes one willing to endure Del Monaco's unpleasant voice.

Angel 3537 has a *Rigoletto* conducted by Serafin that is made outstanding by Gobbi's performance in the title role. Di Stefano sings well in his mannered style; and Callas's singing, occasionally made unpleasant by the shrillness and wobble of her upper range, is often made exciting by the extraordinary timbre and expressive force of the middle and lower range that is still beautiful, and by her unfailing sense for continuity of musical phrase and her power of expressive projection.

Victor LM-6021 had a *Rigoletto* with excellent singing by Warren, Peerce and Berger.

The *Il Trovatore* conducted by Cellini on Victor LM-6008 has superb singing by Bjoerling, Milanov and Warren.

304

The Il Trovatore conducted effectively by Basile on Victor LM-6150 has impressive singing by Price, Elias, Warren and Tozzi, with singing by Tucker that lacks warmth, luster and ease.

The La Scala *Il Trovatore* on Angel 3554 is made outstanding by the playing of the orchestral part under von Karajan's direction—the precision and refinement of execution and tone, the expressiveness of the phrasing, the power of the larger shaping. What was said of Callas's and Di Stefano's singing in *Rigoletto* can be said again here; and Panerai is excellent; but Barbieri's tempestuous singing produces sounds that are unfocussed and clouded by tremolo.

Schippers conducts *Macbeth* on London 4380 with a feeling for the expressive character and style of Verdi's writing—i.e. with an enlivening of the orchestral part and an expansive treatment of melody—that Leinsdorf's conducting of the work on Victor LM-6147 doesn't exhibit. The London performance is therefore the one to acquire in spite of its cuts, and in spite of the superiority of Rysanek's and Warren's singing in the Victor performance to Nilsson's and Taddei's in the London.

In the arias from *Nabucco*, *Ernani*, *Macbeth* and *Don Carlo* on Angel 35763 the upper range of Callas's voice is unpleasantly shrill and wobbly; but in its lower range the strange-timbred voice is beautiful and affecting, and the expressive inflection of phrase is powerful. Concerning the Sleepwalking Scene from *Macbeth* I must add that I find the tempo over-deliberate and the expressive inflection in the early portion exaggerated to the point of hamming.

It is astonishing to hear, on Seraphim 60014, that the voice and art of Fischer-Dieskau which are overwhelming in German songs do not work convincingly in the Verdi arias he sings with the Berlin Philharmonic under Erede.

Victor LM-2506 has Price's performances of Leonora's two arias from the complete *Trovatore*, and her additional beautiful performances of *Ritorna vincitor* and *O patria mia* from *Aida*.

Victor LM-2262 had Rysanek's beautiful performances of arias from *Aida*, *La Forza del Destino* and *Otello*.

London 5520 has Tebaldi's lovely and expansive singing in excerpts from complete recordings of *La Forza del Destino*, *Il Trovatore* and *Otello*.

London 5912 has Tebaldi's performances of arias from *Giovanna d'Arco*, *Un Ballo in Maschera* and *Don Carlo*, in which her voice, even without its earlier bloom, is still a superb one that she deploys spaciously with impressive effect.

See also in Chapter 27: Bjoerling, De Luca, Hempel, Kipnis, Lemnitz, Matzenauer, Pinza, Ponselle, Rethberg, Roswaenge, Schipa, Slezak, Steber, Urlus, Wildbrunn, and under MISCELLANEOUS COLLECTIONS: *The Age of Bel Canto*, Callas, Evans, Farrell, Ghiaurov, Horne, Simionato, Sutherland, Tebaldi.

Choral Works. Toscanini's definitive performance of the *Requiem* is the one to acquire; but one possible alternative is Giulini's performance on Angel 3649, which is paced effectively for the most part and offers superb playing and singing by the Philharmonia Orchestra and Chorus, but has an occasional ineffective tempo—in the *Sanctus*, for example—and soloists whose voices, except for Ghiaurov's richly sonorous bass, are not well suited to the warm, impassioned music.

Giulini's excellent performance of the *Four Sacred Pieces* with the Philharmonia Orchestra and Chorus, on Angel 36125, enables one to hear—in addition to the marvelously beautiful *Te Deum* that Toscanini performed—the *Stabat Mater*, with beautiful but more diffuse choral and orchestral writing; the *Laudi alla Vergine Maria*, with its lovely *a cappella* writing for women's voices; and the *Ave Maria*, a strange-sounding but impressive *a cappella* contrapuntal exercise around a *scala enigmatica* that interested Verdi.

VICTORIA

Masses *O Quam Gloriosum* and *O Magnum Mysterium*. Sung well by the Choir of the Carmelite Priory, London, under McCarthy on Oiseau-Lyre 270.

Officium Defunctorum (Mass for the Dead) and other pieces. Sung beautifully by the Netherlands Chamber Choir under De Nobel on Angel 35668.

Missa Quarti Toni, Motet *O Vos Omnes* and other pieces. Sung well, on Music Guild 143, by the Schola du Grand Scholasticat des Pères du Saint-Esprit du Chevilly under L. Deiss, and the Chorale Sant-Jordi of Barcelona under O. Martorell.

See also under MISCELLANEOUS COLLECTIONS: Welch Chorale.

VIVALDI

L'Estro Armonico. Bach Guild 143/5 offers excellent performances of the twelve concertos by a Vienna State Opera chamber group under Rossi, with Tomasow and Boskovsky as violin soloists.

The Four Seasons. Angel 35877 has the fine performance of the Virtuosi di Roma; Angel 35216 a beautiful performance of a different kind by Giulini with the strings of the Philharmonia Orchestra, and with Dart providing an unusually inventive realization of the continuo on the harpsichord.

Collections. The Virtuosi di Roma, on Decca 9729, plays the superb No. 8 from *L'Estro Armonico*, a Concerto in G minor for two violins and cello obbligato, and Concertos in C minor (*Il Sospetto*) and E for violin.

I Musici, on Angel 35087, plays the Concertos in D minor (*Madrigalesco*) and A for strings, in D for violin, and in D minor for viola d'amore.

The Virtuosi di Roma, on Decca 9679, plays the same Concerto in D minor for viola d'amore and the Concertos in B flat for strings, in D minor for oboe, and in C for violin and two cellos.

Bach Guild 538 offers Nos. 3 and 11 from *L'Estro Armonico*, the equally lovely Op. 12 No. 1 for violin, and the charming Op. 10 No. 3 (*Bullfinch*) for flute, excellently performed by a Vienna State Opera chamber group under Golschmann.

The Sonata No. 5 for cello, with the realization of its figured bass arranged for strings, is performed beautifully by Fournier with Festival Strings Lucerne under Baumgartner on Deutsche Grammophon 18-986 (with Couperin's *Pièces en concert*).

See also under MISCELLANEOUS COLLECTIONS: I Musici, Virtuosi di Roma.

WAGNER

Die Meistersinger. Angel 3572 has the performance to acquire, conducted effectively by Kempe, with excellent singing by Grümmer, Schock, Frantz and the others, and with beautiful playing by the Berlin Philharmonic.

Tristan und Isolde. The performance conducted by Furtwängler (see in Chapter 27), with Flagstad and Suthaus, is unequalled, and

307

the one to acquire. (In the performance on Deutsche Grammophon 39-221/5 Böhm's conducting hasn't the relaxed, spacious
and sensitive lyricism of Furtwängler's; Nilsson's voice hasn't the
beauty, and her singing hasn't the musical sensitiveness, of Flagstad's; and the same may be said of Windgassen's voice and singing as against Suthaus's.)

Collections of Excerpts. In addition to Toscanini's performances
there are, on Angel 36188, Klemperer's of the Prelude and Finale
of *Tristan und Isolde* and the Funeral Music from *Die Götterdämmerung* with the Philharmonia, which approximate Toscanini's
in tension and power, and the one of the Prelude to *Lohengrin*,
which is more relaxed and comes off the record more beautiful
in sound than Toscanini's.

Wesendonck Songs. In addition to Flagstad's performance (see in
Chapter 27), there is Farrell's with the New York Philharmonic
under Bernstein on Columbia ML-5733—most of the time quiet,
intimate singing in *mezza voce*, with richly detailed inflection of
the line of lovely vocal sound that is spun out in long-breathed
phrases; but now and then excited singing in which the voice becomes lusterless and tremulous, and the phrasing explosive and
jagged.

See also in Chapter 27: Flagstad, Gerhardt, Leider, Lotte
Lehmann, Lemnitz, Matzenauer, Roswaenge, Schorr, Sobinov,
Urlus, Wildbrunn.

WALTHER

The *Concerto del Sigr. Meck* and four chorale-preludes for organ are
on Overtone 8 (with works of Pachelbel)—one's pleasure from
the early-eighteenth-century music increased by the playing of
Noss and the sound of the Holtkamp organ in Yale's Battell
Chapel.

WALTON

Façade. This early parodistic and otherwise humorous music for
Edith Sitwell's poems seems to me Walton's most impressive
achievement. On London 4104 the poems recited by their author
and Peter Pears often blanket the music performed by a small
group under Collins; in the old performance on Columbia
ML-5241, in which Dame Edith recites all the poems, the group
conducted by Prausnitz is more clearly audible.

308

WEELKES

See under MISCELLANEOUS COLLECTIONS: Collegium Musicum, Deller Consort.

WILBYE

Bach Guild 578 has a number of lovely madrigals, sung beautifully by the Deller Consort.

See also under MISCELLANEOUS COLLECTIONS: Deller Consort.

WOLF

Decca 9632 had Fischer-Dieskau's performances of sixteen songs of the *Italian Song Book*, including a number of the finest.

Decca 9743 had Seefried's finely spun performances of twenty-two songs of the *Italian Song Book*, which included examples of the Wolf song that is remarkable in its relation to the poem but not in addition a moving or attractive piece of music.

Angel 35838 has Fischer-Dieskau's performances with Moore of songs of the *Spanish Song Book*—some of them only expressive declamation which carries the words efficiently, some of them in addition moving or attractive as pieces of music.

Angel 35474 has Fischer-Dieskau's performances with Moore of a number of beautiful and affecting songs—*Phänomen, Anakreon's Grab, Verschwiegene Liebe, Lebe wohl, In der Frühe, Fussreise*—in addition to the *Harfenspieler* songs and *Cophtisches Lied* 1 and 2, which are interesting only for their relation to the poems.

See also in Chapter 27: Ferrier, Gerhardt, Kipnis, Lotte Lehmann, Schumann, and under MISCELLANEOUS COLLECTIONS: Ludwig, Schwarzkopf, Seefried.

RECORDED PERFORMANCES
IN MISCELLANEOUS COLLECTIONS
LISTED UNDER NAMES OF
PERFORMERS OR TITLES OF RECORDS

Age of Bel Canto, The. This is an assemblage, on London 4357, of arias, duets and trios from familiar operas of Handel, Mozart, Weber, Rossini and Donizetti, and unfamiliar ones that include Donizetti's *Lucrezia Borgia*, Bellini's *La Straniera* and Verdi's *Attila.* The aria from *Attila* is one of several fine pieces, in addition to a number of engaging or pleasant ones, and a few that are uninteresting. Horne's singing is consistently first-rate; Sutherland's ranges from her superb performance in *Attila* to her mannered moaning in *La Straniera*; the tenor Richard Conrad's is unattractive in vocal sound and unimpressive in musical style.

Albanese. Assembled on Victor LM-2286 are the 78-rpm recordings of performances of the Letter Scene from Tchaikovsky's *Eugene Onegin* (with an orchestra conducted by Stokowski) and arias that include *Deh Vieni* from *Figaro*, *Batti, batti* from *Don Giovanni*, Micaela's aria from *Carmen*, and *Qual guardo il cavaliere* from *Don Pasquale.* The beautiful voice is sometimes dry and afflicted with a strong vibrato; but with the musical taste, the style and the intensity of the singing these are superb and exciting performances.

Berganza. London 5591 offers her impressive use of her fine voice in *Che puro ciel* and *Che farò* from *Orfeo ed Euridice*, *Divinités du Styx* from *Alceste*, *O del mio dolce ardor* from *Elena ed Paride*, *Piangerò la sorta mia* from Handel's *Julius Caesar* and other eighteenth-century arias, with the Covent Garden Orchestra under Gibson.

Callas. Angel 35233 has her in good voice in exciting performances of arias from *The Barber of Seville*, *Dinorah*, *Lakmé*, *I Vespri Siciliani*, and less consequential operas, with the Philharmonia under Serafin.

On Angel 35304 Callas sings an aria from Cherubini's *Medea* and three arias from Spontini's *La Vestale* very impressively; and with these the record has arias from her recordings of *La Sonnambula* and *I Puritani*. Thus it offers the striking and saddening contrast between the steady, agreeable-sounding high B flats in *I Puritani* and the unlovely, wobbly ones recorded a few years later.

Collegium Musicum of Yale University School of Music conducted by Hindemith. Overtone 5 offers works by Perotin, Dufay, Palestrina, Lassus, Jacob Handl and Gabrieli—all lovely and moving, and sung not only with remarkable transparency and beauty of tone, but with exciting animation in phrasing and contrapuntal movement. I am in fact not sure it isn't the superb performance that makes Bach's *Singet dem Herrn ein neues Lied* seem so attractive; but I have no such doubts about the other pieces on Overtone 4: Monteverdi's famous *Lagrime d'Amante al Sepolcro dell' Amata*, two characteristically bold and strange madrigals by Gesualdo, and two lovely ones by Weelkes.

Cuenod. *Elizabethan Love Songs and Harpsichord Pieces*, on Lyrichord 37, includes two especially fine songs by Dowland, *Weep You No More Sad Fountains* and *Sorrow Stay*, and an extraordinary piece by Gibbons, *The Lord of Salisbury His Pavin*. Superb singing of his kind by Cuenod, and good harpsichord performances by Chiasson.

English and French Songs of the 16th and 17th Centuries, on Westminster 9620, offers a number of pleasant French songs, several charming ones by Bartlett, Pilkington and Morley, and Dowland's *Flow My Tears* and *I Saw My Lady Weep*. Superb singing again, with lute accompaniments by Leeb.

Italian and Spanish Songs of the 16th and 17th Centuries, on Westminster 9611, offers very fine songs and performances.

Deller. *Elizabethan and Jacobean Music*, on Bach Guild 539, has songs by Dowland and other composers, of which Dowland's *From Silent Night* and Parson's *Pandolpho* are especially fine; and instrumental pieces which include Jenkins's superb Pavan and Fantasia and a charming Morley Air for viols, and the engaging *My Lady Hunsdon's Puffe* for lute and Farnaby setting of a Johnson Alman for harpsichord. Deller's sensitive singing is admirably supported

311

by Desmond Dupré's lute and, in *From Silent Night*, by the viols; and their performances of the instrumental pieces are excellent.

English Lute Songs, on Bach Guild 576, offers a number of songs by Dowland, Pilkington, Morley, Campion and others, of which Campion's *Care-Charming Sleep* and the anonymous *Have You Seen But a Whyte Lillie Grow* are outstanding. Deller's counter-tenor voice is not always attractive, but his inflection of it is extraordinarily sensitive; and his singing is again admirably supported by Dupré's lute. Several *In Nomines* by Bull, Tomkins, Taverner, Tye and White are played well by the In Nomine Players, a group of viols and cello.

Deller Consort. *The English Madrigal School* Volume 1, on Bach Guild 553, has a number of pieces by Morley, Weelkes, Wilbye, Vautor and others—the gay ones charming, the slow ones, with their dense textures and their chromaticism, deeply affecting—sung with extraordinary refinement of tone and phrasing.

The English Madrigal School Volume 2, on Bach Guild 554, offers on the one hand a number of fine examples of the fully matured form by Weelkes and Wilbye, two of which are outstanding: Weelkes's *Thule the Period of Cosmography*, with its rich texture and its unusual and wonderfully expressive harmonic progressions; and Wilbye's *Lady When I Behold*, with wonderful harmonic progressions too. And on the other hand a number of earlier pieces by Tallis, Edwards, Johnson, Shepherd and anonymous composers, most of which are lovely, and a couple—Johnson's *Defiled Is My Name* and the anonymous *The Bitter Sweet*—poignant and moving. The performances again are extraordinary in their refinement of tone and phrasing.

The old French, Italian and English madrigals that are sung beautifully on Bach Guild 604 include fine pieces by Monteverdi, Gesualdo, Morley and Tomkins.

The additional English madrigals on Bach Guild 624 include Gibbons's *The Silver Swan*, *What Is Our Life?* and *Ah! Dear Heart*, and a number of other fine pieces by Pilkington, Byrd and Ward.

Monteverdi's *Lagrime d'Amante al Sepolcro dell' Amata* and other fine pieces by Monteverdi, Marenzio and Gesualdo, among others, are sung beautifully on Bach Guild 639, even with the unattractive timbre of Deller's counter-tenor that is prominent now and then.

312

Monteverdi's *Lamento d'Adrianna* and other madrigals of Monteverdi, Gesualdo, Marenzio, Lassus, Josquin and Jannequin are sung beautifully on Bach Guild 671.

De los Angeles. *Five Centuries of Spanish Song*, on Capitol G-7155, offers a number of fine songs from the Gothic, Renaissance and Baroque periods, which De los Angeles makes now moving and now delightful with her lovely voice, her musical taste, and her personal warmth and charm.

The Spanish songs of the Renaissance on Angel 35888 are individually very fine, but collectively sound very much alike, and are therefore best listened to a few at a time. They are sung exquisitely to accompaniments by Ars Musicae, a group of players of old instruments.

De los Angeles's voice is unsuited to the concluding section of Schubert's *Der Tod und das Mädchen*, but she does lovely singing, on Angel 35971, in Scarlatti's *Le Violette*, Handel's *Oh! Had I Jubal's Lyre*, Schubert's *An die Musik* and *Wohin*, and songs of Brahms, Fauré and Spanish composers that I find less interesting.

Evans. London 5994 has impressive performances of *L'onore!* from *Falstaff*, the *Credo* from *Otello*, *Un fuoco insolito* from *Don Pasquale*, Pizarro's monologue from *Fidelio*, Papageno's first song from *The Magic Flute*, the Catalogue Aria from *Don Giovanni*, *Non più andrai* from *Figaro*, and a couple of Handel arias.

Farrell. In the performances of arias from *Alceste*, *Oberon*, *Ernani*, Tchaikovsky's *Jeanne d'Arc* and less consequential operas on Angel 35589, Farrell's voice and her way of using it place her among the greats of our time.

Columbia ML-5408 had superb performances of *Abscheulicher!* from *Fidelio*, Beethoven's *Ah, perfido*, arias from *Der Freischütz*, Neris's aria from *Medea*, and an aria from *Alceste*.

Ghiaurov. The fresh, powerful voice is used impressively, on London 5769, in *Ella giammai m'amò* from *Don Carlo*, the Catalogue Aria from *Don Giovanni*, and Pimen's narrative from *Boris Godunov*, among other things.

History of Music in Sound. Each of the ten volumes is accompanied by a booklet with material from the corresponding volume of the Oxford University Press's *New Oxford History of Music.* Victor issued the volumes as follows:

Volume 1, *Ancient and Oriental Music*, on LM-6057

Volume 2, *Early Medieval Music up to 1300*, on LM-6015
Volume 3, *Ars Nova and the Renaissance*, on LM-6016
Volume 4, *The Age of Humanism*, on LM-6029
Volume 5, *Opera and Church Music*, on LM-6030
Volume 6, *The Growth of Instrumental Music*, on LM-6031
Volume 7, *The Symphonic Outlook*, on LM-6137
Volume 8, *The Age of Beethoven (1790-1830)*, on LM-6146
Volume 9, *Romanticism (1830-90)*, on LM-6153
Volume 10, *Modern Music*, LM-6092

In his introduction to the booklet of Volume 2 Dom Anselm Hughes contends that the music "should not be regarded merely as a collection of interesting but dead museum pieces"; but I must report that among the pieces in this volume and on the first two sides of Volume 3 only very few have more than historic interest for me. But on the third and fourth sides of Volume 3 are pieces by Dufay, Ockeghem, Obrecht, Pierre de la Rue, Josquin, and their English contemporaries including Fayrfax and Taverner, that are lovely, charming and impressive to present-day ears. So with many of the pieces in Volume 4—the madrigals of Marenzio, Luzzaschi, Wilbye, Greaves, Weelkes; the French chansons; the church pieces of Victoria, de Monte, Palestrina, Lassus, Gallus, Tallis, Byrd, Gibbons, Morley (an especially beautiful *Agnus Dei*), Praetorius, Giovanni Gabrieli; the French, Spanish and English solo songs; a few of the instrumental pieces. And so with many of the pieces in Volume 5—the excerpts from operas of Cavalli, Cesti, Stradella, Alessandro Scarlatti, Handel, Logroscino, Lully, Rameau, Blow, Keiser; from oratorios of Carissimi and Marcello; from the church music of Rameau, Scarlatti, Pelham Humphrey, Greene, Schütz, Buxtehude and Bach. But except for a superb chorus from Handel's oratorio *Susanna*, the pieces in Volume 6 seem to me poorly chosen—i.e. not the most beautiful or impressive examples of the writing of Purcell, Domenico Scarlatti, the French harpsichordists, Vivaldi, Bach. And though Volume 7 has excerpts from operas of Gluck and Mozart and movements from instrumental works of Haydn and Carl Philipp Emanuel Bach that are musically impressive, it has other excerpts from operas of Dittersdorf and Grétry and movements from instrumental works of Boyce, Stamitz, Monn and Johann Christian Bach that have little but historic interest.

Volume 8 has excerpts from Cherubini's opera *Les Deux Journées*, Méhul's *Joseph*, Spontini's *La Vestale*, Spohr's *Jessonda*, Weber's *Euryanthe*, and Rossini's *Otello;* songs by Zumsteeg, Schubert and Loewe; chamber music by Spohr, Field and Prince Louis Ferdinand; piano pieces by Tomásek, Dussek, Clementi and Hummel.

Volume 9, which cannot provide complete documentation of its period, offers music that is presumed to be unfamiliar: passages from Meyerbeer's *Les Huguenots*, Berlioz's *Les Troyens*, Marschner's *Hans Heiling*, Smetana's *Libuse*, Glinka's *Ruslan and Ludmila* and Musorgsky's *Boris Godunov* (the original); songs by Schumann, Liszt, Franz, Cornelius, Wolf, Borodin, Musorgsky, Duparc, Chausson and Fauré; piano pieces by Liszt, Brahms and Grieg; chamber music by Mendelssohn, Schumann and Fauré.

Volume 10 offers partial documentation of impressionism with small pieces by Debussy and Falla; of late romanticism with pieces by Scriabin, Strauss, Reger, Schönberg and Berg; of the anti-romantic reaction with pieces by Satie, Bliss, Milhaud, Stravinsky, Bartok, Janáček and Hindemith; 12-note music with pieces by Schönberg and Dallapiccola; eclecticism with pieces by Roussel, Shostakovich, Copland, Rubbra and Rawsthorne (the English origin of the project accounts for space being given to Bliss, Rubbra and Rawsthorne that is not given to Mahler, Prokofiev and Webern).

The performances are for the most part excellent.

Horne. The beautiful voice, the secure and accurate florid singing, the phrasing and style that created a sensation in a concert performance of *Semiramide* a few years ago are heard on London 5910 in arias from *Semiramide*, *La Cenerentola*, *L'Italiana in Algeri*, *Les Huguenots*, *Le Prophète*, *The Daughter of the Regiment* and *La Clemenza di Tito*.

On London 4263 the voice has less luster in its upper range, and produces a few growling low notes for dramatic effect, but is still extraordinary in its beauty, range, power and agility; and the use of it is magnificent most of the time in the performances of familiar and unfamiliar arias from *Orfeo ed Euridice*, *Fidelio*, *Le Prophète*, *The Barber of Seville*, *L'Italiana in Algeri*, *Tancredi*, *Otello* (Rossini's), *Semiramide*, Bellini's *I Capuleti ed i Montecchi*, Gounod's *Sapho*, and *Il Trovatore*.

315

See also *The Age of Bel Canto*.

Jurinac. The lovely voice and affecting singing are heard, on imported Odeon HQM-1024, in superb performances of Ilia's two arias from the 1951 Glyndebourne *Idomeneo* conducted by Busch, Cherubino's two arias from the 1950 *Figaro* conducted by von Karajan, the Countess's two arias from the 1955 Glyndebourne *Figaro* conducted by Gui, Marzelline's aria from the lethargic 1953 Furtwängler *Fidelio*, and excerpts from *The Bartered Bride* and Tchaikovsky's *Joan of Arc*.

Kulenkampf and Solti. The conductor Solti's powers as ensemble pianist are demonstrated impressively in his superb playing with the violinist Kulenkampf in Mozart's Sonata K.454 and Beethoven's Op. 47 (*Kreutzer*), on London 7218 (with the three Brahms sonatas).

Ludwig. Seraphim 60034 has this remarkable singing actress's affecting performances of songs which include Schubert's *Fischerweise*, Brahms's *Sapphische Ode*, Wolf's *Gesang Weylas* and *Auf einer Wanderung*, Strauss's *Die Nacht*, and Mahler's *Ich bin der Welt abhanden* and *Des Antonius von Padua Fischpredigt*.

Masterpieces of Music Before 1750. Haydn Society 9038/40 enable one to hear in living sound the pieces—from Gregorian chant to Bach—that are given in short score in Parrish and Ohl's book of the same title. The authors claim that their primary requirement in selecting each piece was that it "be in itself an interesting and beautiful piece of music"; and many of the early pieces on the first two records are in fact interesting and beautiful, but a few are neither; and listening to the later pieces on the third record one wonders why certain examples—e.g. of the Scarlatti harpsichord sonata, the Handel concerto—were chosen in preference to the more interesting and beautiful ones that were available. Most of the performances by Danish soloists and ensembles are good; but some are not. There is distortion near the ends of the last three sides.

Motets of the 15th and 16th Centuries. See Welch Chorale.

I Musici. The group's incandescent execution, tone and phrasing are heard, on Angel 35253, in the well-known Concerto Grosso No. 11 from Vivaldi's *L'Estro Armonico* and three fine unfamiliar pieces: Vivaldi's Concerto in A for viola d'amore, Corelli's Concerto Grosso Op. 6 No. 1, and Martini's Concerto in F for harpsichord.

Netherlands Chamber Choir conducted by De Nobel. Angel 35667 offers beautiful singing of the lovely vocal polyphony of Palestrina's *Sicut Cervus, Soave Fia Morir* and *O Beata et Benedicta,* and the more dramatic *Lamento d'Arianna: Lasciatemi Morire* and *Ch'Io T'Amo.*

Philadelphia Orchestra conducted by Ormandy. *First Chair,* Columbia ML-4629, presents the orchestra of ten years ago, with its great solo oboe, Marcel Tabuteau, in Handel's beautiful Concerto No. 3; its great solo flute, William Kincaid, in Griffes's *Poem;* its excellent solo horn, Mason Jones, in an engaging Larghetto by Chabrier; its brilliant solo trumpet, Samuel Krauss, in Purcell's *Trumpet Voluntary;* its fine solo clarinet, Anthony Gigliotti, in the inconsequential Weber Concertino; its excellent solo bassoon, Sol Schoenbach, in an inconsequential *Concert Piece* by Burrell Phillips; its solo cello, Lorne Monroe, in an engaging Weber Adagio and Rondo in which his technique is dazzling but his tone is made edged and brash by the recording; and its concert-master. Jacob Krachmalnick, in Beethoven's uninteresting Romance No. 2 in which his tone also is poorly reproduced.

Schwarzkopf. Angel 35023 offers lovely and charming songs by Bach, Gluck, Mozart, Beethoven, Schubert, Schumann, Brahms, Wolf and Strauss, including a few—Schubert's *Litanei,* Schumann's *Aufträge* and *Der Nussbaum*—that are outstanding. The performances range from the exquisite sustained singing in *Litanei,* in *Der Nussbaum,* in Wolf's *Wiegenlied,* to the excessively arch and staccato delivery of *Aufträge,* the excessively dramatized delivery of Brahms's *Vergebliches Ständchen,* the excessively finely spun delivery of Schubert's *Ungeduld.* Fine piano accompaniments by Moore.

Seefried. Imported Deutsche Grammophon 19-050 (France) has the superb performances that were on Decca 9809—of Schubert's *Auf dem Wasser zu singen* and *Lachen und weinen,* Wolf's *Das verlassene Mägdlein* and *Begegnung,* Strauss's *Ständchen,* and Musorgsky's cycle, *The Nursery,* with songs of Brahms and Bartók.

Simionato. The lovely voice, the superb style in ornamented cantilena, the brilliant bravura style in florid writing are most impressive, on London 5269, in arias from *The Barber of Seville, La*

317

Cenerentola, Don Carlo, and the unfamiliar *I Capuleti ed i Montecchi* of Bellini.

Stader. Though the voice, on Deutsche Grammophon 19-261, hasn't the loveliness it has in the earlier recordings of Mozart operas, it is still a fine one, which is used with musical skill in beautifully shaped phrases in the arias from Bach's *St. John* and *St. Matthew Passions,* Handel's *Messiah,* Haydn's *The Creation* and *The Seasons,* and Mendelssohn's *Elijah* that she sings with the Munich Bach Orchestra under Richter.

Sutherland. The breathtaking ease, accuracy, tonal brilliance and style of Sutherland's execution of florid writing, and her musical phrasing of cantilena, are heard in her performances of arias from *Lucia, Linda di Chamounix, Ernani* and *I Vespri Siciliani,* on London 5515, and of arias from *The Abduction from the Seraglio, Norma, I Puritani, La Traviata, Otello* and lesser works, on London 4241.

The later London 5776 offers a curious miscellany: on one side familiar arias from *Oberon, Dinorah, Le Cid* and *I Pagliacci;* on the other, unfamiliar and interesting arias from Verdi's *I Masnadieri* and *Luisa Miller,* Rossini's *Le Cambiale di Matrimonio,* and Bellini's *Beatrice di Tenda.* And in these it offers her remarkable and at times spectacular control of a voice that is attractively bright only in its upper range; the impressive sense for shape of phrase and style that operates in her use of the voice much of the time; the mannerisms—the little moans, the little explosions of tone— that she falls into at other times.

See also *The Age of Bel Canto.*

Tebaldi. London 5007 offers a fresh and lovely voice, occasionally a little tremulous and shrill, in arias from *Aïda, Il Trovatore, Faust* (with a sustained note in place of the trill at the beginning of the Jewel Song) and other operas. Erede conducts the veiled-sounding Orchestre de la Suisse Romande.

Interesting, on London 5202, is the simple, unaffected phrasing in *Porgi amor* and *Dove sono* from *Figaro;* and interesting also is the change in the singing—the increase not only in emotional warmth but in the beauty of the voice itself—in *Selva opaca* from Rossini's *William Tell,* in which Tebaldi evidently feels more at home than in the Mozart arias. Interesting too is the fact revealed once more at the end of *Dove sono*—that Tebaldi cannot

318

trill. The other pieces on the record are by Mascagni, Cilea, Catalani and Refice.

The group of three songs entitled *La Regata Veneziana*—three of the many charming small vocal and instrumental pieces that Rossini wrote in the years after *William Tell*, his last opera—is included among the songs and arias by Alessandro Scarlatti, Handel, Mozart, Bellini and others that Tebaldi sings in ear-ravishing fashion on London 5394.

Tourel. Decca 9981 has fine performances of Tchaikovsky's songs *At the Ball, So Soon Forgotten, None but the Lonely Heart* and *When Spring Was in the Air,* and songs by Glinka, Dargomizhsky, Balakirev, Gretchaninov, Rimsky-Korsakov and Rachmaninov.

Valletti. Cetra 55002 had his beautiful singing in arias from *Don Giovanni, The Barber of Seville, L'Italiana in Algeri* and *La Sonnambula,* among others.

Virtuosi di Roma. Decca 9674 offers superlative performances of Rossini's charming Sonata No. 3 for violins, cello and bass; a fine Oboe Concerto in C minor by an anonymous Venetian composer; an impressive Recitative for violin and strings by Bonporti; and a less interesting Piano Concerto in G by Cambini.

Decca 9649 has Corelli's beautiful *Christmas* Concerto Grosso Op. 6 No. 8, part of the *Spring* concerto from Vivaldi's *The Four Seasons,* and other engaging pieces by Torelli, Boccherini and Scarlatti—the last played on the piano by Ornella Santoliquido.

Welch Chorale. *Motets of the 15th and 16th Centuries,* on Lyrichord 52, offers good singing of an outstanding piece by Palestrina, *Super Flumina Babylonis,* Victoria's *Tantum Ergo* and *Vere Languoris,* the powerful *Tenebrae Factae Sunt* of Marc Antonio Ingegneri, and fine pieces by Dufay, Josquin, Dunstable, Byrd and others.

Wolfe. *English Keyboard Music,* on Experiences Anonymes EA-0013, offers on one side a large number of small pieces, some of them too short to make any effect, most of them engaging, and two—a Pavan by Newman and Tallis's *O Ye Tender Babes*—outstandingly beautiful. More satisfying are the long pieces on the other side: Bull's *In Nomine,* Byrd's *Ut Re My Fa Sol La,* and—especially fine —Tomkins's *The Perpetual Round* and *Fortune My Foe.* Good playing by Wolfe on an excellent-sounding harpsichord.

INDEX OF

MUSICAL PROCEDURES,

FORMS AND TERMS

GENERAL INDEX

INDEX OF PERFORMERS

ACKNOWLEDGMENTS

I am indebted to

Mel Evans, for the initial idea of *The Listener's Musical Companion* (1956), of which the present book is a new version.

Charles B. Farrell, for the information about the Boccherini Cello Concerto in B flat and other such matters.

333